COMMUNITY AND CARING

*Older Persons, Intergenerational Relations, and
Change in an Urban Community*

Harley Carl Schreck

University Press of America, ® Inc.
Lanham • New York • Oxford

Copyright © 2000 by
University Press of America
4720 Boston Way
Lanham, Maryland 20706

12 Hid's Copse Rd.
Cumnor Hill, Oxford OX2 9JJ

British Library Cataloging in Publication Information Available
A division of University Press of America
Library of Congress Cataloging-in-Publication Data

Schreck, Harley Carl.
Community and caring : older persons, integenerational relations,
and change in an urban community / Harley Carl Schreck.
p. cm.
Includes bibliographical references and index.
1. Aged—Minnesota—Minneapolis—Case studies. 2. City and town life—
Minnesota—Minneapolis—Case studies. 3. Social change—Minnesota—
Minneapolis—Case studies. 4. Intergenerational relations—Minnesota—
Minneapolis—Case studies. 5. Minneapolis (Minn.)—Social conditions—Case
studies. I. Title.
HQ1064.U6M5869   2000   305.26'09776'579—dc21   00-042318 CIP

ISBN 0-7618-1772-7 (pbk: alk. ppr.)

To Janice, Carl, and Miriam,
with much love

Table of Contents

Table of Figures

Acknowledgments

Ethnographic research is always a community affair, and this book could not have been written without the generous help of many living in Northeast Minneapolis. The twenty-one persons who put up with long hours of interviewing are the main stars of this work. They shared information generously and were highly committed to the telling of the story of Northeast Minneapolis. I thank them profusely and trust that my telling of their stories is clear and accurate. There are many others living in Northeast who put up with my questions, and I thank them for their patience and interest.

My sister, Priscilla Cunningham, contributed her skills as a writer and teacher to give me feedback when editing this book. I thank her for this and our lifelong friendship. Chelsea DeArmond was a wonderful partner as she prepared this text for publication. I deeply appreciate her interest and kind advice.

My students at Bethel College have been the first audiences for many of these stories and descriptions. I thank them for their patience. More than this, I also thank them for their interest, fellowship, and partnering as we have trudged the streets of Northeast together.

My family is the most wonderful support a researcher and author could have. They put up with the strange life of an anthropologist, including having to explain this to friends at school and in the neighborhood. Carl and Miriam are the best research companions, and I hope that you look back at various forays into Northeast homes, coffee shops, bakeries, and other exotic locations as fun and interesting. It was always more enjoyable for me when you were there. Janice, you are my friend and companion who never complains about the inconvenience of fieldwork, with its missed suppers and rushed appointments. Thank you much for your love and support.

Many have supported this work, given valuable feedback, and sped it to its completion. Any errors or gaps in the work, however, are only to be attributed to me.

Chapter 1

Older Persons and Cities

Many people spend all their lives in cities. Some live all their years in single urban neighborhoods. They are born, encounter and learn from their surrounding social worlds as young children, develop and grow into adulthood, marry, beget and raise children of their own, and grow old in the same neighborhoods. As such, the city, as it is known by them, is largely presented through the neighborhoods in which they live. For these lifelong residents, the city becomes immediate and manageable in neighborhood size terms.

Cities are collages of neighborhoods which often constitute immediate and manageable social worlds for their inhabitants. Cities are also centers of population, power, and wealth wherein large, powerful social, economic, political, and cultural forces are at play. Some accident of nature or history encourages centralization and allows the birth and growth of a city. People are pulled in from surrounding and more distant areas. They arrive with their skills, desires, histories, and cultures. The city changes them and shapes them into urban dwellers. They, in turn, shape the city as they live out and express their skills and intentions and apply that which their own personal histories and cultures of origin have imbued in them. The result is a dance between a city and its dwellers. As persons move into a city, they add new steps and the dance flows on, constantly moving and constantly changing.

Older persons who are life-long residents in urban neighborhoods have participated in this dance for a long time. They have learned well and have survived life's challenges to arrive at and live in the present. The ways in which they understand the world, interact with others, and carry on with their daily lives have been learned over a lifetime. This book focuses on the crucial area of such learning which has to do with care-giving and receiving and is based on the life stories of older persons who are long-term residents of Northeast Minneapolis, a well defined portion of the city of Minneapolis, Minnesota (see Appendices 1 and 2). Older persons who are lifelong residents of urban neighborhoods have had much experience in giving and receiving help as they, or those with whom they are closely connected, have faced crises and challenges. They have learned appropriate ways to give and receive care. They have learned to whom they are connected through strands of obligation and affection. Even as they were learning this, the cities and neighborhoods in which they have lived have changed around them, making it possible that the caregiving knowledge and skills they have learned have become outdated and that those culturally appropriate ways of interacting with others and culturally shaped ways of understanding that are learned in a person's earlier years might come to be less appropriate in that person's later years.

In conversations with lifelong residents of Northeast Minneapolis, a central focus was the knowledge and patterns of interaction which have defined care giving and receiving over their lifetimes. We begin this study with the story of one woman's life. Phyllis[1] is a woman who has lived almost all of her life in Northeast Minneapolis. She has faced and endured many crises. As she has done this she has relied upon and received help from others and used knowledge and skills that she has learned throughout her life.

Phyllis' Story

Eighty-three years is a long time. It stretches back to 1912 and meanders through sixteen presidents, four "big U.S. wars" and countless campaigns and police actions, vastly changing technology, religious trends, new roles for women, rapidly transforming demographic and cultural makeup of our nation, and innumerable fads and failures in American academic life. It is a long time.

For Phyllis, it seems like only a blink of an eye. Eighty three years—seventy of which were spent in one house, just an easy walk from her church, grocer, and butcher. Phyllis is not a native of Northeast Minne-apolis. She moved there when she was not quite two years old, but she counts herself as an early member of the cradle roll at the church that she still attends. It seems like only a day or two since she was walking home from church with her father, mother, two sisters, and three brothers. Soon there would be food on the table and relatives would gather to eat and talk, often in Swedish. Swedish was often spoken in the home by her par-ents and their friends. It was also the language of her church. She under-stood some of it, but much went over her head. Sunday was the highlight of the week. After attending church and cleaning up after dinner, Phyllis would play with her favorite cousins. There were always lots of cousins in her house after church on Sundays.

School was another center of her life in those years. She remembers it as great fun but "strict." Her grade school is torn down now, but Edison High school is still standing. The building looks the same, but the stu-dents are entirely different. Phyllis cannot quite understand why they wan-der around so much. Do they ever go to class? She remembers the panic of heading for a class that was on the second floor only to find she had gone to the wrong end of the building where the "down only" staircase was found. She hurried to the other end of the building, always trying not to run, and bounded up the staircase in a mad hope to make it to class on time. The last thing she needed was her dad to hear that she had been late to class.

After graduating from Edison in 1930, Phyllis dearly wished to become a nurse. Yet her father told her that this would be unfair to the family. Phyllis's mother needed help with such a big house, and more income was needed for the family during the hard times of the 1930s. Besides, the boys still had to finish Edison. So Phyllis found a job with a construction com-pany in downtown Minneapolis where her secretarial courses taken at Edison came in handy.

She worked there for fourteen years. In many other ways, her life did not change. She helped her mother with the housework and was active in church. Her social life was enhanced by her involvement in the Baptist Young Peoples Union (BYPU). This was organized for young persons in Baptist General Conference churches across Minneapolis and St. Paul. There were meetings and social events of many types. As Phyllis grew older she found that she did not feel comfortable in BYPU. She quit her in-volvement there and joined the same women's missionary circle as her mother. Phyllis had passed through her youth to an adult stage of life.

In 1944, Phyllis wanted a change of pace. She went to California with a girlfriend to seek work. There were many jobs there because of World War Two and not enough workers to fill them. She loved California. After a month Phyllis called home. She remembers the phone conversation with her father. Her brothers were gone. The housework was too much for her mother. Her dad had to slow down at work and was making less money. She just had to come home. It was unfair for her to take off by herself and live in California. She had responsibilities.

Phyllis came home and was re-hired at her old job. She continued to attend the family church, but it had changed. English was now used in all the services. It was losing some of its emphasis on Swedish heritage. Phyllis's role in the church had also changed. Her old friends were still active in the church, but she found it hard to fit into their friendship circles. The Sunday School class for her age group was called "Home Builders," and the socials were for people who were married. Much of the conversation dwelt on raising children. There was little Phyllis could contribute. She loved her mission circle and found it to be her main touchpoint in the church. In 1952, the pastor decided that the church was old fashioned and needed modernizing. In particular, mission circles were from an earlier time and needed to be replaced with women's groups in which every woman in the church was involved. The mission circles were disbanded, and twelve new groups were organized. Phyllis's old mission circle was split up, and the members were distributed across the new circles. The new groups only lasted a year. Later, new groups were formed. But they were always short term. There was no replacement for the mission circle to which Phyllis had belonged for so long. This was a lonely time for Phyllis. She had lost her most important connection with the church, and she found most of her friends consumed with family duties and responsibilities.

In the 1960s, her mother and father died. Phyllis continued to live in the family home with her two older sisters. Her brothers had married, established families, and were living elsewhere. Phyllis decided she had worked hard and long enough. She quit and stayed home to take care of the house. The three sisters remained active in the church. It was good to live with her sisters, and this was a quiet time in her life. In 1983, Phyllis's oldest sister announced that she thought it was time to sell the house. The neighborhood was going downhill and the house was too much for them to maintain.

They sold the house, split up the furniture, and moved into three separate apartments in a new senior high rise just a few blocks from the family home. They continued to attend church, but now there was a church van that picked them up. It was easier to find friends at church now. Many of the women were losing their husbands and seem to have more time for Phyllis and her sisters.

Six months after they moved into the high rise, Phyllis's older sister died. It was sudden. Soon after that happened her younger sister became very sick. Phyllis described herself as living on the staircase—running up and down between her own apartment and that of her sister. After months of illness, her younger sister died.

Phyllis packed up the apartments of her sisters and sorted through their belongings, making sure that her brothers, nieces and nephews received valued family treasures. She settled into her new life alone. Her brothers were married, had children and grandchildren, and were starting to retire. They lived in the southern and western parts of the metro. She saw them a couple of times a month and spent holidays with their families.

She continued at church and made some new friends in the high rise. For a while she was secretary to the resident's association. Then the city decided to allow younger persons to live at the high rise, and the proportion of older people decreased. Younger and angrier people moved in. The meetings were stressful, and it seemed that the older people did not get to speak any more. She stopped going to the meetings. She also stopped using the stairs. She was not sure who would be there or what would happen.

In fact, much of Northeast Minneapolis was changing. Phyllis used to do most of her shopping on Central Avenue. Now she does not shop there much anymore. There are new types of people there—people from other countries. She does not know what they sell or what she would do with the things she could buy there. She just does not know much about them, and this makes her uncomfortable.

Phyllis continues to live in her apartment with its walls covered with pictures of her father, mother, sisters, and brothers. She is especially fond of picture of a her parents. Her mother is beautiful. Her father is handsome and strong. She loves them and knew that they always wanted only the best for her. Pictures of her brothers and their families, taken up at the lake or on vacation, sit on end tables. She is proud of her nieces and nephews. They all are doing so well.

Phyllis still goes to church and never misses a Sunday service or a social event. Wednesday night services are a little harder to attend. Her friends do not get out much now. Many of her friends are often sick. Some have died.

One friend, in particular, is bed bound. She fell and broke her hip while out with Phyllis. Phyllis feels terrible about this and blames herself. She talked her friend into going out that day. She spends almost every morning at her friend's apartment, helping her get ready for the day. It is the least she could do.

Phyllis has lived most of her life in Northeast Minneapolis. She was born in a world before widespread use of automobiles and easy access to electricity and has lived through much change. All along this journey, she has had to cope with crises, such as the death of parents, grandparents, siblings and friends, economic stresses, wars and national emergencies, unfulfilled dreams, and declining health. As Phyllis has coped with these things, she has been enmeshed in a certain context. Part of this context makes up her "effective community," or that portion of her social world that is accessible to her as possible sources of support. In a positive sense, this effective community has been crucial to Phyllis' ability to weather crises and transitions. It is the source of instrumental, affective, and, often, spiritual support. Members of Phyllis' effective community have helped her find jobs, bury her parents, and reach decisions about housing options. They have offered shoulders to lean on and listening ears to her stories and concerns. There is also a negative side to "support." At times, members of her effective community have limited her and presented demands that were onerous and heavy. In negative or positive ways, they have made up her immediate social world, constituted the effective community in which she has lived, and helped determine the quality and direction of Phyllis' life.

Cities are filled with people like Phyllis. They are long-term residents in neighborhoods that have gone through and continue to go through massive change. These persons were born and raised in strikingly different social, cultural, and technological settings than those in which they now live. They have learned how to cope with challenges and changes brought on by crises, such as deaths of friends or family members, job losses, illnesses, or divorces. Part of this coping has entailed providing or receiving support from members of their effective communities. Yet these communities have been greatly affected by the many changes through which these persons have lived. Such changes have often altered the composition of these effective communities and the way help is given or received.

Understanding effective communities, how they are constructed and change, and the forces that shape them will allow us to understand something about the nature of aging in an urban neighborhood. In particular, the description and analysis of linkages with the surrounding social world will allow us to speak to how older persons are faring in this environment. As such, it will provide an understanding as to the changing nature of community in urban areas—communities that are in many ways constructed on the basis of interaction and networks built up through such interaction. Understanding effective communities will help us understand the ability of urban communities to be places of healing that provide the number and types of support needed by older persons facing transitions and crises. To be able to carry out this analysis and achieve this understanding, we need a useful model of community as it applies to the city.

Seeing urban communities

Community is used is many different ways by those who study urban life. It often refers to large scale social phenomena, such as the entire city. Bellah and Adams, for example, critique North American cities as valuing production over community and disregarding the nurturing of a moral dimension. They call for a recognition that cities need strong institutions to become communities that are more than

> just the free-floating groups banded together for narrow political gain, but an intelligent form of life requiring the constant engagement of its members in discussion and decision-making, in defining and redefining its goals and purposes. It is a context in which argument—even conflict— can occur, especially about how shared values will be actualized in every-day life, but within the bounds of a commitment to the common good. (Bellah and Adams 1994, 605)

Community, defined in this large sense, can be described in terms of values, institutions, beliefs, and practices and can be seen as constituting the context in which social interaction takes place. At an even higher, more diffuse level, the community is defined by a sense of presumed "likeness," or affinity. This is the imagined community and is defined by a sense of shared meaning and belonging (Calhoun 1991). Imagined communities could include persons who share an ethnic identity, those who claim to be evangelical Christians, persons labeled with a regional identification such as "Westerner," or the nation.

> Members of modern nations cannot possibly know all of their fellow-members, and yet in the minds of each lives the image of their communion...It is imagined as a community, because, regardless of the actual inequality

and exploitation that may prevail in each, the nation is always conceived as a deep, horizontal comradeship. In this view, members of a community internalize an image of the community not as a group of anomic individuals, but as interconnected members who share equally in their fundamental membership in the community. The internalization of the image and a sense of connectedness to the community is as important as actual physical presence in the community. (Chavez 1994, 54)

In the United States, and other large, complex societies, one's sense of identity and belonging is multi-dimensional. Ethnicity interacts with occupation, geography, religion, political life, and other social involvement to create an identity (Jabbour 1993). "Imagined communities" are constructed along these various dimensions. It is clear that a person may belong to a number of such imagined communities at any one time. For example, a person may simultaneously belong to communities defined by nationality, religious belief, professional identity, gender, and lifestyle. He or she could easily move back and forth between these communities in the course of his or her social life with little or no awareness and scarce acknowledgment of conflict or contradiction. Thus, we find conservative, evangelical women professing theological positions that define men as possessing God-given authority over women, while at the same time these women assume positions of power and authority in their professional lives with little sense of conflict or compromise.

These two large scale models of community are useful for understanding the nature of social and cultural life at their respective levels of analysis. However, at the level of the neighborhood and its residents, they do little to help us understand the nature of community defined in terms of support and interaction.

In this book, I am concerned with concrete, small scale communities defined by a sense of identity, belonging, and social interaction. That is, I am looking at communities through which resources flow that affect, in positive or negative ways, individuals who belong to these communities. Even with this more narrow focus, defining urban communities continues to be a difficult task because cities are complex social institutions made up of many kinds of persons and social institutions. They constitute difficult collages of ethnicity, occupation, class, lifestyle, and interests. Yet in the midst of all this we find that most persons build lives of meaning and find the support they need. Most people can identify a group of people whom they would recognize as constituting "their community." These are the persons whom they recognize as being potential candidates for interaction and with whom they share some similarities or interests.

Scholars have questioned whether the concept of community, in this sense, is useful for urban areas. It has been argued that urban life is isolated and fragmented and that the primary bonds of kinship and community have been replaced by secondary, more impersonal relationships (Mitchell 1969; Redfield 1947; Wirth 1947). Urban dwellers essentially are strangers to one another, and, from this viewpoint, city life is seen in negative terms as alienating and anti-community.

This argument has been attacked by those who discovered that communities do exist in the city. Ethnic neighborhoods were found that were homogenous, stable, and cohesive with little evidence of great social distance separating their residents. Urban dwellers were not found to be socially isolated and suffering from anomie. Indeed, some neighborhoods were almost villages in terms of their homogeneity and degree of interaction (Gans 1962). It is not surprising that many of these "urban villages" were discovered in central city neighborhoods in which there were Roman Catholic churches with strong ethnic identities.

> For millions of immigrant Catholics the national parish and parochial school were surrogate associations for the communal village they left behind. Ethno-religious institutions relieved their emotional stress, protected them from the dominant Protestant world, and facilitated their transition to American life. (Swierenga 1994, 131)

Some have turned this discovery of communities in more central city, urban areas into an argument that played one area of the city against another. One version of this states that central city ethnic neighborhoods are places where community is found and that suburban areas are places devoid of community and characterized by alienation, disengagement, and impersonal lifestyles. At times, this becomes quite moralistic, as in the following two examples.

> A prosperous family moving to its "Garden of Eden" sees its move as an individual issue, but the policies which made the move possible are anticommunity, creating suburbs and tearing up communities in the city. (Bakke 1987, 32)

> The gospel of community has always been a central theme of the Christian faith. Love that casts out fear, bearing one another's burdens, loving one's neighbor as one's self—these are the validating norms of historic Christianity. Yet, somewhere along the way to becoming the richest church in history, the gospel of community has faded into near obsolescence. We simply outgrew our need for it. Safety was dealt with through

suburbanization (the withdrawal of neighbors into isolated sanctuaries). Untidy borrowing/lending/sharing involvements were replaced by individualization (I've got mine; you get yours). Self-sufficiency became the measure for good stewardship. Elective therapy-style nurture groups provided intimacy-upon-demand, addressing our affiliation needs without the encumbrances of long-term relationships. (Lupton 1996, 3)

This claim that community does not exist in suburban areas is a mixture of political statement and intellectual blindness. It is akin to earlier arguments, such as Wirth's, that state that urban life was characteristically anomic and chaotic. It and other examples of failure to find community in some or all urban places point to the difficulty in defining urban community in such a way that it makes sense. The problem is that urban communities are constructed realities and take on many different forms. The one form that is easy to see is when people live and interact in neighborhoods that are well-bounded, village-like communities. This seems to conform to a notion of community which presumes homogeneous, seamless social unity. Some consider this sense of oneness to be essential to the nature of community.

The concept of "community" implies consensus. To say that someone is a leader of a community or that an organization is a community group, implies compatibility and unity rather than adversity, conflict, and discontinuity. (Jones 1987, 117)

A model of community that demands consensus and homogeneity has a long history and comes, at least in part, from our understanding of village life. Villages are places where one's entire social and cultural life could be lived out.

Socially, economically, and politically, it was a community…The medieval village…was the primary community to which its people belonged for all life's purposes. There they lived, there they labored, there they socialized, loved, married, brewed and drank ale, sinned, went to church, paid fines…Together they formed an integrated whole, a permanent community organized for agricultural production. (Gies and Gies 1990, 6–7)

The problem is that many, perhaps most, people who live in cities do not live in neighborhoods that conform to this picture of the urban village. They might know their neighbors and might even interact with them to some extent, but they also know and interact with a wide range of persons from other areas of the city. Furthermore, there are neighbors with whom they are not very neighborly and might not interact with at all. They might not even know who they are. Their lives are more dispersed and relationships are more single-stranded than those found in villages or village-like neighborhoods, but they are not living inordinately anomic, isolated, or fragmented lives. Instead, they often live in dispersed communities made up of intimate, primary relationships with other persons who come from neighborhood, church, kin, club, work, and a host of other places and situations in the city. That is, instead of living in geographically defined "villages," they create communities through the maintenance and activation of crosscutting, personal networks (Keefe 1980). Such communities are real and effective in meeting the needs of their members for identification, interaction, and support. Communities defined by interaction are probably more common in urban areas than the homogenous, village-like communities found in some neighborhoods. If community is only defined in terms of the village one is led to false conclusions about the nature of urban life and existence of urban communities.

Thus, to understand urban communities we need better models. These models need to take into account the fact that

> Individuals and groups are simultaneously involved in the structures, activities, and objectives of many different kinds of groupings which, on the surface, may appear contradictory...Thus ethnicity may conflict with class and occupational groupings, political subsystems may clash, trade union membership may accommodate itself to government demands to the disadvantage of the rank and file...Each of these sub-systems, therefore overlap....(Gutkind 1974, 65–66)

This reflects the basic nature of cities. With increasing urbanization, there is an increase in social complexity and cultural heterogeneity which gives the individual relatively more free choice in the selection of appropriate roles and behaviors (van Baal 1981, 283–284; Eames and Goode 1977, 39–42). Urban dwellers select others for their personal networks from the vast range of potential partners. Of course, this is not a totally free choice. It is conditioned by culturally shaped notions of familiarity and safety. Those who are not known by urban dwellers and included in their personal networks are strangers to them. This means that cities, on the whole, are collections of strangers where the overwhelming majority of persons in the city are unknown to one another (Merry 1981, 11–12).

Unfamiliarity often has the connotation of danger. In particular, in American cities unfamiliarity in the form of racial or ethnic differences has historically meant danger, exclusion, or stigmatization. Overt racism is no longer in vogue, but a more sophisticated yet still powerful form of marking danger, exclusion, or stigma is using the medium of cultural or national differences. Often, new immigrants are pointed to as disruptive or undesirable additions to an urban neighborhood because of presumed deep and unwelcome cultural differences (Stolcke 1995).

The mystery of urban life is that in the midst of this aggregate of strangers communities arise. Sometimes this is the village. More often it is a personal network, whose construction depends upon the individual's social status, cultural integration, and personal characteristics. Most importantly for this discussion, communities have the potential of providing rich sources of support and help when persons, particularly older persons, go through crises.

Social support and the older person

Family, friends, neighbors, and other informal sources of support have consistently been shown to be important to the well-being of older persons living in the United States (Comptroller General of the United States 1977; Froland et al. 1981; Stoller 1990; Wang 1979). Healthy social support networks have been shown to have clear linkages with health status and social functioning (Berkman 1983; Berkman and Syme 1979; Cohen et al. 1983; Cohen and Sokolovsky 1980; Eckert 1983; Gallo 1983; Sokolovsky and Cohen 1978). The reason this is so is not clear, and much debate has been concerned with the wisdom of and procedures for taking informal support into account when designing long-term care plans for older persons (Cantor 1983; Chapman and Pancoast 1983; Cohen and Adler 1984; Cohen and Adler 1986; O'Brien and Wagner 1980; Steinmetz 1981; Sussman 1985).

The blending and coordinating of informal and formal sources of support is of interest to many researchers. One set of concerns has to do with the way the formal service sector views and works with the informal sector. For example, the formal service sector is constrained by rules that set standards for professional and ethical work. This includes notions of professionalism that define who is and who is not eligible to give care and define the type of interaction that is appropriate between caregivers and clients. It also includes well-developed understandings of confidentiality and the rights of clients. These are often are at risk of being violated when working with informal sources of support (Chapman and Pancoast 1983).

Another set of concerns pertains to the effects of networks on the likelihood of a person to be served by the formal service system. For example, networks that are dense, highly active webs of interaction primarily be-tween kin-persons or networks that are small, scarcely active and mostly devoid of kin-persons decrease the likelihood that persons would know of and be able to access available services provided by formal sources of support (Chapleski 1989). The first does not have access to further resources that might be needed. The second does not allow the flow of information and help that is needed. There is much more that is needed to be known concerning the appropriate roles and interaction between various sources of support, both formal and informal, in social support networks. Two models have been proposed to explain this. The hierarchical-compensatory model suggests that the persons who play the primary roles at the center of the network are preferred as the source of a variety of types of help. The first choice is kin, followed by friends and then formal organizations. The task-specific model suggests that different sources in a support network will take on specific types of tasks. Connidis and Davies find some support for the task specific model when looking at informal sources of support.

> Children are more apt to be specialists as confidants, while spouses and friends predominate as companions...The most striking observations here are the greater dominance of a spouse in the companion than confidant network among the married, the greater dominance of children in the confidant than companion network among those with children, the greater dominance of friends in the companion than confidant network for all groups, and the greater dominance of siblings and other relatives in the confidant than companion network for all groups. (1990, s147)

Many questions remain concerning how informal sources of support fit into this mix. Although research indicates that formal and informal services complement, not substitute for or displace, one another (Connidis and Davies 1990; Olson 1994, 37), the results are still best seen as tentative. A real fear is that formal care might undermine contributions from infor-mal sources of support. The result would be a weakened social support network. On the other hand, informal care might either limit the appro-priate use of formal care or provide care that is actually detrimental to the well-being of older persons.

For a social support network to effectively help an older person through a crisis, there have to be members in that network who provide positive support. It is clear now that an earlier picture of the isolated, lonely older adult is wrong and that most older adults are enmeshed in relatively large social support networks (Atonucci 1985). Even those whom we suspect to be among the most isolated, such as residents of Single Resident Occupancy Hotels (SROs) in large cities or those with high levels of disability who have suffered the loss of age peers through death, have been shown to interact with others on a consistent basis (Johnson and Troll 1994; Sokolovsky and Cohen 1978).

These optimistic findings need to be tempered by recognition that, if we take age, ethnicity, and family situations into account, there are large differences in the nature and effectiveness of social support among older persons. Those persons who are childless suffer great risk of not receiving needed help.

> Although few respondents need care-giving help until their mid-eighties, by age eighty-five only thirty-six percent of the childless have a family caregiver or some relative potentially available to help. In comparison, eighty-eight percent of the parents have an available caregiver. More telling is the finding that sixty-one percent to sixty-four percent of the childless, irrespective of age, need help on a regular basis but have no one in their informal network to respond. In contrast, only twelve percent of the parents have problems meeting their needs. (Johnson and Troll 1996, 184)

Age differences among the elderly need to be looked at closely in this area. The oldest of the elderly population look very different from younger elderly persons. When extremely advanced age is combined with childlessness, there appears to be little likelihood that other family members will step in to provide the support that might have been provided by children. Ethnic differences have also been found to affect the likelihood of support. In particular, African American older persons seem to enjoy support from a wider array of persons, kin and non-kin than do Whites. This includes more distant relatives and fictive kin who carry out supportive roles often associated with children (Johnson and Troll 1996, 195).

There are many factors that affect the ability of older persons to interact effectively with others in their environment. Johnson and Troll argue that living in a changing neighborhood, widowhood, relocation late in life, having very old friends, reduced physical status, and having a troublesome personality all work to reduce the probability of having rich social support (1994, 83–84). In addition, many older persons suffer reduced financial statuses, making it more difficult to participate in wider social arenas where friends may be found. For many older persons living in urban neighborhoods, the construction and maintenance of social support networks becomes problematical if they are less able to take active roles in interaction with others and thereby "groom" their support networks. The result is social isolation, a deterioration of the older person's social support network, and an increased challenge to the well being of that person.

The importance for understanding these issues becomes more clear when we look at demographic and lifestyle changes in modern American life. The population of our society is rapidly aging, and the fastest growing segment of the population is made up of persons ninety years old and older. Daughters, who have traditionally provided the bulk of care for older persons, are increasingly unavailable as care-givers largely due to increased participation in the work force, fewer children born to women who are now in older age, higher incidence of divorce, and higher rates of mobility.

> Uncertainty involves the traditional support structures within family units (which are, and will likely remain, central to long-term care of elderly persons in the community). In the past, adult daughters were traditionally the ones who provided elderly parents with home care. Today's smaller families, however, eventually will disrupt this custom. Baby boomers, having produced so few offspring, will have few adult children to fill the caregiver role when they grow old next century. Moreover, these prospective caregivers—women now in their twenties—typically hold jobs already, leaving little time for those traditional home responsibilities. Intercohort trends strongly suggest that at least four-fifths of women now in their 20s will be in the labor force when their parents reach old age. Few will be inclined to quit a paying job to become an unpaid caregiver to an elderly parent if any other alternatives exist. (Morrison 1990, 403–404)

At the same time, other informal sources of help, such as neighbors and friends, are more problematical as urban areas become more diverse. Diversity can result in barriers to interaction. It also can mean that there are different cultural understandings and expectations concerning caregiving and receiving. Such differences can include the extent and efficiency of effective communities.

To help us assess the extent of these changes and understand the nature of support, we turn to the question as to why persons offer help to others. Daniels, in an essay on intergenerational responsibility, points to the lack of clear evidence for relying upon "natural feelings" or filial responsibility to persuade younger persons to sacrifice time or money to care for older persons.

> We remain without compelling foundations for filial obligations, even though it still may strike us as rational and fitting and praiseworthy that (most) children want to help their parents. Without such foundations,

however, we cannot specify the content and limits of filial obligations—
and it is clear, given today's demographics and social structure, that there
must be limits if such obligations exist at all. Without agreement on these
limits, filial obligations cannot be made the basis for laws enforcing family
responsibility. (1988, 34)

Furthermore, in a large, complex society, with substantial cultural diversity, there are diverse beliefs about what filial obligations entail. This
makes it difficult to construct social policy. In the United States, the solution has meant an increasing reliance upon publicly funded programs
designed to help older persons. This has not, however, led to a disappear-
ance of help given by family and other informal sources of help.

> In a racially and culturally diverse nation like the United States, official
> policy regarding the care of the elderly cannot be based on a common set
> of norms concerning the family's role in the care of its older members. In
> the United States, the federal government has assumed the major respon-
> sibility for insuring the economic welfare and physical health of the eld-
> erly through Social Security and Medicare. Yet despite this shift in financial
> responsibility, the family continues to provide the majority of day-to-day
> care for older members. (Angel and Angel 1997, xiv)

It is sometimes argued that there used to be a time when families cared
for aged parents in extended families and that the solution to present day
needs is to return to traditional values and social forms. Daniels correctly
points out that it is unlikely that such simple solutions would work due to
the massive demographic, economic, and social changes that have occurred.
It does not seem likely that the clock could be turned back to some mysti-
cal, "family friendly" age[2] (1988, 21–22).

Thus filial responsibility or "natural feelings" do not work to ensure
the proper level of support for older persons in need. Neither do they
explain much of the support that is actually given. A more profitable approach to explaining help giving is to see it as a form of social exchange with
a complete or partial absence of reciprocity. In such an exchange a person is
more likely to help someone without direct reward when the costs of such
help is relatively low, the person in need is seen to share close social distance
with the help giver, and the recipient of the help is seen to be "truly needy,"
in the sense of having a clearly defined need and not being be in a category
that would make the person unworthy to receive help (Schreck 1996).

Specific life circumstances greatly modify this for care-givers and re-
ceivers. For example, we know that wives are heavily invested in the care

of their husbands in time of need. This investment might have deleterious effects on their own support networks in that this often leads to a reduction of interaction with and support given to their own friends (Gallagher and Gerstel 1993). This then harms the ability of these women to stay connected with their own networks, thereby making it less likely that these networks will be strong sources of support when they need help.

As another example, older, childless women were found to have feelings of regret that emerged and intensified in later life. Although these women might have coped well with the many challenges of life and have rich, supportive social networks, as they aged they have reevaluated their own histories and experiences of childlessness. This often leads to the realization that children play unique roles in social support networks and are seen as "the only ones that can be relied upon to provide authentic, morally obligated care" (Alexander et al. 1992, 623).

Preferences and expectations for help are shaped by the larger sociopoltical-economic context. In a study carried out in Norway, the time period from 1969 to 1981 saw a substantial shift on the part of older Norwegians toward preference for help given by public services as opposed to help given by family members. This appears not to be due to a reduction in natural feelings or affection but rather to increased availability of public services and a more general social acceptance of such services. This was combined with a strong preference on the part of the elderly to not be a burden on their children. This shift occurred even though children continued to feel a strong obligation to help their parents in need (Daatland 1990). Edelman and Hughes, however, found that in a North American context the provision of services by formal services and informal caregivers had little effect on each other. Instead, they argue that formal and informal sources of support tended to supplement rather than substitute for each other (1990). Clearly, studies need to consider the larger context in which these decisions and preferences are found.

Friends and neighbors are also important sources of support for older adults. At times they are even preferred over formal sources of support (Smithers 1985). Some have argued that they may be taking increasingly central roles in the support networks of older persons.

> It seems safe to conclude that in American society at present, the family network for older people is only one of at least two support systems. Older friends and neighbors form the second and—on a daily basis, with routine kinds of events—may even form the central support system. Adult offspring feel as if they can be called in for assistance and support but the hope is they will never have to be. (Peterson 1989, 183)

Older adults continue to have positive and valued interaction with friends (Armstrong 1990). It is clear, however, that interaction between friends differs from that among family and kin. For example, some support, such as confiding and sick care, is often unreciprocated when given by children or spouses but rarely so when given by friends (Ingersoll-Dayton and Antonucci 1988).

The nature of help given by friends is modified by the nature of the family and kinship system in which the older person is immersed. In general, if there is a lack of available kin, friends act like kin, in terms of the type of help given and how it is given (Johnson 1988).

People living in cities are surrounded by neighbors who are often involved in providing support to one another. This seems to differ in character from support given by friends or kin-persons.

> Friendship is characterized by intimacy, closeness and mutual support...In contrast, neighbor relationships are characterized by availability, friendliness coupled with respect for privacy and an understanding of potential helpfulness. Relationships with neighbors are more instrumental than the expressive nature of friendship... Both friendship and neighborliness involve an assumption and expectation of reciprocity, but while reciprocity between friends is one-to-one, and may be long-term, reciprocity between neighbors is more generalized, may be serial, (i.e. to some other member of the neighborhood) and more likely to be short term. While friendship is basically a relationship of mutuality, empathy and involvement, neighborliness is a more distant relationship reflecting independence, sympathy and less involved concern. (Wenger 1990, 166)

A good neighbor is friendly and helpful, yet respect for privacy is important. They are important sources of help when there is a need for speed of response, dealing with problems that are based on shared territory, such as a troublesome neighbor, and requiring knowledge or information that is shared among neighbors. Neighbors often help one another, but they have no obligations to do so past norms of helpfulness or reciprocity. Furthermore, the reciprocity tends to be short term and balanced. Perhaps the most important contribution a neighbor provides is to keep an eye on his or her neighbors and become an informal early warning system for the detection of problems or signs of decline (Wenger 1990, 158–163). The operation of networks in times of change needs clarification. Social support networks provide buffers that enhance the possibility of coping with crises. For example, women who in their earlier years were involved in community clubs or associations tend to enjoy better health in later life

(Moen et al. 1992). The link here seems to be between strong social networks and health.

One challenge facing many older persons is their desire to live independently and avoid moving into long-term care facility when faced with the many challenges of aging. Pearlman and Crown found that nursing home placement was associated with the network characteristics of having a care-giving relationship of less than three year's duration and having a primary caregiver who is someone other than a spouse or an adult child (1992). Once a person moves into a nursing home, primary relationships, which are vital to healthy social support networks, are often damaged (Fisher and Tessler 1986; Greene and Monahan 1982). Density and reciprocity of social support networks prior to admission to long-term care facilities have been found to positively affect the duration of ties with relatives and closest others after entrance into long-term care facilities. Interestingly, neither had any effect of the duration of ties with friends (Bear 1990, s159).

Social support has been shown to be clearly associated with the well being of older persons. It also contributes to the ability of older persons to weather change. Not only is the older adult going through change, but the city itself is changing. These changes affect the very nature of community in which older persons live and age.

Community, urban change, and the older person

This book is set in Northeast Minneapolis and is focused on older persons who are life-long residents of this area. Established in the nineteenth century, Northeast Minneapolis was relatively stable through the first half of the twentieth century. A time of rapid change ensued at the end of World War Two and has continued to the present. Older persons who are long time residents of Northeast have seen changes in the cultural and ethnic mix, church life, and economic vitality of the area. Many older persons have seen their roles go from elders of the tribe to "those who have been left behind" as their potential sources of support disappear. A general pattern is that many in the generation following these long-term residents have left Northeast Minneapolis for new housing in suburban parts of the city. In addition, many friends and neighbors who are contemporaries of these older persons have also moved out to suburbs. This pattern is not at all unique to Northeast Minneapolis.

> Most intermetropolitan and rural-urban moves made by the elderly have their destinations in suburban locations. At the intraurban level, as well,

the flow from the central city to the suburbs in the 1970s was approximately three times that of the reverse flow. (Clark and Davies 1990, 432)

Those older persons who live in central city locations differ significantly from those who live in suburbs. In central cities, it is common to find "gray ghettoes" of disadvantaged older persons who are poor and heavily dependent on friends and relatives (Clark and Davies 1990, 433). Older persons who have had more financial success tend to be move out of central city neighborhoods more often than those who are less fortunate. However, depending upon the conditions of life in the particular neighborhood, there is strength in staying in place and being a long-term resident of a neighborhood.

> The social context in which the very old individuals live determines their social resources and their ease of access to friends, neighbors, and community associations....If respondents stayed in the same neighborhood most of their adult lives, and if the neighborhood has remained stable and homogenous, their neighbors can be friends of long standing. They may have shared membership in the same churches and clubs over many years...where neighborhoods changed to a more heterogeneous population, however, friendship with neighbors generally declined. (Johnson and Troll 1994, 83)

Cities are clearly highly dynamic places where major shifts in ethnic composition can occur. This often entails a younger population moving into an area in which an older population already lives. The generational divide separating the two populations opens up a myriad of possibilities for misunderstandings and distrust. Rosenbaum and Button analyzed items from a 1990–1991 Florida public opinion poll having to do with young persons' perceptions of older adults and their cost or benefit to society. They found that

> [there was] a very substantial proportion of younger respondents, ranging from roughly a third to more than half this group, who agreed to a variety of statements suggesting that older residents in their county or city were variously an economic burden, an economically selfish voting bloc, a generationally devised influence, or an unconstructive community element (1993, 488).

When a generational divide also entails ethnic differences between the older and younger populations there are even more risks for misunderstanding, mutual mistrust, and conflict. In some areas, such as California, intergenerational mistrust is happening on such a massive scale that some are calling for the development of a social policy that promotes intergenerational and inter-ethnic justice and interaction (Hayes-Bautista et al. 1988). In other areas, it is happening on a more localized level. In either case, the result can be increased social isolation of older persons.

Angel and Angel point to this danger in terms of the national population:

> The huge preponderance of ethnic whites in the older population hints at what could become a major social problem in the years to come. In the future a larger fraction of the working-age population will consist of blacks and Hispanics, while the older population will remain predominantly non-Hispanic white. It is possible, therefore, that racial and ethnic resentments could override age as a potential source of conflict between the generations, as a white gerontocracy draws upon the resources of a relatively poor black and Hispanic working class. (1997, 4)

It is precisely in cities that the possibility of this cultural and generational divide is most likely to happen. Thus, the scenario painted by the Angels could very well be and, indeed, is taking place in many urban neighborhoods at the current time.

These changes have meant that many older persons are often isolated at a time when they need strong, supportive communities. It has been argued that aging is deeply affected by forces and events in the larger social and cultural context. In addition, aging is a process that involves changes at both the personal and interpersonal level. A perspective that has been developed to account for these changes at various levels is the Life Course Perspective.

The life course perspective and the city

Aging is a process that begins at birth and continues through to death. Along the way, a person is shaped by genetic inheritance, nurturing and early childhood experiences, cultural values and rules, social pressures and forces, physical changes and challenges, personal choices and decisions, accidents, and vicissitudes of all types. In this dynamic and interactive process, the environment both affects and shapes the person and, in turn, the person affects and changes the environment. In Northeast Minneapolis, persons who are older and are life-long residents have had a complex relationship with the surrounding neighborhood.

We need to see aging as a continuum in which persons have lived out their daily lives and faced and met crises over their lifespan (see Figure 1.1). In this process, they have relied upon and used their skills, attitudes, knowl-

FIGURE 1.1: *Aging in context*

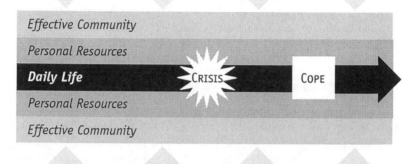

LARGER SOCIO-ECONOMIC-POLITICAL-SPIRITUAL-CULTURAL CONTEXT

Ethnicity   Events   Social Policies

Effective Community

Personal Resources

Daily Life   CRISIS   COPE

Personal Resources

Effective Community

Housing   Jobs   Gender

LARGER SOCIO-ECONOMIC-POLITICAL-SPIRITUAL-CULTURAL CONTEXT

edge, and inner strength. As the long-term residents who are the focus of this book lived out their lives in Northeast Minneapolis, they have interacted with and given and received support from other persons and various institutions. This has made up their effective community, or that portion of the surrounding social world to which the person is connected either directly in primary, personal ties or more indirectly in secondary ties. All of this has taken place in the larger spiritual, socio-cultural, economic, and political context that defined their worlds in Northeast Minneapolis. The life course perspective offers a powerful conceptual model to help us understand aging in such a context.

The Life Course Perspective model was developed in the 1970s to investigate the context in which aging takes place, the interrelationship between the different age stages of a person's life, and the specific events and occurrences that have helped shape the aging process.

> Three life-course themes are relevant: timing, process, and context. Timing relates to the incidence, duration, and sequence of roles throughout the life course....Process focuses on aging as a series of role transitions rather than as a single event....Context, in terms of the personal circumstances of women's lives—their education, marital status, and family size,

as well as their age.…The life-course perspective offers no simple interpretation of the relationship between social integration earlier in life and health in the later years of adulthood. Rather, it suggests that the connection be viewed as a dynamic, and possibly cumulative, process, wherein the roles individuals occupy in early adulthood play out in patterns of involvement over the life course that, in turn, sustain health. (Moen et al. 1992, 1612–1638)

The life course perspective helps us see aging within a larger context. It helps us understand the cumulative advantage that some persons have when favored because of fortuitous positions in terms of class, ethnicity, or gender. It is telling to note that those persons who were so favored early in their lives enjoy substantial advantages throughout their entire lifetimes over those less favored. These advantages are even further extended in oldest age (O'Rand 1996). Three types of developmental processes are taken into account in the Life Course Perspective. First, all cultures give significance to age as a way of assigning roles to its members. Persons of a particular age, or within a range of ages, are expected to behave accordingly. In North American society, persons recognize that there are certain ages at which persons should go through transitions, such as marriage or having children. There seems to be less clarity about the consequences for missing these transitions (Settersten and Hagestad 1996). This might be an expression of American individualism. With strongly held models of individual efficacy and independence it is difficult to recognize social or group phenomena. Many Americans recognize that they pass through life stages, but they see these only in individualistic terms, failing to see cultural or social patterns and sanctions.

Expectations of age appropriate roles create a series of age grades that are marked off, to varying degrees of distinctiveness, in different cultures. Some cultures have very clear markers, whereas others have less distinct markers. In North American society there are clear markers for the earlier age grades and less clear markers for later ones. Yet the age grade system of a society does set up a set of expectations and helps to define the aging process for its members.

A second developmental process has to do with change taking place in the surrounding society. A person is a member of a cohort of persons born around the same time. As this cohort ages, it experiences similar historical changes and forces. Members of this cohort age in ways that are shaped by these changes and forces. This social nature of aging has been modeled as a "social career," in which cultural patterns and individual variation intersect to create the social process of aging (Humphrey 1993). This developmental process interacts with the first type discussed above, a culturally defined series of age grades, in that the actual age grades themselves are shaped by this historical process and can be somewhat specific to a cohort and the era in which it ages. For example, someone in the second decade of life is supposed to be an adolescent. This is seen as a time of growth, exploration, and relative freedom from responsibility. In the first part of this century, adolescence stopped earlier than it does today. Except for the few who could afford to consider post-secondary education, persons in their late teens were expected to enter the job market. At that time they left adolescence and assumed new adult roles. Today this is much less common. Young adults are assumed to be in the adolescent stage of exploration well into their early twenties.

The third developmental process is the individual life experience of the person him or herself. Each person's aging process is unique. A person's physical endowments and challenges, social successes or failures, specific familial and larger cultural milieu, individual choices, and a myriad of other forces and events shape that person and his or her aging process.

The Life Course Perspective model captures these three processes and allows us to see aging as a dynamic, highly interactive process. In this study I looked at the lives of twenty one persons as lived out in Northeast Minneapolis. Since they come from the same general cultural setting, we could expect them to share similar notions of age grades and age appropriate behavior. Furthermore, we might expect them to have learned these notions in the course of being socialized to the culture as they were growing up. Yet older persons who are living today are much more active, generally healthier, and enjoy more financial security than persons who were older when these persons were in their twenties. Age grades and expectations linked to age have changed. Older persons generally expect to be more independent and active today compared with older persons my informants knew when they were young adults. As these older persons have aged in place in Northeast Minneapolis, they have gone through a complex process wherein their understanding of cultural patterns of aging have been shaped by their early socialization and modified throughout their lifetimes as they have been affected by larger social and cultural changes surrounding them. As we look at life in Northeast Minneapolis in the present time, we would expect older persons to have a different understanding of the aging process than those younger persons currently living around them who have not had the same experiences.

The persons whom I interviewed have lived through the same general time period and have remained in the same general social environment of Northeast Minneapolis. There is substantial intra-group variation, however. Firstly, their ages range over a period of twenty-five years. The oldest persons were born in the late 1800s or early 1900s. Younger persons were born in the post World War One era. Conditions in Northeast were strikingly different in these two eras, as we shall see later in this book. Secondly, they lived in different parts of Northeast Minneapolis. In Northeast Minneapolis, residence was closely associated with ethnicity. Those who came from Lower Northeast were often from strong Slavic communities, and others who came from Upper Northeast were more often from areas with ethnicity traced to northern Europe. Lastly, differences in social class adds variability. Persons living Lower Northeast tended to be a bit poorer than those living in Upper Northeast. What this all means is that even within this sample of twenty one persons who were born over a relatively short period of time we can expect to see some differences in their aging processes.

Lastly, individual life experiences and choices affect persons deeply. This is certainly the case with persons in this study. For example, Irene described how her life course was altered dramatically by divorce such that she had vastly different experiences than those women in her neighborhood who did not go through a divorce.

Irene's Story

It must have taken strong reasons to leave all that is familiar and move to a new, unknown land. Poverty is a strong reason. Many young, single persons left Poland in the 1890s to travel by themselves to a place called Minneapolis. They had little knowledge of what they would find. Irene's father was the first to arrive. He was thirty three years old. Her mother came at the age of sixteen. They traveled separately and had not known each other before they met in Minneapolis. They met after both had lived in Northeast Minneapolis for some time. Both fled poverty and bleak futures in Poland and were drawn to America by the dream of the "Golden Land." America offered hope and a future they had not seen in Poland.

Although neither arrived with much money, English skills, or formal education, they came with two essential resources—the names of relatives and a strong willingness to work. The names gave them places to stay in Northeast Minneapolis. Irene's mother lived with her second cousin. Her father lived with his sister. This placed them both solidly in the midst of a strong Polish community clustered around Holy Cross Catholic

Church. Their willingness to work was quickly put to use as jobs were abundant in this fast growing, industrial city.

Irene's mother worked at the Maryland Hotel on Hennepin Avenue. An Italian restaurant and apartment building are now located there. Since she did not speak English, she could not be a waitress. She washed dishes. The conditions were difficult in the kitchen. Wood stoves were used for cooking. There was little ventilation in the kitchen, and in the summer it would be so hot that some of the women would pass out. Irene's mother said that they were lucky because passing out was the only way any of the kitchen staff was able to rest. Otherwise trying to sit down and rest would bring on the ire of the supervisor who would loudly curse them out for being lazy. It was slave labor and low pay, but for Irene's mother it was a start. She had free meals and made enough money to pay room and board.

Irene's father was hired as a mattress maker. He worked at a company on East Hennepin where he and the other workers made mattresses by hand. They used long needles to sew the mattresses after the covers had been stuffed with cotton. Although some mattresses were made with new materials, much of the work was renovating used mattresses. Many were dirty. People had died on some of the mattresses. Like many fellow workers, Irene's father contracted tuberculosis. Irene suspects the cause was renovating mattresses of persons who died of that disease.

Within two years after Irene's mother had arrived, she met her future husband. They shared the same religious beliefs, spoke the same language, and were involved in the Polish Catholic community centered on Holy Cross Catholic Church. Since there was more to unite them than to divide them, they decided to marry. Soon after their marriage they had a house built in Northeast Minneapolis close to University and 20th Street near Holy Cross Catholic Church and many other Polish immigrants.

Irene was born on December 30, 1918, in the same house in which she now lives. She was the third of four children. As with most births in her neighborhood, there was a midwife in attendance. Midwives were often neighbor women who had themselves given birth a number of times. Experience was their only training. Irene's midwife was a Russian immigrant who lived across the street. Irene was born during the 1918 influenza epidemic. Many persons were dying. Irene's mother was sick with the flu at the time of her birth. The family was concerned for the health of this new baby. Both mother and baby were strong and survived.

Irene was born in a Polish immigrant world. Most of her friends were Polish Catholic. Many of the families, including Irene's , spoke only Polish at home. This was America, however, and there were clear expectations from the larger society that these new immigrants should become Americans. This included learning to speak English. Irene's parents, like most of the adults in the area, attended night school to learn English and study for citizenship tests. Eventually, her parents learned English, yet they always retained a strong Polish accent. The children, who grew up speaking Polish at home, quickly learned English. They heard and used it when playing with their neighborhood friends, at programs at the neighborhood park and the Neighborhood House, and in school.

Holy Cross Catholic Church was the center of life for this Polish immigrant community. Irene's family attended but was not as active in church activities as those who were more prominent as parish leaders. Irene's mother complained that the church was run by cliques, and Irene's parents felt like outsiders in a church run by "big shots" with more money and bigger houses. The church leaders were often the owners of neighborhood stores and businesses. Within the church, they were leaders of many groups such as the various sodalities, the Mother's Club, the Holy Name Society, and the usher corps.

If the church was the center of Polish culture, Northeast Neighborhood House, one of the many settlement houses in the Twin Cities, and Bottineau Park, the neighborhood park, were centers of American culture. These were used heavily by Irene and her friends. She participated in cooking, dancing, and drama lessons and played basketball, volleyball, baseball, and tennis at Neighborhood House.

Irene knew everybody in the neighborhood. She knew their names, ethnic backgrounds, and what was happening to the various families in the neighborhood. The neighborhood was a well known, safe place. Although most of the adults were immigrants from Poland, there were other non-Polish families. Slovaks attended St. Cyrils of Methodius Catholic Church, and "Russians" went to St. Mary's and St. John's. Children of all background freely played together. Irene's friends included children from Polish, Slovakian, and Russian families. Ethnicity did not separate them but did offer material for teasing and jokes.

Irene's world was a small one. Almost everything was within walking distance. Shopping was done locally. There was a grocery store just a block down on University. Another grocery store was just a short distance away on 2nd Street and 22nd. The first grocery store sold meat which was prepared by a butcher who worked at the store. The second only sold groceries. There were neighborhood drug stores. Four blocks away, on 4th Street and 17th Avenue, there was a small clothing store. There was little need to shop outside the neighborhood. The store owners lived in the neighborhood, so customers and merchants knew each other well.

Many other services came directly to the house. The "Raleigh Man" sold ointments, salve, and liniment, and the "Watkins Man" sold spices. Irene's mother used lineament as a cure all. Coal was delivered to the house. It was dumped it in the driveway and then shoveled through a basement window leading to a coal bin. The workers would be black from coal dust and used to tease the children by trying to hug and kiss them. This sent the children away screaming.

Central Avenue was not visited often by those in Irene's neighborhood. Ten blocks was too far to walk. Besides, Central Avenue stores did not have much that could not be obtained in the neighborhood. Practicality reigned, as Irene pointed out, "Who is going to haul a couple bags of groceries [ten blocks]? My mother used to buy flour by the fifty pound sacks. That wasn't the kind of stuff you liked to haul."

Irene attended preschool at Northeast Neighborhood House. From the beginning, she loved school. Kindergarten followed at Schiller Elementary School at California and 27th. When she reached first grade she switched to parochial schools. She attended at Holy Cross where she finished eight years of elementary school there. Holy Cross required students to learn to read, write and spell in Polish and English. They also learned to read and pray in Latin. It would have been hard to fit in at Holy Cross if one were not of Polish heritage. Holy Cross had high standards and demanded much work from the students. This paid off. When Irene attended Edison High School she excelled and was named to the National Honor Society.

She chose Edison High School over vocational school because she wanted an academic education. She was practical, however, and enrolled in secretarial classes while at Edison.

Irene enjoyed Edison and made friends from all parts of Northeast. She soon saw that the students who lived east of Central Avenue seemed to have more money and wore more fashionable clothes and shoes. She felt poor for the first time in her life. Irene was determined to prove herself equal to them and remembered that "I couldn't see that they were any better than I was. They all had one head, and two arms and two legs."

Graduation was a big deal for Irene. She liked wearing a cap and gown. There was a senior prom where Irene wore her first formal dress. When the ceremonies were over she found she had graduated right in the middle of the Depression. It was 1936. Work was hard to find. College was out of the question for her. It was only for the wealthy.

After some time, Irene found employment doing housework for a Jewish couple who lived in South Minneapolis. She cleaned house, washed and ironed clothes, and cooked supper. She was able to eat there, and after cleaning up from supper she would return to sleep at her parents' house. The food was better there than she had ever eaten. They had enough money to buy good, expensive food. They had Matzo bread. She had never seen it before and would eat it with jelly, even though her employer told her that was not the way to eat it. Irene enjoyed working for them. They were only in their twenties and were nice to her. The women gave Irene her castoff clothes, which were very fashionable.

After working there one year, Irene was hired at the Strutwear Factory, which made lingerie and knit clothes. She operated huge knitting machines. The room in which she worked was filled with many co-workers attending machines which were fed by spools of thread. Often the threads would break, and Irene and her co-workers would have to tie the ends of the threads together. The machines could not be shut down. As the women attempted to retie them the fine silk threads would run through their fingers causing many small, cuts. It was hard work and the conditions were dirty and smelly. She made eight dollars a week. Although this was three dollars more than she made doing housework, Irene hated working there.

All of the workers attending the machines were women. There was one man who worked on the floor. He was the supervisor. If he thought someone was wasting time or slowing down he would shout at the worker to speed up. It was worse than being disciplined in school. After three months the boss asked her how she liked working there. She said, "I hate it here. The minute I can get an office job I am leaving." The next pay check came with termination papers.

Irene then found work in a typing pool at Pillsbury Flour Mills. Her secretarial courses had finally paid off. She typed eight hours a day in a large room filled with many female typists and a male supervisor. He sat at a desk, like a teacher in high school, and watched the women work. If someone stopped typing for a minute he would come up and ask, "Don't you have anything to do?"

Meanwhile, Irene continued to live at home. She was the only child still living there. She gave half of her pay to her mother to help with household expenses. One brother had been drafted into the Army. Her other brother and sister were married and lived elsewhere in Northeast Minneapolis. These were good years. Even though it was the tail end of the Depression, Irene was hardly aware of it. Once she had a job, she did not lack anything. Irene continued to participate in sports, such as hiking, skating, skiing, and tennis. She loved tennis and played with a girlfriend that lived next door. They were good. She stopped playing after she began to date the man she eventually married. She played against her future husband once. Unfortunately, she won, and he refused to play again.

On October 18, 1941, Irene married. Her husband soon left for military service and was gone, with one brief furlough, until 1945. Irene continued to live with her parents. Pillsbury would normally terminate employment for women once they were married, but the war was on and many men were leaving for military duty. This created a labor shortage in Northeast. Pillsbury allowed her to continue to work. She became pregnant after her husband's furlough, however, and Pillsbury forced her to resign.

Her first child, a daughter, was born in 1942. Irene was fortunate in that her daughter was born within nine months of the time she left Pillsbury. This meant that her insurance was obligated to cover the birth. Irene only had to pay two dollars. This included ten days of hospital stay.

After her daughter was born, Irene moved in with her sister and brother-in-law in Southeast Minneapolis, at her sister's request. She soon was hired at a real estate office. This was an ideal job since it was close enough to walk to work. She worked there until the end of the war. In 1945 her father died, and her husband came home.

Her husband found a job in South St. Paul. Irene and her husband bought a bungalow nearby. This was a good time. The neighborhood was filled with young people just like Irene and her husband. Irene quit work and was a full time housewife. Her second child, a son, was born in 1947. The women in the neighborhood had much in common. They all had young children and would often get together for social events.

Irene's life was on the path she had expected to follow. In 1950, everything changed when her husband announced that he wanted a divorce. Irene and her two children moved in with her mother in a small, two room flat on the second floor of her mother's house. She made contact with her former boss at the real estate office who immediately offered her employment. She accepted and worked for him until 1970.

In 1950 the community looked down on divorce. The church in which she had grown up and become active was now a place of pain. Even though she felt the sting of rejection and condemnation, Irene decided she was going to survive. She joined various clubs at the church in spite of obvious disapproval on the part of many other women. She remembers that she "…didn't care what they thought. I figured the ones that didn't like me, so what. They weren't the church. They were just some people in it." Even though many of her friends dropped her and discontinued their friendships, she kept some old friends and began to make new ones through her involvement in various social clubs and activities.

As a divorced mother of two, she worked hard. No help came from her husband, "When he [her husband] divorced, he divorced us all. So, I took care of the kids." Irene did not even think of applying for any type of governmental support, "My son and daughter were my children, and I had to take care of them." Days were long. She worked all day at the office and then would come home to wash clothes, make supper, clean house, and help the children with their homework. Finally, she would read to them and put them to bed. In the morning she started all over again by making breakfast, sending her children to school, and going back to work. Sunday was a family day when the three would go to a lake to swim or on a picnic.

Irene was helped immensely by her family. Her younger brother was single and lived downstairs with Irene's mother. He was the surrogate father for the kids. In fact, Irene's son went into heating and air conditioning work, just as her brother. Irene's mother took care of the children when they would come from school until Irene came home from work.

Irene's brother lived downstairs until Irene's mother died in 1968. Her brother then married and moved to a different house but continued the close relationship with Irene and her children. The children eventually graduated from high school, married, and now live in the Twin Cities. In fact, her son and his family live on the first floor of the house in which Irene was born, in which she has lived most of her life, and where Irene continues to live in the second floor apartment that was prepared for her after the divorce in 1950.

In 1970, her boss at the real estate office was close to eighty years old. Irene realized she was fifty two and needed work longer than her boss could continue his business. She began to look for a new, more secure job and took a test to qualify to employment with Hennepin County. She did well. Irene was offered two different secretarial positions. She accepted a position as a secretary to the head of the juvenile probation office. Later she transferred to the domestic relations division where she supervised thirteen clerical workers. On March 20, 1984, she retired.

Retirement has been good. At first she had little to do and went on a "cleaning frenzy." She soon found many activities to keep her busy. She tutored at the local school, joined a hiking club, and continues to meet regularly with friends. One of her favorite activities has been traveling. She takes one grandchild on every trip. She took the oldest granddaughter to Hawaii and others to California and Florida. On a trip to Poland she reconnected with her heritage and found that she still was fairly fluent in Polish.

As Irene looks around her current neighborhood, she notes that those she knew as a young child are all gone. Some of them are dead. Others have moved. She does not know the new neighbors. They are younger. They work. There is no reason to interact, but she thinks that most of them are just about the same as those who lived there earlier. Most are homeowners. There is one rental across the street, however. The renters have been a source of complaints. Sometimes they have all night, loud parties. Yet most people in the neighborhood are still solid and hard working. They probably earn more today than those who lived there when she was growing up, but everything costs more. They have better education and training and do not have to work at menial jobs.

Irene thinks that people in Northeast are not as aware of ethnicity today compared to when she was growing up. She does not know the nationality of the people next door. When she was younger she knew the ethnic background of every family. The neighborhood is still a good place to live, but she is more cautious and does not go out at night. Still, she is not afraid to live in Northeast. This has been her home for a long time, and she will continue to make it so.

Irene's life took a predictable path until 1950. She had followed a normal life course for a woman born in her situation. She veered off course when she divorced. This was relatively rare in 1950 and seen as an error, aberration, or personal failure. In her own words, Irene was "stigmatized." This event shaped the rest of her aging process. She was excluded from many activities that drew mothers and wives. She lost some of her friends. On the positive side, she became more independent and was deeply enfolded into a circle of support provided by her mother and siblings. She now feels deep satisfaction with her life. She is close to her children and siblings. Irene is a participant in clubs and associations that interest her. She weathered the crisis of divorce and came out stronger. Her personal strength and the support of her family helped her through. As we look at Irene's life, we can see how the three developmental forces of culturally prescribed life stages, historical change, and personal experiences have worked together to shape her aging process.

The life course perspective helps us pull together the concepts of social support, urban change, and patterns of care giving and receiving. The task remaining is to investigate these issues through the lives of older persons who are life long residents of Northeast Minneapolis. The central question is whether the patterns that have been learned and that have been effective over a lifetime can continue to be effective today.

Researching the lives of older persons in Northeast Minneapolis

The monograph is based on an ethnography of aging in Northeast Minneapolis. The purposes of the research have been to arrive at a richly contextualized understanding of the matrices of social support in which older persons live, the ways in which older persons interact with and groom their social support networks, the contribution of local churches to the lives of older persons, and the way this has changed over time. Further, the impact on social support by neighborhood level and larger social and cultural changes has been of interest and a focus of the research.

This is a continuing project. I first started working in Northeast Minneapolis in the fall of 1993 as a participant observer. I am still involved in this and have been able to work in a wide range of settings and formats, including attending various meetings and functions in the area, giving community service presentations in nursing homes, ministerial meetings, and service club luncheons, volunteering at local agencies, and interacting with people from Northeast in more informal settings. As I have continued to work in this area, I find that I have moved into a set of roles that include being a friend to some and researcher and consultant to others. In all this, I have tried to situate my work in such a way that I frequently bring the results of the work back to the community in appropriate ways. This has included writing reports, giving addresses and presentations, and sharing results in many conversations with a wide variety of persons in Northeast Minneapolis.

Cities are rich places in terms of interaction, institutions, plans and programs, cultures and subcultures, and schemes of all types. In North America, a highly literate and technological society, there is also the added richness of documentation and publications. I have carried out archival research with newspapers, church records, high school annuals and accounts of class reunions, and personal papers.

The work has also entailed numerous interviews and conversations with various persons living in Northeast. A specific effort that is relied upon for this book is a survey I conducted with the thirty-five churches in the area (fourteen Roman Catholic, nineteen Protestant, and two Orthodox). This was followed with focus groups with key leaders in local churches. The focus of these activities was the types, range, and nature of church-based programs of assistance and advocacy for older persons.

During this time period I have taught an undergraduate qualitative methods course four times in the spring semesters of 1993, 1994, 1996, and 1997. The courses focused on Northeast Minneapolis. These classes have worked in partnership with churches in Northeast Minneapolis that have wanted to better understand their neighborhoods. In the course of this research, students have carried out observations, conducted interviews, facilitated focus groups, and used surveys. Their work has been collected into four volumes of papers. Copies of these have been given to the partner churches. This work has produced valuable data and insights into Northeast Minneapolis, and some of it is incorporated in this monograph.

The primary data for this particular monograph has come from life history interviews with long time residents of Northeast Minneapolis. I worked intensively with twenty one persons (described in Figure 1.2). In these interviews I asked persons about their lives, their expectations of aging, and the matrices of social support in which they had lived. These interviews entailed from two to six meetings. I took extensive notes and tape-recorded the sessions. These were later transcribed. I then compiled the notes for each person, edited them for coherency and sensitivity, and gave each person a copy of his or her interview. I asked the persons interviewed to correct mistakes and return these to me. I then made corrections, as appropriate, and returned final copies to them.

This work has generated a wide range of data, from stories to statistics. The data is used to tell the stories of these persons and to place their stories into a larger context. The goal of this is to better understand the reality of aging in Northeast Minneapolis in terms of care-giving and receiving during times of need or crisis. This study examines these issues through the lives of older persons who have lived most, if not all, of their lives in Northeast Minneapolis. The next four chapters focus on the four eras of life of these persons in Northeast Minneapolis. Following these chapters, the attention turns to a consideration of care-giving and receiving and how it has changed over time in the lives of these persons and others in Northeast Minneapolis. Finally, I look at the lessons that have been learned from this exploration.

FIGURE 1.2: *Characteristics of long term residents who were interviewed for life history research*

Ages	68 to 96 (1927 to 1899)
Gender	10 men and 11 women
Ethnicity	Austro-Hungarian, French Canadian, German, Lithuanian, Polish, Russian, Slovakian, Swedish
Immigrant Status	16 are 1st generation born in USA 5 are 2nd or more (3 are 2nd)
Neighborhoods	3 north of Lowry and west of Central 3 north of Lowry and east of Central 8 south of Lowry and west of Central 6 south of Lowry and east of Central
Marital Status	4 have never been married 9 are presently married 7 are widows or widowers
Time in Northeast	1 moved to Northeast at 2 1 moved to Northeast at 18 (from Mora) 1 moved to Northeast at 18 (from North Minneapolis) 18 were born in Northeast

Chapter 2

Early Beginnings

The city of Minneapolis straddles a waterfall. In fact, its height at sixty five feet makes the Falls of St. Anthony the most severe drop in the entire course of the Mississippi River. This waterfall was long known, revered, and respected by Native Americans, the first and most long standing inhabitants of this area. Their appreciation of the waterfall was not for its commercial purposes, as it was for Euro-Americans who were late arrivals to the area. The aspects of it that drew the attention of Native Americans can be seen in the names they gave it. The Chippewa called it *Kakabikah* (the severed rock). The Lakota called it *Minirara* (curling water) or *Owahmenah* (falling water) (Kane 1987, 2).

In 1680, it was named the Falls of St. Anthony of Padua by the first European to see the falls, Father Louis Hennepin, a Recollet Priest from the Spanish Netherlands (now Belgium). He named the falls in honor of his ecclesiastical province. Given the settlement of this area by Euro-Americans and resultant political and economic domination of Native Americans, St. Anthony Falls became the permanent name and the more descriptive, colorful names were lost (Hazel 1977, 5).

St. Anthony Falls turned out to be one of those vital assets that birthed a city. It defined the upper limits of practical navigation by large steamboats on the Mississippi. Milled wheat and other grains from the upper midwest and sawn lumber from the extensive pine forests of northern

Minnesota were shipped from the loading docks of Minneapolis' twin city sister, St. Paul, to the rest of the nation and many other areas of the world. Most importantly for St. Anthony itself, it provided an abundant source of power for flour mills and saw mills. These, in turn, provided jobs.[1]

After Father Louis Hennepin, further Euro-American settlement and development waited almost two hundred years until the first white settler, Franklin Steele, built a log house in 1837 on the east bank of the Mississippi at the foot of the bluffs opposite the falls. In 1848, Steele and David Stanchfield established the first lumber mill at the falls, and the rush was on (Hazel 1977, 8). By 1850, fifty Whites had settled near the falls on the east side of the river. The city of St. Anthony quickly grew on the east bank of the Mississippi. Minneapolis formed on the west bank. Industry, based on water power, was established and urban growth took off. From its very beginning, Northeast Minneapolis, as St. Anthony was soon to be called, was a Euro-American city. Native Americans, long time residents of the area, were barely acknowledged by those building this new, industrial city. This was a Euro-American reality that can be traced back to 1837 when the Sioux and Chippewa Indians ceded by treaty all land between the St. Croix and Mississippi Rivers to the United States government, which was the same year Franklin Steele built his house near the falls. The full transition to this new reality is evidenced by the fact that none of my informants, of the earliest of whose memories reached back to within ten years of the turn of the century, recalled Native Americans living in or traveling through Northeast Minneapolis.

Population growth came from the inflow of persons seeking work. Some of the earliest were French Canadians. In the first census of St. Anthony, conducted in September, 1850, there were 600 persons, most of whom were French Canadians (Hazel 1977, 8). Already a dynamic was set in place that continues to this day. In the minds of the business elite, those who owned and financed the mills, the New England manufacturing town was the model for this fast growing city. Their intentions were that St. Anthony was to be solidly in the mainstream of American cultural life as defined by Anglo-oriented New England.[2] Many of the arriving workers were outside of that cultural tradition. They came from Ireland, French Canada, Germany, Italy, and many areas in eastern Europe and moved into neighborhoods in which they built churches, spoke languages, and interacted in ways that did not closely conform to the "all American" ideal of the business elites who were building the city.

St. Anthony grew rapidly. The first church, St. Anthony of Padua Catholic Church, was established in 1849, and the first newspaper, the weekly *St.*

Anthony Express, was published on May 31, 1851. The city of Minneapolis, its west bank rival, soon outpaced St. Anthony. In 1872, the two consolidated, and St. Anthony became a part of Minneapolis. It was renamed Northeast Minneapolis and continued to be an industrial stronghold with its many mills and factories built to take advantage of St. Anthony Falls. Minneapolis developed quickly. From the first white settler in 1837, Minneapolis grew to be the eighteenth largest city in the nation in 1890 when Minneapolis-St. Paul had a population of 297,894 and contained twenty-three percent of the state's inhabitants (Wiberg 1995, 7).

Population flowed into Northeast Minneapolis from other parts of North America and many areas in Europe. New Englanders tended to dominate the commercial, political, and social life of the area. Immigration into Northeast Minneapolis follows the general pattern for immigration into the state of Minnesota.

> As the first sizable wave of settlement reached Minnesota in the 1850s and 1860s, the town-site developers, timber speculators, small businessmen, grassroots politicians, and organizers of churches and schools were often New England Yankees. They flocked to Minnesota Territory, which was established in 1849, hoping to create a New England of the West. (Holmquist 1981, 2)

Quickly following New Englanders came immigrants from western Europe. French, Irish, Swiss, and British immigrants came in large numbers up until 1890. Many Germans arrived between 1875 and 1900. A substantial number of French Canadians arrived from 1875 through 1900. Northern Europeans came next—Norwegians from 1875 through 1910, Danes from 1885 through 1920, and Swedes from 1885 through 1910. Eastern and southern Europeans followed. Poles came from 1895 through 1910. Hungarians came from around 1900 to 1910. Italians arrived right after 1910 through 1920 (Holmquist 1981, 3). Eastern Slavs, including Ruthenians and Russians, arrived in greatest numbers from 1905 to 1916. A later, smaller migration of Ruthenians occurred in the 1920s (Dryud 1981, 407).

A significant difference between the statewide pattern of immigration and what was found in Northeast Minneapolis was that there was a greater concentration of immigrants from eastern Europe in Northeast Minneapolis. The first such immigrants arrived early in Northeast's history. The first Russian immigrant settled in Northeast Minneapolis in 1877, and in 1878 the first Ukrainian immigrant arrived in Minneapolis (Megets 1996, 3).

New arrivals swelled the population of Northeast Minneapolis and fueled a building boom. New homes were constructed in neighborhoods that stretched north from the Falls of St. Anthony. Waves of French Canadians, Germans, Swedes, Norwegians, Poles, Russians, Rutheans, and Italians continued to arrive and settle in Northeast Minneapolis. As these immigrants arrived, they often settled close to persons from the same areas of origin and begin to establish the shape of Northeast Minneapolis. Beltrami Park Neighborhood was Swedish. Later, it became Italian. St. Anthony West was German and Irish. Marshall and Sheridan were Polish or Russian, depending on the specific area. Windom Park and Audubon Park were Scandinavian or German. The character of these neighborhoods was often determined by the ethnicity of the persons who lived in them.

Throughout the 1800s and into the early part of the 1900s, newly arrived individuals and families continued to settle in neighborhoods and join churches that reflected their ethnicity and spoke their languages. These churches were started by the earlier waves of immigrants and provided rich support for later arrivals. Importantly, they offered the recognition and affirmation of ethnicity. This allowed a strong sense of identity and belonging, for these immigrants who had recently moved away from their native villages and safe moorings of kin and friends.

Churches were a means toward incorporation into American life. For example, they offered English classes for their members as a way for these new arrivals to gain a vital tool for full participation in American life. Churches also established libraries to encourage literacy. Last, they allowed the formation of political strongholds for politicians who claimed to represent the populations the churches were serving.

Meanwhile, economic growth was rapid, and Northeast Minneapolis prospered. Commerce and industry thrived. Residential and commercial properties were quickly developed. Already by the late 1800s, a vibrant business district developed along Central Avenue. This area was originally called New Boston, reflecting the intentions of the founding fathers. New Boston was soon renamed Northeast Minneapolis. Central Avenue was called Elmwood Avenue for a short time period when elm trees were planted along the streets (*Sun Newspapers* 1976, 12–13). Eventually, the more prosaic, but descriptive, name of Central Avenue was appended to the street.

By the early 1900s, Northeast Minneapolis assumed its present character in terms of residential and industrial mix. This included a continuing tension between those who wanted a Yankee flavor and were part of the business-oriented elite and the residents of non-Anglo ethnic neighborhoods. Central Avenue was the all-American street while the adjacent neighborhoods were solidly ethnic with their Swedish Baptist, Russian Orthodox, or Polish Roman Catholic churches, neighborhood stores that sold ethnic specialties, such as Polish sausages, and where languages other than English were often spoken.[3]

The strength of ethnic identity varied, depending upon degree of residential clustering, actions of key institutions, and ease with which an ethnic group could meet the demands for Anglo-conformity in American life. Russians lived in relatively homogenous areas in the western part of Northeast Minneapolis and were constantly reminded of who they were through their church, St. Mary's Russian Orthodox Cathedral, with its many programs and use of Slavonic as a language of worship. There continues to be a strong sense of shared identity among those in the Northeast who claim Russian descent. Lithuanians, on the other hand, were less well defined, due in part to the fact that there were fewer of them and they were more scattered throughout the entire Twin Cities area. Still others, such as Germans and Swedes, found it much easier to conform to the majority Anglo culture of the United States. They moved relatively quickly from a strong identification with an Old World ethnicity to an enthusiastic adoption of a new American identification.

Even for those for whom ethnicity was less salient, the neighborhoods in which they lived made up the most vital parts of their social and cultural worlds. It was in these neighborhoods that they bought or built homes and established families. These children are the persons who are now the senior generation in Northeast Minneapolis, and it is to their stories that I now turn.

Ten of the twenty one persons with whom I spoke were born before the end of World War One, yet the period from 1899 to 1918 was a time of beginning for all of them. The families into which they were born were established in this time period, and their parents were finding employment, participating in churches, and learning to be neighbors in Northeast Minneapolis. The familial, cultural, and social settings in which my informants were to be born and develop were being formed.

Fred's family was among the earlier arrivals to Minneapolis from eastern Europe. They found an already established "Russian" community clustered around St. Mary's Parish, which was later more elegantly named as St. Mary's Russian Orthodox Cathedral.[4]

Fred's Story

A thriving Russian[5] community clustered around St. Mary's Parish by 1900. In a house still standing as a material link to the past, located within shouting distance of St. Mary's, Fred was born on September 28, 1909. As many others in this community, Fred's parents came from a part of Austria-Hungary which is now in Slovakia. They moved from a small mountain village where life was difficult and the people were poor. There was no chance that they knew each other there. Fred's father was ten years older than his mother, and he had left for America before she was born.

Two deaths shaped Fred's early years. One occurred long before he was born. His maternal grandfather had immigrated to America, leaving a wife and young daughter behind. He died soon after he arrived. Fred's grandmother, upon hearing the news, left her daughter with relatives and came to America. She moved in with relatives in Northeast Minneapolis. Eventually she married a grocer who shared her ethnic background. After the marriage, she sent for her daughter, Fred's mother, who arrived in America in 1902 at the age of twelve.

The second death occurred in 1913. Fred's mother had met and married a man who worked for the Soo Line Railroad. Fred was born soon after. When Fred was four years old his father was crushed to death between two rail cars at the Soo Line railyards. Fred has few memories of his father outside of the times when he brought him pink peppermint candies. Fred and his mother moved in with his maternal grandparents on 22nd Avenue between 2nd Street and 3rd Street Northeast.

After a short time, Fred's mother remarried. Fred's stepfather had also immigrated from Austria-Hungary. His mother and stepfather met through their involvement at St. Mary's. The newly formed family, which included Fred, a sister born shortly before the death of Fred's father, his mother, and the new stepfather, moved three blocks east to a newly built house. Fred's parents borrowed the money from a lodge at St. Mary's which was organized to provide credit and insurance to parishioners. Over the next few years, three more children, two boys and a girl, were added to the family.

The neighborhood was largely made up of immigrants. It was mostly Russian but also included Swedish, Polish, Irish, and French-Canadian families. Fred's family spoke Russian in the home until his stepfather gained fluency in English. At that time they switched almost exclusively to English. Fred's family, as many in the neighborhood, were in a hurry to become American.

The church was the center of the Russian community. It offered financial support, provided a school where children learned Slavonic for use in worship, and even built the first library for the neighborhood on an empty lot across the street from Fred's home.

The neighborhood in which Fred was allowed to play was defined by railroad tracks. On the east side was the Soo Line Railroad. On the west side there was the Great Northern Railroad. As he grew older, his neighborhood expanded so that the Mississippi River became the boundary on the west, Columbia Park defined the northern boundary, the southern boundary was around 8th Avenue, and the Soo Line tracks continued to define the eastern boundary.

For a young boy growing up in Northeast Minneapolis, parks and open lots meant there was always a place to play ball. The most heavily used park was Bottineau Park. Jackson Park was used less frequently because the children had to cross the railroad tracks. Sandy Lake still existed, since Columbia Park, whose construction required the lake to be filled in, had not yet been established. The lake was shallow and swampy, but there was a creek with fireflies and pieces of lumber to be scavenged from industrial yards along the southern edge of the lake. Fred found all he needed for many adventures.

Factories and grain elevators provided other, albeit more dangerous, opportunities for Fred and his friends. To the north of Fred's home was a grain elevator. Somehow Fred and his friends talked the watchman into letting them play there. One of the favorite sports was running over the rollers that moved the grain around from one elevator to the other.

Fred began to work at an early age. He helped his grandfather deliver groceries by horse and wagon. His grandfather was a strong influence on him. He was the head of an extended family and carried out his role with a firm hand. He was also generous to Fred and others in the family. This generosity was extended to the neighborhood as he freely gave credit to many who could not pay with cash. As a good businessman, he carefully recorded these transactions.

Fred attended Schiller Elementary School, where he was called "Skippy," reflecting his fondness for running and skipping. The principal, Mrs. Martin, was a strict disciplinarian. She also was a strong supporter of athletics who insisted on everybody going out for some sport. Fred played basketball for awhile. He found it hard to compete against highly skilled players who learned to play together at Northeast Neighborhood House. Fred switched to track where he enjoyed more success.

In the years before Fred attended high school there were many changes in the neighborhood. Although the main street were already paved, the side streets were packed dirt when Fred was young. These were paved in this time period. Empty lots were being filled with new homes. Existing homes were continually being added on to as residents felt the need for more room to house growing families or gain additional income brought in by renters who occupied apartments created by these additions.

Fred attended Edison High School and soon discovered an interest that later became his life's work. Fred enjoyed botany classes and was put in charge of the high school greenhouse. He graduated from Edison in January, 1928, and took a job as a billing clerk with Wyman's Sash and Door Company on Central Avenue and 8th Street. Fred lost this position when the business closed in 1932 due to the harsh economic conditions of the Depression. Utilizing money that had been set aside when his father had been killed, he enrolled in the University of Minnesota to study forestry.

After three years of studies, he was hired by the United States Forest Service and began to work in Wisconsin where his first assignment was to direct a Civil Conservation Corps crew as it built a dam which formed a trout pond. He did a variety of things after that, but his favorite job was cruising timber.

Two years later Fred returned to his studies at the University of Minnesota. He began to feel financial pressures, however, and, after one year, decided to move to Detroit, Michigan, in an attempt to find work. This was in 1939. He was not successful and returned home to Northeast Minneapolis.

By this time, World War Two had started. Fred joined the Navy in 1940 and was sent to the Great Lakes Naval Training Station. Eventually, he was sent to aeronautical school in Seattle, Washington, where he was trained to become an aerologist. In the spirit of patriotism that was typical during World War Two, he tired of being a noncombatant and told his commander that he wanted to be on a ship and join the "real Navy." This must have pushed the wrong button because the commander said, "Okay, we will send you to Attu—a real hell hole."

This threat never came about. An officer that Fred knew had received orders to the U.S.S. Lexington. He arranged it so that Fred also received orders there. Before he could report, the U.S.S. Lexington was taken out of service. Fred was then assigned to the U.S.S. Barnes, which was an aircraft carrier used as an auxiliary ship to carry planes, pilots and support staff, marines, and Seabees.

On the U.S.S. Barnes he was the air officer's "talker" who passed orders over the radio to the pilots while in-flight. The ship eventually set course out into the South Pacific and was involved in battle at Tarawa. At the end of the war the ship came back to San Diego. Fred was transferred to an aerology department on shore. He was discharged in 1946 at the Great

Lakes Naval Training School and moved back with his parents in the house where he was born. Two sisters were also living there.

Fred found a job with a plumbing company where he worked in the supply room. From there he went to work for a manufacturing business in a similar position. Finally, he found work in a greenhouse and returned to the interest first discovered in high school. He worked there until he retired.

He continued to live at home. In 1971, his stepfather's health began to fail. At the age of sixty two, Fred retired to be able to attend to the many needs at home as his stepfather's health continued to deteriorate. At this time he shared the house with his stepfather, mother, and younger brother.

Fred's stepfather died when Fred was sixty-eight years old. Fred remained in the house with his mother and younger brother. His mother broke her hip, and her health began to suffer. When Fred was seventy-three, she died. Fred and his brother continued to live at home. His brother developed Parkinson's disease, and Fred took on the role of primary caregiver for a third time. When Fred was eighty five his brother died. Shortly thereafter he sold the family home and moved into a senior housing complex.

Fred is still active at St. Mary's Russian Orthodox Cathedral, which has been a central pillar for him and the Russian community in which he has been immersed for all of his life. Family is still important. Fred often sees his sisters and their families at frequent visits and family get-togethers.

A new area of interest is volunteer work in hospitals, through which he has made many friends among the nurses and doctors with whom he has worked. Fred began volunteering in 1982. At that time he had bypass surgery at what was then called Mt. Sinai Hospital (now called Hennepin County Medical Center). He thought the program was so good that he volunteered in the rehabilitation unit. His task was to repair equipment. He now volunteers at Hennepin County Medical Clinic where he works on special projects. This mostly involves collating information gathered by doctors and nurses. He also records information about how patients are reacting to the various procedures.

Fred sees many changes in Northeast. Stores are now large. Most of the smaller grocery stores have closed. The two banks on Central Avenue are now part of large banking chains. His old neighborhood has not changed as much. Some of the stores became apartment houses. For a time period there were younger people living in them who caused trouble. That made people in the neighborhood nervous. In response, they put up fences around their backyards. Some even fenced in their front yards. In the past, fences were built because people had chickens and rabbits that had to be contained. Now they are built for protection. There are more cars parked on the street. The police come around more often. Unlike the past, Fred says that today he does not know any of the policemen. There is no chance to meet them. They are never on the sidewalks. The police are always in cars, either going to or coming from someplace.

The neighborhoods are not neighborhoods any more. They are just places where people stay. Very few people know their neighbors. What they do know of each other is bad. Fred no longer knows people he sees on the streets. He misses seeing children using parks and involved in sports programs. He also misses band concerts that used be held in parks. The neighborhood looks the same, but the people are changing.

Fred was born and raised in the middle of a cohesive, well defined ethnic community centered around St. Mary's Russian Orthodox Cathedral. He learned to speak, read, and write Russian, participated in rituals, ceremonies, and events that reinforced a sense of identity and belonging, and frequently interacted with friends and family, most of whom were from the same community. This provided a reference point and sense of security for Fred. Within this community there was also a strong urge to become thoroughly American and participate fully in the larger society. Fred's family abandoned Russian for English as the language used at home. The children attended public schools and made friendships that crossed the many ethnic boundaries in Northeast Minneapolis and, by the time they were adults, they were prepared to take positions in businesses, industry, and government in Northeast Minneapolis, throughout the Twin Cities, and elsewhere. The ethnic community in which Fred lived was a vital part of this preparation. In this fast developing industrial city, Northeast ethnic communities played vital roles in the preparing their members to participate in the economic, social, and political life of the area.

Northeast Minneapolis is being built

Initial development in Northeast Minneapolis took place along the north and east banks of the Mississippi, adjacent to St. Anthony Falls, where industries could take advantage of water power. The first major industry was lumber milling. This declined precipitously around 1920 due to the fact that by that time most of the easily available stands of trees in northern Minnesota had been cut. Flour milling began soon after the first lumber mills were established and was in high production throughout this time period.

Most of my informants' fathers worked either in these mills or in the numerous small factories that were established in the area. This was hard and, often, dangerous work. Conditions were terrible. This was especially true in the mills where workers faced noise, powerful equipment, and clouds of lung-filling dust. Many of these long-term residents report that their mothers worked out of the home. This was often at low paying jobs set aside for immigrants with no or poorly developed English skills. Many worked in kitchens, and my informants remember stories of heat and overwork.

This was also a time of fires as lumber and flour mills burnt down in spectacular infernos. Eventually, all of the lumber mills were destroyed. Some of my informants described the excitement of horse drawn fire engines careening down the streets and hills of Northeast. One man recalled the time a fire engine sped down Lowry Avenue and attempted to turn the corner onto Central Avenue. The end of the engine swung wide and hit a lamp post, killing the fireman on the back of the rig. Another man recalled the excitement and horror of the fire that burnt a livery stable on Central Avenue where fire horses were kept. This occurred in 1914, and he said that he could clearly remember the screaming of the horses caught in the blaze. The stables were located where Central Norwest Bank now stands and were never rebuilt.

Early in this period most roads were still unpaved. One man recalled that when the rains came these roads turned into mud pits. Horses would get stuck up to their bellies in the deep mud. He told of one attempt to deal with this by paving part of Lowry Avenue with asphalt bricks. This was done both to take care of the mud and to avoid the noise the horses made on cobble stones. This turned out to be a bad idea. With the first heavy rain the asphalt bricks washed away.

Cars and trucks were rare, and electricity did not reach out into the neighborhoods until the latter part of this time period. One man recalled:

> In my time it was a change from horses to motorcars. Most of the streets were unpaved. Streets like Lowry Avenue were paved [because of] the bridges [across the Mississippi River]...That is one of the streets on which the honey wagons used to go. That is when they still had privies outside the city. That is when they had to clean out the privies. You would see those wagons every now and then coming down Lowry and going down to the river. I imagine they dumped it in the river. They did not come where we lived because we had sewers. It [the change from horses to mo-

torcars] must have been a sudden change because when I was young, at my grandfather's store, we still took groceries around [by horse and wagon]. And then he had a car shortly after that.

Automobiles began to appear during this time period. One man recalled that the first car he knew of was an electric car owned by a German doctor who served the people in his neighborhood. The strength of this memory might have been reinforced by the fact that the doctor would give money to children in the neighborhood as he was leaving after making a home visit.

Another man recalled seeing his first automobile in 1920, which was the year he lost his hearing due to scarlet fever. When he was younger many neighbors used horses and wagons, but it was made illegal to keep horses in the city around 1910 to 1915. Even outlying areas of Northeast Minneapolis were changing in character from rural to more urban. Before World War One, most of the area east of Johnson Avenue was farmland.

Although Thomas Lowry had laid tracks for a streetcar line running from the Hennepin Avenue Suspension Bridge to the University of Minnesota earlier, the first streetcar to serve Northeast Minneapolis was a one horse bob-tail streetcar that ran on a line was laid in 1892 with tracks running to 40th Avenue Northeast and Central and west along 40th to Jefferson (Fuehrer 1991, 7; Wiberg 1996, 7). From the layout of lines it is clear that they were meant to bring workers from the newly forming neighborhoods to work at the mills and factories along the Mississippi.

This was an era when the essential shape of Northeast Minneapolis was established. As one man, born in 1909, recalled, "There were a lot of spaces around. There was a park across from the store where we lived [between Broadway and Lowry and west of Central]…There were more empty spaces than there was houses."

Empty lots were gradually filled in with new homes. Yet the oldest of my informants recalled that even in the 1910s there were many empty lots on which no buildings had been constructed. By 1875, Thomas Lowry had platted and developed a residential area that contained 100 homes near Central Avenue and Lowry. He named this New Boston (Fuehrer 1991, 7). Five major streets and arterials provided the basic framework for the layout of Northeast Minneapolis. Hennepin Avenue established the southern border. University and Central Avenues ran north and south, and Broadway and Lowry Avenues ran west and east. The northern border of Northeast was established by Columbia Park. Industrial areas followed the Mississippi River on the west and south, clustered near the Soo Line railroad yards on the north, and were scattered more thinly along Central Avenue and in areas to the east of Central. University, Hennepin, and Central Avenues were major commercial streets and traffic corridors. Broadway and Lowry carried traffic across the river to North Minneapolis or to eastern, still rural parts of the growing Twin Cities metropolitan area. Residential neighborhoods filled in the spaces in between these major features.

My older informants remembered a life that was firmly focused on the neighborhood, family, and hard work. This was, and continued to be for many years, a working class area. In the pre-World War One era, wages were low, living conditions were sufficient but not luxurious, and expectations of material goods and comforts were basic. Few class differences existed. My informants remembered that most of the families seemed to have the same basic living standards and material goods. Many pleasures were home-grown. Neighborhood ball games were often played with a ball made of rolled up twine and a recycled sash used as a bat. Social life was rich and often built on close family ties and frequent interaction with relatives.

Toward the end of this time period changes began to accelerate. One woman recalled:

> East of Central I remember having kerosene lamps and we had the lamp lighters that would come by along around five or six o'clock. They would light the lights on either end of the block. Nothing in the middle, but on the ends of the block. And we had the ice man that came by. And we had the Watkins man. They sold tea, coffee, and herbs. And the Jewell Tea man did the same thing. And my mother couldn't decide which one she wanted. She liked them both. So she ordered from both of them. I remember when the gas lights came. Oh, that really was something terrific—when the gas lights came on in the home. We had kerosene lamps [before that]. Then we had gas. We had the mantles. And we had to be careful not to stomp too hard because the mantles, after they were once lit, were very fragile. And then the plumbing came in. We did have running water. But there was no plumbing outside of that. I remember my mother taking the clothes closet that was in the dining room [and making a bathroom]. My cousin made a window in there. And all we could have in there was the [toilet] seat. Were we ever proud. Oh, we thought that was absolutely wonderful.

By 1918, the present day configuration of neighborhoods was set. As today, Northeast Minneapolis neighborhoods were defined by perceived boundaries and key institutions. Perceptions were shaped by the range of one's activities, physical features such as roads and railroad tracks, and the types of people one might encounter in various areas. The ethnic character of Northeast neighborhoods was firmly established by the end of this time period. Key institutions included parks, churches, and schools.

Key institutions

Schools help define neighborhoods and stand out strongly in the memories of long-term residents. One woman remembered how her mother and other neighborhood women would bake special treats for the teachers at Sheridan School, which was located directly across the street from her home. This close interaction had mixed blessings. If she acted up in school she was sure to find that her mother had received a visit from the teacher before she came home. A stern look and spanking greeted her arrival from school. The relationship between teachers and the family was long lasting. In 1931, when this same woman was twenty-two years old, her father was killed in a construction accident. Even though she had been out of school for many years, the teachers and principal of Sheridan Elementary School marched in the funeral procession of her deceased father.

Neighborhood parks have a long history in Northeast Minneapolis and were often used by long-term residents to define neighborhoods. Logan Park was established as the first park in the city of Minneapolis in 1883. Its character was entirely different from that of a modern, neighborhood park. At its center was a fountain. Walking paths were lined with benches. When first established, Logan Park was a place of rest and relief from urban life and urban crowding. Gradually, parks were reshaped to provide recreational activities for children and room for social events for adults.[6]

The third neighborhood pillar was the church. St. Anthony of Padua Roman Catholic Church is located in Northeast and was the first church established in Minneapolis. Mass was first conducted in 1849 (*Sun Newspapers* 1976, 30). The period ending in 1918 saw the establishment of most of the active churches in present day Northeast Minneapolis (see Figure 2.1).

Another key institution in Northeast Minneapolis was the settlement house. In 1912, the Minnesota League of Catholic Women established the Margaret Berry House to provide services for the growing Italian immigrant population in the Beltrami Park neighborhood. In 1915, the Northeast Neighborhood House, a larger facility with much more extensive programming, was established in the largely Polish area of Northeast Minneapolis located just south of Lowry and east of University Avenue (Bolin 1976, 60).

The YMCA had an early presence in Northeast Minneapolis. In May, 1886, the YMCA rented a room on the third floor of a building at Central

FIGURE 2.1: *Northeast Minneapolis churches established by 1918*

1854	First Universalist Society of St. Anthony (since disbanded; its building was acquired by a congregation of French Canadian settlers in 1877 who established Our Lady of Lourdes)
1854	First Congregational Church of St. Anthony (since disbanded)
1858	St. Boniface Catholic Church
1877	Our Lady of Lourdes Catholic church
1880	St. Mary Russian Orthodox Greek Catholic Church (building constructed in 1889)
1882	Trinity Methodist
1884	Church of the Holy Cross
1884	Emanuel Lutheran
1887	House of Faith Presbyterian
1888	Salem Swedish Mission Church
1888	Elim Swedish Baptist Church
1890	St. Paul's Lutheran
1891	St. Matthew's Episcopal
1893	St. Cyrils of Methodius Catholic Church
1895	St. Clements Catholic Church
1905	Grace Methodist
1906	St. John the Baptist Catholic Church (Byzantine Rite)
1912	St. Constantine Ukrainian Catholic Church
1914	Gustavus Adolphus Lutheran
1914	Sacred Heart of Jesus Polish National Catholic Church
1914	Salvation Army Corps
1916	All Saints Catholic Church

Avenue Northeast and University to establish programs in the area. In 1887, this closed due to a lack of resources, yet, even prior to the establishment of a permanent program in Northeast Minneapolis, the YMCA continued to offer services to this area of the city. In 1906, it provided health education classes on topics such as diet, sleep, teeth care, and sexual hygiene. In 1912, it offered English classes for Russian, Rutheanian, and Sybrian people in churches serving this population. Eventually, there were five locations, one of which was at the Northeast Settlement House. Beginning in 1914, it organized an annual "Health Week." Finally, an office was established above Danielsons' Drug Store at 24th and Central. This was aided greatly by a highly successful fund-raising campaign in 1916 that raised moneys to support YMCA programs throughout the city. One hundred thousand dollars was given to support programming in Northeast and programs such as an inter-church older boys' cabinet, a "learn-to-swim" program, a "grow-your-own fruit" campaign, and various industrial activities (Ashmore 1990, 12).

Many fraternal organizations were established in this time period. Masonic Arcana Lodge was established in 1887. The first meeting was held in a hall over the J. H. Moody's Drug Store at 2423 Central (Olson 1996, 10). In 1900, the Sons of Norway was established (*Sun Newspapers* 1976, 31). The Polish White Eagle Society began in 1906 with the three objectives being: "To promote unity and fraternity within its community; to openly express loyalty and appreciation to their adopted country, the United States of America, by being worthwhile citizens; thirdly, to make it possible for their fellowman to participate in a program offering death benefits to beneficiaries designated in their plan and later in their policies, at low premiums" (Polish White Eagle Society 1981, 10).

Commercial and business life

The first major commercial street in Minneapolis on the east side of the Mississippi was Main Street. Hennepin Avenue soon outstripped Main Street in terms of commercial importance. By the end of this first time period, Central Avenue had become the most important commercial and shopping street for those living in Northeast. Only those persons living south of Broadway and west of Central continued to shop more on Hennepin than they did on Central. Hennepin, however, still attracted residents from other parts of Northeast Minneapolis seeking more exclusive, expensive goods. In particular, a number of men remembered buying fine clothes at Eklunds Clothing Store on Hennepin.

On the southern end of Central numerous factories and industries were established. The Aaron Carlson Millwork company began its operations in 1890 at its present location just north of Broadway on the east side of Central Avenue. It is now run by a third generation of Carlsons. One man who grew up attending Salem Covenant Church recalls that many men from Salem worked there.

Many commercial institutions were located on Central. For example, Olson Hospital, a private hospital was established at 18 ½ and Central in 1913 by Dr. John Olson. The first bank on Central Avenue opened in 1907.

It was located at 2401 Central Avenue Northeast and opened with total deposits of $111,069.16 (*Sun Newspapers* 976, 13, 16).

Daily life in Northeast Minneapolis

The parents of many of these long-term residents were immigrants who arrived as single persons and settled in among fellow immigrants. Often this meant living with relatives or persons from the same region or village in Europe. They met their future spouses through friendship networks or in churches that were predominantly filled by fellow immigrants.

Whether immigrant or native born, the challenge faced by the parents of my informants was to find work, secure housing, and begin the process of building a family in Northeast Minneapolis. All of the persons with whom I talked who were born in this time period were birthed at home where their mothers were attended by midwives. The midwives were women who lived in the neighborhoods and received most of their training "on the job." One woman who was born in 1899 recalled:

> No hospital in those days [at child birth]. There was a midwife that lived down the block from us. She brought all the babies in the neighborhood. She rode around in the winter in a cutter. And in the summer, wagon and one horse. They could have horses in town in those days. Four wheeled with one seat.

There was an African American woman who was well known in the southeast part of Northeast for her skills as a midwife. Neighborhood children would follow her as she made her way through the neighborhood to a delivery. The children were certain that there was a baby in the black suitcase she carried on these rounds. One woman remembered being disappointed when she found out that it held much less exciting supplies needed for assisting with the delivery. According to these long-term residents, women in their neighborhoods began to go hospitals to deliver late in this time period. This reflects changes in birthing practices and increased affluence among Northeast families.

Northeast Minneapolis was already known as a working class area of Minneapolis. Jobs were readily available at the many mills, factories, and railyards in Northeast. Many men worked for the Soo Lines Railway or in the flour and lumber mills alongside St. Anthony Falls. Few married women worked outside the home in this time period. The pattern seems to be that immigrant women did work outside the house when they first arrived. However, as families settled in and became more stable financially and as children began to arrive they stopped working outside the home

The ethnic layout of Northeast was well established by the turn of the century. Before World War One, Germans were visible and numerous. For example, German Lutherans founded Trinity Lutheran Church in St. Anthony in 1856, the oldest Missouri Synod congregation in the state, and the earliest German Methodist church in Minneapolis was established in Northeast in 1870. By 1880, Germans made up over forty percent of the population of St. Anthony West, an area of Northeast south of Broadway and west of Central (Johnson 1981, 170–171). With the outbreak of World War One, German ancestry was not well accepted in Northeast, as in general for the rest of the United States. Thus, there is little mention of German identity in Northeast after 1914. However, even up until the present, a sizable portion of the population of Northeast Minneapolis continues to have German ancestors in its background.

Some ethnic populations that were highly visible earlier had started to disperse and no longer remained a presence in Northeast by the end of this time period. Among the first arrivals to Northeast Minneapolis were French Canadians. They eventually made up a good proportion of the population. One woman, with French Canadian heritage, lived in an area located east of Central and south of Lowry from her birth in 1910 to around 1917. At that time this neighborhood was largely French Canadian. Both she and her parents were married at Our lady of Lourdes Catholic Church, which was a church with a heavy emphasis on French Canadian heritage. She, her brothers and sisters, and all of her children were baptized, went through catechism, were confirmed, and made their first communion there. She also was educated at Our Lady Lourdes Catholic School. Even though English had replaced French as the language of instruction in 1906, many of her teachers were Catholic nuns who had immigrated from French speaking areas of Canada. The neighborhood changed around the time of World War One when many French Canadian families moved to other areas of the Minneapolis or St. Paul in a search of better housing. Her family moved across Central Avenue to the St. Anthony West neighborhood. This resulted in the loss of a French Canadian population presence in Northeast.

Irish Americans began to cluster around St. Anthony of Padua in St. Anthony West by the 1860s. By World War One, they had moved out of Northeast. Many left to live in South Minneapolis (Regan 1981, 142). Again, by World War One, there was no well defined Irish American community in Northeast Minneapolis.

By World War One, the most visible ethnicities in Northeast were Italian, Slavic, and Scandinavian. The 1913 Northeast Side Survey found that thirty-eight percent of the population was of foreign birth and forty-two percent were born of parents who were of foreign birth. Thirteen percent of the population were native Scandinavians, and ten percent had been born in Slavic countries. Due to higher birthrates, second generation Slavic persons already outnumbered second generation Scandinavians by this time. Altogether, twenty-six percent of the population was Slavic (Bolin 1976, 59).

As a general pattern, Slavic neighborhoods were found west of Central, and Scandinavian neighborhoods were found around Logan Park and east of Central. Due to the influence of St. Mary's, persons identifying themselves as Russian were tightly clustered in the western part of Northeast Minneapolis in a area near the intersection of 5th and 17th. Russian was used at St. Mary's until 1905 when English began to be used in church services. A man who lived east of Central, between Broadway and Lowry, recalled that there were many Scandinavians in his neighborhood. Indeed, a hill at Lincoln and 29th was known as Norwegian Hill. Italians were concentrated south in the Beltrami neighborhood.

Not only were the ethnic populations well defined in terms of geographic concentration, but they were well defined by stereotypes that the various ethnic groups held of each other. A man who claimed English descent said that his parents would not let him go to parts of Northeast that contained many Polish persons. They saw Polish neighborhoods as dangerous with much violence and heavy, public drinking. His sister claimed that in the 1920s many homes in Polish neighborhoods were extensively remodeled. She said that it was assumed by those in her neighborhood that this was done with money made from selling bootlegged liquor.

Even though ethnicity was a dominant feature of their social worlds, this was also a time of intensive "Americanization" of newly arriving immigrants and their families. Public policy strongly advocated the assimilation of the large number of European immigrants who were flooding into America. This was reflected in the lives of my informants. They learned and used English even if their parents or other relatives spoke Polish, German, some other non-English language. One woman recalled that her German-born, maternal grandmother lived with them during certain parts of the year. She only spoke German. Although my informant could speak and understand German, she would only answer in English. This infuriated the grandmother. As a child who was growing up in an atmosphere that stressed the need to become "American," my informant resented the fact that she was expected to speak in a "lesser language."

As the children were learning English in schools, at park and settlement house programs, and in play with neighborhood friends, their immigrant parents were also learning skills needed for success in America.
Some attended night school at places like Holland Public School. These
classes were organized to help prepare immigrants for citizenship exams
and were organized by Minneapolis Public Schools.[7] They offered classes
on English, American history and culture, and skills, such as arithmetic,
which were needed by the modern, industrial worker.

Ethnicity and church were closely intertwined. A number of the
churches held services in languages other than English. Many customs
and traditions found in Northeast Minneapolis churches had Old World
origins. Some of the churches were highly influenced by church polity
and changes that were taking place in Europe. This became very complex.
For example, the history of the Orthodox church in Northeast Minneapolis is closely related to the "Old World."

> Many families [of Slavic descent] bought land "bordering the city on 7th
> Avenue Northeast near the Mississippi River, built homes and gardens and
> went to German and Polish parish priests" until 1887, when there were
> enough of them to begin organizing their own Byzantine Catholic con-
> gregation. The existence of this congregation and the small frame church
> its members built in Northeast Minneapolis touched off a controversial
> series of events which were to affect East Slavs in both the United States
> and Europe, events which ultimately involved the highest policy-making
> levels in Austria-Hungary, Russia, and the Vatican. At the heart of the con-
> troversy was the effort to establish the Byzantine Rite in the United States.
> Like many other immigrant groups, the Minneapolis Ruthenians wished
> to continue to practice their faith in the new country. Thus in 1888 they
> completed St. Mary's Greek Catholic Church on the corner of 17th Avenue
> and 5th Street in the Northeast Minneapolis neighborhood where many
> of them lived. (Dyrud 1981, 409)

When St. Mary's was formed in 1888 the congregation asked Bishop
Ireland to accept Father Toth (a priest sent from Hungary by the Bishop
of Presov at the request of the congregation). Bishop Ireland refused because Father Toth had been married and, in general, he did not want a
church following the Byzantine Rite to be formed. He ordered members
of the church to attend a Roman Catholic Church. The church escaped the
control of Bishop Ireland by becoming St. Mary's Russian Orthodox church
in October, 1892 (its current name of St. Mary's Russian Orthodox Greek
Catholic Church reflects its origin). This development was politically and

financially supported by the Russian government and Russian Orthodox Church. Of course, this support ceased with the Russian Revolution.

Meanwhile, Hungarian leaders (church and lay) were concerned about the conversion of Greek Catholic immigrants to Russian Orthodoxy. They proposed to establish a Byzantine Rite church in Northeast Minneapolis. In 1902, a papal representative (Andor Hodobay) visited and recommended that a Byzantine Rite church be established to slow down the conversion of Greek Orthodox to Russian Orthodox Christianity. Bishop Ireland agreed. As a result, St. John the Baptist Eastern Rite Catholic Church was organized in 1907 (Dyrud 1981, 408–410).[8]

While all this was keeping their parents very busy, my informants were young children. For them, this was a time of growing up, learning how to be a responsible members of the community, and much play. One man born in 1902 recalled a pretty normal childhood in his neighborhood located east of Central and between Broadway and Lowry. This included chores, such as mowing the lawn, washing windows, and hauling out the coal ashes. It also include much play, Although he was not involved in organized sports, he remembered that schools offered sports programs. Most play, however, was informally organized by neighborhood children. Play often utilized whatever was available. For example, he used to play baseball using a ball of rolled twine and a sash for a bat.

During this time period there was much building going on in Northeast. There were numerous pits from the excavation of limestone used for construction. These sometimes filled with water and were abandoned. One man recalled one that was located at the site of the present day post office. These made tempting swimming holes. Unfortunately, they were dangerous swimming holes. He recalled that children died yearly in these swimming outings.

Neighborhoods were small. Most needs, such as church, shopping, friendships, and, quite often, employment, could be met within walking distance. As these long-term residents looked back, they remember neighborhoods where crime was rare and life was quiet. Few people locked their doors. Strangers were rarely seen, outside of the occasional hoboes seen in those areas close to the Soo Line railroad tracks. Hoboes went go door to door and asking for something to eat. If they found an offer of free food they could be seen sitting on the front steps as they waited for a meal.

These long-term residents spoke of their neighborhoods as neighborly. For children, this meant that there were many playmates and little about the neighborhood that was dangerous or off limits. For adults, it meant that neighbors knew each other, reached out to one another in friendship, and provided help when needed. One woman who lived east of Central and between Broadway and Lowry described a neighborhood in which families met frequently for meals and dances. These were organized by her father and were held in her house. Her father played a homemade hammered dulcimer. He made the body out of wood, strung it, and fashioned hammers out of his wife's corset stays and cork. The cork strikers were wrapped with leather. He played and called for square dances. Neighbors and relatives came over to her house on a Saturday night, bringing wieners, potato salad, home-baked beans, coffee, and milk for the children. They would roll up the rugs and dance. The amount of socializing in this neighborhood is probably somewhat unique and might be explained by the high concentration of French Canadians. Her family was French Canadian, and she believed that dancing and music were important familial and cultural traditions.

World War One broke out at the end of this time period. This was a time for residents of Northeast Minneapolis to demonstrate their patriotism. Many families saw sons join the military. They hung banners with red borders outside their house if they had sons in the war, with a blue star for each son in the service and gold stars for sons killed in action. Northeast Minneapolis, with its many ethnic groups, was becoming an all-American town.

Hard times and helping

In this time period there were few formal programs designed to help people who were going through hard times. The first line of support was the immediate family. Churches and neighbors helped out to a more limited extent. One woman recalled that when her father died in 1906, her church helped with the funeral. Meals were provided to the family by neighbors and relatives in the weeks immediately following the death. Past this meager help, the family survived through hard work. Her two older brothers left school and went to work to keep their father's small broom factory going. Just nine years later, her mother died. At this point the remaining family broke up. She moved in with an aunt and uncle and lived with them for two years while she finished high school. Her brothers went different directions. After high school she found a job and moved in with a married cousin. She repaid her aunt and uncle all the costs they incurred when raising her.

There were no pensions and Social Security did not exist during this time period. Older persons continued to work as long as possible. If they could not work and needed help, most turned to family. Many of my informants could remember grandparents or other older relatives living with their families. In most cases this involved an older person living with the family of an adult child. Some families arranged this so that the older person would rotate between the homes of a number of his or her children.

Churches were important sources of help for this largely immigrant community. Salem Swedish Mission Church was established in 1888. Wiberg recounts cases in which the church helped those in its congregation who were in need.

> There were no safety nets such as Social Security, Medicare, or any other welfare entitlement programs. Nor was there easy access into the social life of the American community [for Swedish immigrants]. They were resident aliens who had become outsiders to the people they had left and were still outsiders among the people to whom they had come. How the church was able not only to provide the means of drawing mind and thought away from the struggle for survival, but also to give aid and support in that struggle, is an engaging story.
>
> Despite their own poverty and lack of social status, the people of the revival—and Mission Friends in particular—were richly endowed with gifts of biblical knowledge and folk leadership to exercise both a practical and a spiritual priesthood in caring for the sick and poor among them. Early minutes of congregational meetings reveal this priestly care and how the struggle for survival shaped the mission. (Wiberg 1995, 36–38)

Wiberg, in personal communication, noted that this pattern of caring was seen as late as 1900, but it seemed to decline after that as churches were less often turned to in times of need. He attributed this to a change in role for many churches as immigrant communities became more established. When immigrants first arrived, they turned to the church as a source of many forms of help. As the community developed and many persons moved into more secure positions in their new chosen land, this help was not needed and, indeed, not sought

For those persons without sufficient family resources or to whom local churches had not responded, life could be very difficult. For the elderly, this often meant spending the last years in poverty or as low paid workers. For women, this often meant domestic work. Indeed, the needs of indigent elderly persons was so evident that the Women's Relief Society established the first nursing home in Northeast Minneapolis in 1906. This was the Scandinavian Relief House and was located just east of Central on Lowry Avenue. It continues to operate today as the Union Home for the Aged.

This was a formative time for these long-term residents. Northeast Minneapolis was being built. Neighborhoods were being formed and took on a shape that lasted until the 1950s. Immigrants and their children were becoming Americans. Ethnicity, however, continued to define many of the neighborhoods in Northeast Minneapolis.

Chapter 3

Growing Up Between Two World Wars

The second era began in 1918, as World War One ended, and extends to 1941, with the entry of the United States into World War Two. Young men were returning from the armed services, and businesses and industries were booming. The oldest persons in the study were about to enter into adulthood while the youngest were still children or about to be born. This second era, located between two world wars, began in hope, moved into prosperity, experienced the failed American social experiment with prohibition, and sank into the hard times of the Great Depression. This era was truly formative in the lives of the persons with whom I spoke. Cultural and social patterns that defined Northeast Minneapolis were developed and incorporated in their lives.

Northeast Minneapolis was going through an economic boom in the 1920s. In the first part of this era flour mills were in full swing. This soon changed as mills at the Falls of St. Anthony began to close when milling companies moved their operations to Buffalo, New York, or Kansas City, Missouri, because of more favorable fright rates and closer proximity to new areas of wheat production (Baerwald 1989, 41). Yet business life was expanding rapidly. Much of the commercial activity took place along Central Avenue. My informants remember the first part of this second time period as being one of activity, prosperity, and excitement. In the 1920s, some of the excitement came from bootleggers who many of my informants claimed to have worked out of Northeast during prohibition, although none could name a specific person or share any firsthand knowledge of bootlegging activities. They only knew of bootlegging through stories and rumors which often identified bootleggers as members of some ethnic group considered to be lower on an informally transmitted scale of social acceptability. One woman, who lived in the Polish neighborhood around Holy Cross Catholic Church, recalled:

> I can remember the stories. There are certain families in the neighborhood that would sell alcohol…There was a little settlement of Greek men that worked on the railroad just on the other side of the bridge on St. Anthony Boulevard. They were the best customers. I know they used to bring it down from Canada.

On the other hand, persons from the mostly Scandinavian "Upper Northeast" assumed that the Polish community in "Lower Northeast" did most of the bootlegging.

If this era began with prosperity, it was largely defined by the Depression of the 1930s. The impact was enormous. People were thrown out of work, and businesses began to falter. Many of the residents of Northeast had to use all their survival skills during this time.

The immediate effects of the Depression on the persons in the study depended somewhat on their ages. The older subjects remembered this time as being tough. They were trying to work, buy homes, and start families. For example, one woman recounted how her husband lost his job at the start of the Depression. They lost the home they had just bought and were forced to move into her parents' duplex, where they lived for over ten years. Only her parents' generosity and occasional odd jobs allowed them to survive. Her husband finally found full time employment with the rapid economic upturn associated with World War Two.

Subjects who were younger remembered it as being a time of deprivation and "having to do without." Many said that since everyone was poor they did not really notice how bad things really were. For those whose parents were weathering this crisis less well than others, there were more noticeable hardships. One man whose father experienced a good deal of job insecurity talked about his mother's skill in economizing. Some of this was easier to live with than others:

> My mother took two pairs of pants with one worn out knee each, cut them in half and sewed them [together] in the middle so there were two different colors. Nowadays that would be wonderful and right in style. I was so proud of them when I wore them to school, then all the kids teased me. I didn't

expect that. They were just like a new pair of pants [to me].

The effects of the Depression were mitigated by the specific circumstances of each family. Those with steady work endured it well. According to one woman:

> During the Depression people who worked for the railroad were far better off than most because they had jobs. Policemen and firemen were also considered very fortunate because they had the security no other private job had.

It might have been during this period that Soo Line railroad workers became to be seen as a source of steady, employed workers for Northeast Minneapolis. They continued to work during the Depression and brought stability in troubled times.

This second time period was a time of hard work, substantial challenges, and hard lessons for these long-term residents. John's story illustrates how the Northeast ethos, as defined by work ethnic, self reliance, and loyalty, helped shape a young man as he grew into adulthood during this time period.

John's Story

In a time period when the border between Germany and Poland shifted toward the east, making his village part of Poland, John's paternal grandfather left Europe to seek his fortune in America. At first, he and his wife settled in Michigan. Later, they moved to Wisconsin. John's father was born in Wisconsin. His mother came from Illinois and was of Slovakian heritage.

Both of John's parents found their way to Minneapolis, where they met, married, and settled into Northeast Minneapolis. John's father was a cabinet maker by trade and worked in a cabinetry shop. He was a hard worker who was promoted to plant superintendent before he retired. As a Democrat, he was also a strong supporter of unions.

John's mother took in boarders in their large home on Monroe Street between 7th and 8th Avenues Northeast. She cooked for them, did their laundry, and cleaned their rooms. When the family moved into a smaller home the children were happy to leave the boarders behind. Not all of the borders liked the children. The children reciprocated and strongly disliked them. A few of the borders went past dislike and used to push the children around. Sometimes they would even discipline them, delivering a slap or spanking every now and then. Once in the new home, John's mother worked in the evening as part of the cleaning crew at the Foshay

Tower located in downtown Minneapolis. She started work at six o'clock in the evening and finished around ten o'clock.

John was born on September 26, 1921, in a house on Monroe Street. It has since been destroyed by fire, but a backyard shed still stands. He painfully remembered the shed from visits he and his father made when he was growing up. Discipline was firmly and quickly delivered in those years. As was common in 1921, his mother was assisted by a midwife during John's birth. His mother used to tell him that she was cutting grass with a push mower at one o'clock in the afternoon on that day. A neighbor called out, "So, when are you going to have your baby?" "I had him this morning," she replied. John's mother was five feet and two inches tall and weighed between 250 to 300 pounds. She told John that a few pounds did not make much of a difference, which made it difficult for someone walking by to know that she had the baby.

John was the youngest of four children. He had two sisters and a brother. All four were born within five years. In spite of the fact that his mother was a staunch Catholic and knew that birth control was strictly forbidden by the church, she took action so that no more children were born.

John was very close to his mother, "…I just cried my eyes out when she died. I thought I lost one very, very best friend. She was always good to me." His relationship with his father was more contentious. John brought some of this on himself by raising controversial subjects such as whether he should be a Catholic or become a Protestant. His sister used to kick him under the dinner table so he would shut up when arguments with his father became too heated.

His father was the king or boss over everything in the household. There were absolutely no questions allowed, and his wife and children were not allowed to challenge him. Adults who were not members of the family were treated differently. He was well respected and acted warm and friendly toward his peers. Children, especially his own, were to be seen and not heard. They were pushed aside whenever an adult would come to visit. His father was dedicated to fulfilling his obligations as a family man. These were to feed his children, clothe them and provide a warm house. He was also the disciplinarian. Affection was rarely given and not expected.

When his father was gone John's mother was in charge. The worst thing his mother could ever say was, "Wait until your father comes home, he will take care of this." That was just like waiting for the death sentence. When he did something at 2:00 in the afternoon he would have to wait in dread until his dad got home at 5:00.

In 1926, John's family moved three blocks to a duplex they bought on Adams Street. He remembered carrying a little bird cage with an artificial bird to the new house. John's family bought the duplex from a lady who then rented the upstairs unit from them. She financed the mortgage. Part of the mortgage payment was offset by rent she paid them. His parents paid her around fifteen dollars a month on the mortgage. She was an "Irish Old Maid," as the family used to call her, and a friend of the family. Years later, after she moved into a nursing home, John and his wife would take her shopping and help her in other ways. They would spend four to six hours a week visiting her. When John was young he shoveled snow off the open stairway to her apartment in the wintertime. She would give him a nickel. John credited her with helping to awaken a desire in him to make money. He respected her for her good business mind.

The family always shopped at Brinda's Grocery Store on Monroe Street. They had a credit arrangement with the owner. John would often be sent to the store with a list from his mother. Sometimes the owner would not give them every thing on the list because they were at the end of their credit. Every week they paid on the grocery bill. John does not think they ever paid off the remaining balance with these weekly payments. Paying on the bill had its own benefits for John. When John would be sent with the payment, Mr. Brinda would often give him a free ice cream cone. Ice cream was kept in tin cans about eight inches in diameter. Four such cans were packed in ice and kept in the cooler. A company would deliver the ice, smash it, mix it with rock salt, and pack it around the containers. At other times, John would be sent by his mother with a bowl, a dish cloth, and a quarter to buy ice cream. Mr. Brinda would scoop out the ice cream, place in the bowl, and cover it with the dish cloth.

John was intrigued with all the things in Mr. Brinda's store. There would be dry goods, grocery items, kerosene, and all sorts of things. To John it seemed Mr. Brinda could have anything he wanted. As a child, John did not realize that Mr. Brinda had to pay for these goods

John's mother was clear about whom he and his siblings could play with and whom they had to avoid. A family who lived in a duplex located just behind their house across the alley was declared off limits by his mother. His mother was concerned that the children not mix with the "wrong people." There was a Lebanese family living a half block down the street. John remembers his mother saying, "You don't play with those children. They are not the quality of people that we are." She was also concerned that the children keep to Catholicism. All of the family friends were Catholic.

He attended Webster Elementary School and was overwhelmed with the oak floors and stairway. The children would sing Christmas songs on a landing between the two floors. At Webster, John saw his first movie. This was a silent movie shown in the gym. There were pleasant memories, but discipline was firm. John definitively remembered when his teacher, Miss Anderson, put soap in his mouth because of bad language. In spite of this, he thought she was beautiful, and John fell in love with her.

This was a time period when new technology was entering into the daily lives of the people living in Northeast. John's family bought a Maytag washing machine. He sat behind that Maytag looking the mechanism, following it through the whole cycle. The mechanism fascinated it him. Of course, it was also warm in that corner because of the hot water in the machine.

A neighbor, Mr. Grounder, was a strong influence on John. He thought the Grounders were the ideal family. Mr. Grounder was a shoe maker. Mrs. Grounder was an attractive lady. John's family and the Grounders did much together. Mr. Grounder was funny, had good morals, and was a hard worker. He was also a good businessman. John learned much about business and how to act as a responsible man from him.

A more negative example came from one of John's relatives. His uncle and aunt were relatively wealthy and lived on Knox and Lowry in North Minneapolis, an area of impressive homes. He worked for Goodyear Tire and Rubber Company as a warehouse superintendent. He also owned an automobile repair shop and gas station. One day John and his father went to pick up their car at his uncle's station where it was being fixed. As he father paid the twelve dollars he owed, his uncle put eight dollars in the till and four in his pocket. He told John this was so the IRS would not tax the four dollars. John thought it was wrong and dishonest.

John's family was Polish-Catholic and went to the All Saints Roman Catholic Church. He stated, "…we were not an in-Polish Catholic family. We were a poor Polish Catholic family…I don't think we were accepted socially at church at all. They had their own cliques, you know. They were the people who did the Novena, and they did all these things together. They had women's clubs and men's clubs. We went to church as bottom-of-the-line Catholics."

John's mother and father took different approaches to church. His father seldom went to church, yet he demanded that the children go. His mother went to church as often as she could.

John's own relationship to church was one of awe. Festivals affected him deeply. The forty days of Lent were strictly kept in his house, which included a ban on playing the radio, singing, and eating meat. A major feast was held on Good Friday. The children received new clothes on Christmas and Easter. He studied the Catholic catechism at the Margaret Berry House which on Broadway in the Beltrami neighborhood. There was a Catholic priest from Southeast Minneapolis who said mass and led the catechism class. His first communion was in the priest's parish in Southeast Minneapolis.

John was serious about religion when he was young. He considered priesthood when he was about eight or ten years of age. As many young boys who were religious, he wanted to be an altar boy. It was a great disappointment to find out that since he did not attend a Catholic school he was not eligible for this. This left a sour taste in his mouth and made him question his allegiance. He was also struck by the disrespect shown his family by the children from the parochial school who cut through their backyard on their way home or to school. When they did this they would often call his mother dirty names. These experiences began to drive a wedge between John and the Catholic Church.

Some future directions clarified for John when he was eight years old. He began to make money. John and his brother sold magazines such as *Liberty, Ladies Home Journal,* and *Saturday Evening Post.* They developed a route beginning at their house, down 5th street to East Hennepin, and along East Hennepin to downtown Minneapolis. They would stop at offices and stores. They began the route immediately after school, three days a week. As John looked back at this time he recognized that his play life stopped and he entered a new phase of life focused on work.

John's brother soon ran into trouble. He spent the money received from customers instead of paying the distributors. This put the family in debt with the magazine company (the distributor). This had to be paid back. At first, John worked alone on the route to get rid of the debt. Later his younger sister helped. They cleared around fifty to sixty cents a week. Eventually, they settled the debt and began to be able to contribute some of their income to the family. In those years, children were expected to contribute a portion of their income to help with household expenses or needs. Being able to do this was a point of pride for John. He continued the magazine route until he found a newspaper route at the age of twelve, which he continued until he graduated from high school.

After Webster John went to Sheridan Junior High and later to Edison High School. He was "not a good student." There was little opportunity to study in a home with no privacy and noise constantly coming from active children and a blaring radio. In spite of this, John was the only child in the family to finish high school.

When he graduated from high school he led the class to the baccalaureate. He described himself as the "proudest guy in the world." His dad would not go because he heard that a Protestant minister was giving the prayer.

During high school, John was deeply involved in Hi Y, which was a program developed by the YMCA for young men in Northeast Minneapolis. His father opposed this involvement. He argued that the YMCA was anti-Catholic. John persisted and made some of his best and most enduring friends through Hi Y.

John's involvement with Hi Y reflected a growing conflict between his father and John, his sisters, and his brother. The four children were making friends and having experiences that led them to question their connection to the Catholic church. Later, they all married non-Catholics. John's father did not attend any of the weddings.

When John graduated from high school in 1940, he decided to go on for more education. The option of working with his dad at the cabinet factory did not appeal to him. He wanted to have a better chance at financial success. Another reason he wanted to avoid his father's occupation was that even in these years John was a Republican and did not like the pro-union, Democratic atmosphere of the shops in which his father worked. John went to Minneapolis Business College. He studied banking, bookkeeping and typing. He also met his future wife while studying there.

Soon after John began his post-secondary studies the Japanese attack on Pearl Harbor occurred. John realized that he was likely to be drafted. The idea of living in the field as a ground soldier did not appeal to him, so he went to see a recruiter for the Navy about becoming an officer in naval aviation. Since he was not twenty-one, he had to get his mother's permission in order to enlist. She refused at first, but relented after he received a draft notice. Four months later, in the spring of 1942, he enlisted in the Navy.

He was assigned to Naval Air to become a pilot. To achieve this assignment he had to cheat on his hearing test in order to pass. He was assigned to fly torpedo bombers and called to duty in January, 1943. John started at a prep school located on the campus of the University of Washington in Seattle, Washington. Following this, he was assigned to St. Mary's College, just outside of Oakland, California. There he completed preflight school. Next he was in flight school at Olethia, Kansas. He was commissioned as an Ensign in Corpus Christi, Texas, while in the final phase of flight training. Finally, he was assigned to a squadron in Fort Lauderdale, Florida. He had been given orders that would send him to the Pacific. Before these could be executed, the war ended. John was discharged in 1945.

While he was at St. Mary's , John attended religious classes led by a Catholic priest. John was full of questions and had many conversations with the priest. He found that he was increasingly dissatisfied with what he heard. This fed the unease he felt toward the church that had been developing since he was a young boy living on Adams Street in Northeast.

After the Navy he was hired by a major, international corporation. He began in 1945 as an accountant and stayed with this company for his entire career. John described his career as a case of perfect timing and good luck. Things were exploding. This corporation is now one of the largest in the world. John's career rode along with the growth of his company. He continued to admire the company for which he worked and has stayed on with it after retirement in a volunteer, emeritus status.

He moved back with his parents and finally got his own bedroom as he was the only child at home. There was a lot of evening work. This continued throughout his career. He was a company man and thoroughly loyal.

Throughout the war he had been in close communication with a woman he met during business college and who was to become his wife. They talked of marriage. She told him that she would not marry during the war because she did not want someone with one arm as her husband. When he came back she said she would not marry anyone without a job. Finally, all the pieces came together and they decided to marry. This created a problem with his parents since she was not Catholic. They liked her but would not attend the ceremony which was held at Central Lutheran Church in downtown Minneapolis in March of 1946.

John and his wife moved to South Minneapolis. They lived in a furnished apartment for forty dollars a month. They attended Central Lutheran Church, where they were active, even organizing the first young married couples club, and made many friends from church. These, along with John's Hi Y friends, made up their social group.

Holidays were spent either at his wife's parents' farm or his parents' house on Adams Street. Indeed, the visits to John's parents soon became their only link to Northeast Minneapolis. Their lives began to take shape and were defined by work, their friends, and church involvement. Unlike others with whom I spoke, John did not feel comfortable in Northeast after he returned from the service in World War Two. As he stated it, "I suppose I had been exposed to so much more. My whole life [before I went into the Navy] was [spent with] in three or four miles, until I went into the Navy. My friends. Even my newspaper and magazine businesses. The church. The school…[after I got out] Yeah. I certainly felt nothing about Northeast. And I have tried to redevelop some of these acquaintances with the neighbor boys. It's never worked out.…I had seen some old friends at funerals. But nothing has ever developed other than my High Y group. And that is still together. That was upper Northeast. That made the difference in my life. I remember my parents were looking at a house up on Lowry. Dad had many big dreams, and he just could not afford it. I was excited about that. I think that was my most exciting childhood thought. I would get to move up there."

In 1949, John received a transfer to Memphis, Tennessee. He and his wife packed everything they had into a brand new Chevrolet and moved. In the next twenty one years they moved from Memphis, Tennessee, to Buffalo, New York, San Francisco, California, and finally back to Minneapolis. John had a highly successful career. Much happened with his family during that time. They had two children, and John's mother and father both died. They visited John's family every two years during that time period. These visits were important for renewing friendships with the group of men that John had met in Hi Y.

In 1968, John took a position in the central corporate offices in the Twin Cities. His son was still in high school, and John and his wife thought it important that he graduate before they moved. So, John moved to Minneapolis while his wife and children stayed in San Francisco until 1970. After his son had graduated, John's wife and daughter joined John in the Twin Cities. From 1968 to 1970, he lived by himself in an apartment in the western suburbs. He worked two jobs to be able to afford frequent flights back to San Francisco to visit his family.

When John and his wife were talking about where to live in the Twin Cities, the only stipulations that his wife made were that she would not live in Northeast and they would not buy a summer lake house. John said that he felt no great need or desire to live in Northeast. In fact, to do so seemed like a step down in terms of social class and type of people with whom they would live. They ended up living in New Brighton, a 1970s era suburb five miles north of Northeast Minneapolis. They moved into their present home in September, 1970.

John retired in 1982 at the age of 61. The first thing he did was to empty his desk. Then he threw away his pipes and tobacco. He also threw away his razor and grew a beard.

With retirement he found that the prestige he had built up at work disappeared. The day he walked out the door he was a nobody, and he found he had an adjustment to make. He still works with his old company as a volunteer. This is primarily with other retirees. Other than that, he does not socialize with former coworkers. He and his wife are active in volunteer work with a variety of organizations in the Twin Cities and heavily involved in a nearby Lutheran church.

Their social life now is made up mostly of their children and their families and the friends that John first made in his Hi Y involvement. Oddly enough, there are few friends that come from his days of employment or from their travels around the country. Instead, Northeast continues to be part of his life through these long enduring friendships.

As John looked back on his life he deemed it a success. He received a good, practical education, built a successful career with a major firm, married well, and raised two children to be productive members of society. He attributes much of his success to good mentoring from key individuals early in his life, a strong work ethic gained while growing up in Northeast Minneapolis, a supportive marriage, and extraordinary good luck. From his early childhood through his early twenties he lived in Northeast. He was shaped to be a person who valued work and loyalty. His work ethic paid off. His loyalty has been rewarded with lifetime friendships that were first formed in Northeast through involvement in sports and a high school YMCA program.

Northeast Minneapolis is built

By the start of this time period, the basic outline of Northeast Minneapolis had been determined. Throughout the 1920s and 1930s, houses were climbing northward up the hill toward Columbia Heights, one of the first ring suburbs of Minneapolis, and eastward to the other side of Johnson Avenue. The most northeast portion of Northeast Minneapolis, Waite Park, was built between 1934 and 1955. The shape of Northeast Minneapolis in this time period is closely linked to the streetcar network that had been built. This followed a typical pattern where businesses followed streetcar lines up main thoroughfares, like Central and University Avenues. The flow of passengers helped determine the density and types of businesses along these thoroughfares. For example, large buildings and businesses were located at major junctions (Baerwald 1989, 41).

Paved streets, electricity, water and sewer lines, and indoor plumbing reached most of Northeast Minneapolis by World War Two. These were momentous and exciting changes for those living in Northeast. My informants spoke of improvements in comfort, health, and safety. In particular, the arrival of electricity and indoor plumbing were occasions for pride and optimism. These changes defined life in Northeast Minneapolis as progressive and hopeful.

Neighborhoods were still well bounded and small. One woman described her neighborhood north of Lowry and west of Central as a "shouting neighborhood." Children could play within a range extending to the limits of their parents' shouting voices or whistles. Effectively, this was an area extending one or two blocks north and south and into the backyards of the houses along the street and front yards of houses across the street.

Life in Northeast neighborhoods in this time period was relatively stable, even though economic conditions were rough. People moved less often and, in general, the people owned the properties in which they lived.

> Most of the houses around there were owned by people who lived in them. They were small houses to begin with, [but] they added on. Either because of more kids coming or because they wanted to have some money. [from renters]. But they lived in the houses too.

A general perception developed among those who lived in Northeast that there was a distinct difference between neighborhoods. My informants thought that neighborhoods became better and more prestigious further north of Lowry and east of Central. One woman wrote in a letter to me:

> It was often joked that people west of Central dreamed of moving east of Central, that those people east of Central dreamed of moving east of Johnson. They were the elite of Northeast. But even they had a dream—to move to a suburb, first to St. Anthony, then to New Brighton. By and large, the people east of Central were better off financially and educationally.

In reality, there were distinct differences in neighborhoods, defined by ages of the houses and social standings of the residents. St. Anthony Boulevard, or "the Boulevard," and Stinson Avenue emerged as two of the more prestigious addresses during this time period. In the most general terms, it was accepted by many that the more one moved in a northeast direction, the more affluent the neighborhood. Conversely, moving in a southwest direction meant moving to less affluent neighborhoods. These two directions roughly correspond to "Upper Northeast" and "Lower Northeast." They also correspond to newer and older parts of Northeast Minneapolis. This pattern is accurate at the more general level, but, in reality, persons of wealth lived scattered through the neighborhoods and were not absolutely confined to certain parts of Northeast. There are some striking properties in "Lower Northeast" that were well known and in which families of wealth and power lived.

Northeast was often compared to South or Southeast Minneapolis. One woman talked about the excitement of meeting good, Swedish young men while attending dances at ballrooms in South Minneapolis. Others remembered their reactions when these young men discovered that my informants were from Northeast Minneapolis. They were surprised that the young women from Northeast did not speak with accents and were well educated. To many outsiders, Northeast as seen as being an industrial, working class part of town, populated with uneducated immigrants, and less prestigious than other parts of the city. Some bristled when they remembered how those in more affluent neighborhoods would refer to Northeast Minneapolis as "Nordeast," which stigmatized Northeast and characterized the people who lived there as uneducated immigrants.[1]

Key institutions

During this time period key institutions that continue to the present to help define neighborhood life were established. Edison High School was built in 1922 (*Sun Newspapers* 1976, 18). Edison turned out to be a vital force in shaping the social world of Northeast Minneapolis. It thoroughly represented the ethnic variety of the neighborhood in terms of who attended, "The 1933 yearbook staff noted that Edison students came from twenty-three different [European most assuredly] nations" (Olson 1997, 5). Evidence of the Swedish population in Northeast is shown by the fact that in 1923 there were so many Johnsons that a club called the "Johnsons" was formed to included all with that last name. According to a member of this club, it had fifty-seven members.

Edison High School also turned out to be strong force of assimilation for its students, many of whom were first generation born in the United States. At Edison High School young persons from "Lower Northeast" and "Upper Northeast" met and, often, became friends. They encountered ethnic, religious, and class differences and grew to accept a closer affinity with American culture. For some of my informants, this was a powerful and dramatic realization. This was especially true for those from "Lower Northeast." Some of those whom I interviewed who lived in these areas clearly remembered the fear they felt as they envisioned being in class with those they assumed to be wealthier. They also remembered when they realized that they could successfully compete with those from "Upper Northeast" in academics and sports. This meant that they too were fully American and able to succeed in the greater society.

Parks were established early in Northeast Minneapolis's history. Long-term residents spoke of parks as important parts of their youth and young adult years. One man, who is one of my older informants, remembered playing in parks during this time period. Indeed, the alternatives he mentioned may have encouraged the redesign of parks as playgrounds.

> To the north of us a little bit, across from Lowry Avenue, there was a grain elevator. They owned a lot of property over there. And that's where all the kids hung out. At least, after they got a little past grade school. That's where we played ball. Kicked everything around. We didn't bother anything over there. The backstop for baseball was a storage place for records for the elevator. We could often go into the elevator in the evening. The watchman let us come in there. We could run over the rollers that move the grain around from one elevator to the other. Columbia Park came later. There was Sandy Lake out there. On the south side of Sandy Lake was the Soo Line Railroad yards and a big pole yard. Telephone poles and that sort of stuff. For us it was a huge place. There were no signs or anybody saying you couldn't this or do that, and so forth. It was also a place where hoboes came to stay occasionally over there. It was always on the south side of the lake. Between the pole yards and the railroad yards over there. We built a dugout and used scrap lumber from the pole yard and any other place we could it over there. And it lasted for a long time until somebody burned it down. I never swam. I don't know of anybody ever swimming in the lake over there. There was a creek and a lot of fireflies. It was a very shallow lake. It was a swamp around it over there. It was drained by the Park Board to make a golf course in the mid-1920s.

He and his friends would also go to Logan Park for ice skating, Bottineau and Jackson Park for ball games, and Windom Park for church picnics. He did not mention swimming pools. In fact, the absence of a swimming pool in Northeast has long been a sore point for many in Northeast. In a July 26, 1935 *Argus* editorial the writer called for a swimming pool and recalls that demands for one had been heard for years. The article goes on to state that, "…each quarry or river drowning raises the chorus anew…meanwhile children continued to walk weary miles to the Camden pool or risk their lives in the Mississippi and unguarded quarry pools (quoted in *Northeaster* 1995, 16).

Community concerts were held in neighborhood parks. These were well attended. One man recalls going to Windom Park for outdoor concerts. He guessed that 400 to 500 people would come to hear the fifteen to twenty piece band play under the open skies. Popcorn buggies were lined up along the park. People sang along with the band while it played popular music of the day. Another man who grew up in the same neighborhood remembers that at 1:00 on the day of the concert the popcorn, ice cream, and peanut vendors would arrive with their one horse-drawn wagons. Soon the popcorn poppers would be banging away. If a popcorn vendor saw a child lounging on a doorstep he might offer a free bag of popcorn (most likely from yesterday's batch) in exchange for watering his horse. This man remembered that he was often that lucky child.

Parks were centers of neighborhoods. My informants recalled that the park boundaries were well-known in terms of which neighborhoods were to be served. For example, one woman was very active in programs at Bottineau Park. She outlined the area from which children came as bounded by 13th on the south, Lowry on the north, the river on the west, and 6th on the east. Children living south of 13th would utilize Logan Park.

Although most churches were established prior to World War Two, this period saw the establishment of some key churches in Northeast Minneapolis (see Figure 3.1). Churches continued to draw heavily from the immediate neighborhoods and were still strong shapers of neighborhood and community life. One man, who is a life-long member of Salem Covenant Church, reported that the Windom Park Neighborhood was heavily populated with members of the church. In fact, he estimates that in this

FIGURE 3.1: *Northeast Minneapolis churches established from 1920 to 1940*

1925	Concordia Lutheran Church (Governor Theodore Christianson spoke at its dedication)
1926	Elmwood Lutheran Church
1926	Ukrainian Orthodox Autocephalic Parish of St. Michael the Archangel
1936	Mt. Carmel Roman Catholic Church
1936	First Wesleyan Methodist Church of Minneapolis (now Waite Park Wesleyan Methodist Church)
1938	St. Charles Borromeo
1940	First Ukrainian Evangelical Baptist Church (shared building with Elim Baptist)

time period around one half of the homes that faced the park were owned and lived in by persons who attended Salem.

It was in this time period that immigrant churches became Americanized and defined in terms of church life and structures as found in North America. For example, Elim Baptist and Salem Covenant churches started out as Swedish Baptist and Swedish Mission churches, respectively. When they were established in 1888 and 1889, they clearly reflected ethnicity and European cultural patterns. Drinking alcohol and smoking were not considered to be improper around the turn of the century. Gradually, they were redefined in terms of stricter American Protestant patterns and were recast as fundamentalist churches, with all of their expectations of behavior and certain types of conformity. This meant that playing cards, going to movies, smoking, dancing, and drinking alcohol were prohibited. One man remembers that at Salem Covenant it was considered improper for women to cut their hair. If a young woman bobbed her hair she could not attend Sunday School.

Northeast Neighborhood House continued its work as an active settlement house. It continued to purpose to meet the needs of new immigrants and their families and help them to become "good Americans." This was attempted through such mundane programs as lessons and programs in dancing, drama, and cooking. In addition, there were Campfire Girls meetings, Halloween parties, daycare, preschool (or pre-kindergarten), and, of course, sports.

> I remember the kids from the Northeast Neighborhood House area. They called it the Nut House. They learned to play together and participate together in sports…those guys, because they had a gym, they developed some good athletes down there. Those guys from the Nut House would come to Edison and they'd been playing together for years. It was tough for someone on the hill to break in. You had to be good to break that barrier.

A man who played sports at Northeast Neighborhood House recalled the organized league play. Teams from other communities and schools from all over the city played each other. The competition was fierce, and there was much neighborhood pride at stake. Northeast Neighborhood House teams dominated these leagues and were known as powerhouses. Edison High School sports teams were led by stars who grew up playing at Northeast Neighborhood House.

The children and youth who participated in programs at Northeast Neighborhood House came from neighborhoods that were west of Central Avenue, which was the line of demarcation between largely Southern and Eastern European, Catholic or Orthodox neighborhoods and Northern and Western European, Protestant neighborhoods. Children and youth from neighborhoods east of Central were more likely to participate in an extensive YMCA church league basketball program that established in Protestant churches. There was organized league play with games were played in church and school gymnasiums. Churches built in this time period included gymnasiums, as they were seen as essential for attracting young persons. The young men who played in this league were required to attended Sunday school at least three times a month in a local church. Given this requirement, it is not surprising that few Roman Catholics participated in this program.

Another influential program was the High Y club. Edison High School had an active group. This was a program for young men and attempted to shape them into productive, godly adults. There was strong emphasis on character building and leadership development. A number of men reported that their closest and most important life-long friends came from this group. Active members of the Edison High Y club moved into business, church, and community leadership and were strong forces in Northeast Minneapolis over the next fifty years.

Key to the success of the High Y program were young men who made up the staff. Many were part time workers who attended colleges in the area. Ed Willow, in particular, stands out as a key leader and role model. Ed Willow began working at the Northeast YMCA in 1927 as a twenty-two year old and spent his entire professional life working there. At that time he was name Ed Wribtzky and later changed his last name to Willow in a move that reflected the general interest in being "All American" (*Northeaster* 1990, 17). Some of my informants remembered that Mr. Willow personally mentored them, encouraging them to succeed in school, live according to strict morals, and think about preparing for future careers.

Fraternal lodges and community service organizations continued to be active. The Arcana Lodge of the Masons had 362 members by January 1, 1921 (Olson 1996, 11). The Knights of Columbus and Merchants associations were also active. Some of these organizations were based upon ethnicity. The Ukrainian Educational Home was established at Jackson and Summer in 1925 and offered a drama society, folk dance ensemble, and an orchestra. In 1927, the Polanie Club was established for women with Polish background (*Sun Newspapers* 1976, 34). The Polish White Eagle Association filed articles of incorporation on August 5, 1926, with the State

of Minnesota. This enabled it to receive a charter from the State of Minnesota Insurance Department permitting it to sell life insurance. In 1941 it
bought and moved into its present building at 1300 Northeast Second
Street. Policies were restricted to those persons who were Roman Catholic and of Slavic origin. It also served a social function. For example, in
1935, its baseball team played in and won the championship in the top city
Senior Division (Polish White Eagle Association 1981, 10, 38).

In 1928, a second institution was established for the care of older persons. Aaron Carlson, a member of Salem Covenant Church, donated his
home at Hayes and 23rd Street Northeast for this purpose. It was dedicated
as a "resort for older pilgrims" and eventually became known as Bethany
Covenant Home (Wiberg 1995, 40). It continues today as a long-term care
facility in newer brick buildings that replaced the original Carlson home.

Commercial and business life

By this time period, Central Avenue was the primary commercial and
retail street of Northeast Minneapolis. It continued to be a walking street
where one saw many persons going from store to store and walking home
with their purchases. The automobile was becoming an important part of
urban life, and Central developed as a significant carrier of auto traffic. It
provided easy access to the downtown area, South Minneapolis, and Northern Minnesota. As Central Avenue continued north it eventually turned
into Highway 65, stretching to the northern towns of Cambridge, Mora,
and McGregor.

A good portion of the lives of some of my informants took place around
or on Central Avenue. They visited doctors or dentists, bought school
clothes, dated their future spouses, opened saving accounts or applied for
loans at banks, and just strolled the "Ave."

Central Avenue was above all a shopping street. One man remembered
that in the 1920s, "Central was a thriving business street. There were five
or six grocery stores. There were also around four drug stores." Others
spoke of jewelry stores, like Gustafsons, Gabchar, and Earle Nordland's
on Lowry and Central. Another man spoke of hardware stores, "The hardware stores were fine operations. Carlsons on 24th and Central. Anderson
on 19th and Central."

While more expensive, fine clothing was usually bought at stores on
Hennepin or in downtown Minneapolis, Central Avenue clothing stores
were well-known and patronized. In a conversation with two women, I
heard them reminisce, "How about the ladies' wear shop up here? They

had Johnson Sisters. Johnson Sisters was an excellent store. 22nd and Central...Simonson's Dry Goods Store...We had several shoe stores too." One woman said she did most of her clothes shopping on Central, "If Johnsons didn't have it, we went to O. E. Larsons. They gave good service and they always gave us good prices."

Another person said, "You could get just about anything—hardware, clothes." She went on to describe that

> we had a grocery store, of course, and everything right within two blocks, everything was right in the neighborhood...but our main shopping area was Central Avenue. That was a big excursion. We would go on Saturday. Some three or four of us would walk to Central. That was quite a shopping area at that time. There was a very nice store. The Mrs. Johnson's department. It was a lovely lady's store. That was the store on Central. And there was a men's store down the...in fact, they were in there until very recently. Finally, finally, closed up. It was a thriving avenue.

For many people, Central was a place to shop for certain types of goods. "Most of my shopping on Central was for clothes and things of that sort. I'll shop at the same places over there. Our dentist was there. It was the place where we banked....That was where my shopping was done. I think my brothers too....We could walk down there."

Services of many types could be found on Central Avenue. Banks have long been a feature on Central. From their first beginnings, they grew to be substantial institutions. In 1927, Central Bank had deposits totaling $1,491,591.89 (*Sun Newspapers* 1976, i). They were pillars of the community. One man described this as:

> The two banks were fine operations. They really drew people from all over the city. They had a lot of commercial accounts. Central and Fidelity both. People from outside the area.

Many spoke of a certain character to the business community. One woman described it as, "An active business community. Very active. Very friendly, sort of small town feeling about it." Another man said, "I remember the Central Avenue Merchant's Association. That was a going outfit." A woman agreed, "Yes. Very much so. Everybody on the avenue belonged." One man remembered that:

> In the old days Central was a shopping area. Our best season was Christmas. People would actually walk up and down Central Avenue, shopping. We would open up three weeks until Christmas and be open every night

until 9:00. There were times we would have people three or four deep in the store. We would have extra help. From the normal four waiting on people we would have eight waiting on people. There were several apparel stores, hardware stores, and furniture stores. Gradually you lost that type of store....We had small grocery stores that were more or less run out by the big ones....We used to have a lot of dentists and doctors on Central Avenue. Lowry and Central. 23rd and Central. Like Dr. Arlander and Olson. They built on Jackson and 23rd.

A strong characteristic of life in Northeast was that people knew each other. This extended to relationships between customers and merchants on Central. When asked if he knew people in shops along Central, one man replied:

Oh yes. I knew all. Most of them were owners that owned the places over there....I think most of them [customers] went to the same places all the time. Drug stores that were there we went to all the time. The were a couple of them there across from each other. But you always went to the same one.

The merchants who owned stores along Central Avenue lived in Northeast Minneapolis and were highly committed to Northeast as a community. One man said that merchants were, "community minded." Another man said, "And they supported the area. Much more so than they have now."

Central Avenue was used and seen differently by people in Northeast. Not everyone saw it as merely a place to shop. For some, the Arion Movie Theater was an attraction. For others, Central was the place to see and be seen by others. Walking the Avenue was a favorite occupation for some teenagers in Northeast Minneapolis.

Walk to Central? Oh yes, we walked all over. We didn't have a ride in those days. If you want to go some place you walked or you didn't go...And the kids from school, we'd walk up there. The library was there. The fire station was there....Yes. For a malted milk. five cents. Danielson's Drug Store. Then we got malts in there for five cents.

One woman described this:

I remember going to the Argus Publishing. We knew everybody there. Everybody would stop in there all the time. Just to see what's new in the newspaper....It was like our own little community....I remember there was a place along here too where you could go get malted milk for a nickel, I think. But you always went to the same little stores.

This depended, to some extent, on where one lived in Northeast Minneapolis. Those who lived further west frequented Central Avenue less often. One woman who lived closer to University remembered that she spent more time in the area of the Ritz Theater on 13th and University Avenue. In addition to the theater, a hamburger shop attracted young people to that area. Another person who lived west of Central said:

It was [a shopping area] but we didn't go there because that was almost a ten block walk. And they didn't have anything there that we couldn't get closer in. You know without a car. No [it was not the area in which we used to shop]. Who is going to haul a couple bags of groceries. My mother used to buy flour by the fifty pound sacks. That wasn't the kind of stuff you liked to haul.

Central was also a symbol of differences within Northeast and helped define different communities. One man recalled that:

The east [neighborhoods east of Central] was the newest part at that time...[but] It was more of a mental boundary. When you think of all these immigrants. Accounting for the growth of the Sons of Norway and the Odd fellows and the Swedes. They were kind of buffer groups for people that came over to maintain a relationship. That led to a certain amount of clannishness.

Johnson Avenue also emerged as an important, but smaller, commercial area at this time. For example, the Hollywood Theater located on Johnson Avenue north of Lowry, opened in 1935.[2]

Central and Johnson were two of the major commercial streets in Northeast, but, for many, neighborhood stores provided almost everything that was needed.

There were so many stores around the place. You didn't have to walk far. We would always go down to Grandfather's place [a store]. But there was a store just across the street, the Ptaks' Store, on the corner of 23rd. There was one on 4th Street, two of them on 4th Street in that block. Another two blocks away on 5th Street. One of our relatives, my mother's sister, was married to a butcher and they had a butcher shop on 5th Street. You didn't have to go very far to buy things you needed.

Some residents of Northeast would shop at a number of different neighborhood stores.

We had two here. One on the corner of Grand and 30th. And one over here on 30th and California. It was wonderful. Jalinksys specialized in meat products, like Polish sausage. They would have notions like your thread and so on. Whereas the store on Grand had the canned goods and the ice cream and the candy and this sort of thing. They were open on Sunday whereas Jalinskys wasn't.

One often shopped at a store because of its proximity, not on the basis of pricing or service. Residents pointed out that this was a time when one walked to stores, churches, schools, and places of entertainment. The determination of which store a family patronized was also largely a function of a complex, multi-stranded relationship, built on friendship, common church participation, shared ethnicity, creditor-creditee ties, and merchant-customer connections. For example, one woman noted that her sister worked at a local store. This forced the family had to shop there, even though there was no employee's discount and other stores were more conveniently located and less expensive. Credit also was a huge factor that helped shape the decision as to where to shop. In this time period a line of credit provided some stability in being able to obtain needed supplies.

One man helped his parents with a family owned, neighborhood store. He recalled that in his neighborhood most of the residents were either Polish or Russian. His father's specialty was Polish sausage: "My dad made his own Polish sausage. He was well known for his sausage making. Smoked his own. Had his own smoke house. Mixed up his own spices…He was an outstanding butcher."

During the Easter season there would be a lineup of people waiting to order Polish sausage. As seemed to be the case for many trades and skills that men had during this time period, his father's butchering and sausage making skills were self taught.

Central Avenue and neighborhood stores were not the only places where retail activity took place in Northeast Minneapolis. Vendors and salespersons were frequent visitors and often seen on the front porches of Northeast homes. A Jewish man collected items to be discarded. He went door to door in neighborhoods east of Central, filling his horse drawn wagon with rags and other recyclable materials. Others vendors included milkmen, icemen, waffle wagons, ice cream vendors, farmers with produce, kerosene lamp lighters, the Watkins man who sold coffee, tea, and herbs, and the Jewell Tea Salesman.

Another commercial institution that was found in Northeast neighborhoods was the neighborhood bar or tavern. These were only found in the western part of Northeast. This was the result of city policy which aimed to cluster bars and taverns in certain locations in Minneapolis.

Daily life in Northeast Minneapolis

Life in Northeast continued to be small scale and face to face, centering on family, church, and neighborhood. In American cities there is a close connection between transportation technology and the shape and nature of the city. Northeast Minneapolis reflects this. In this time period, widespread acceptance and use of the automobile was just emerging. Much of life was still limited to areas within walking distance. Neighborhood residents walked to stores to shop, churches to worship, and theaters, like the Arion or the Ritz, malt shops, or taverns to socialize.

Indeed, as these long-term residents described their neighborhoods and neighborhood life, the neighborhoods started to sound like villages. Everyone was known, consensus on how to live was widespread, and life was familiar. It was rare to see a stranger in one's neighborhood.

There was a commonly accepted sense of safety in Northeast Minneapolis. My informants contrasted this with their lives today. As one woman recalled:

We always walked [to church]...we would kind of run sometimes. But there wasn't that much fear. I don't ever remember ever hearing of anybody that was molested...If we had heard [of any trouble], my parents wouldn't have let us go...[It is different today] Even around here with all that we have...I don't go out much at night. I take the car [when I do go out] and pull the [garage] door shut [when I return].

Life was safe and familiar. Neighbors knew one another. Entertaining or visiting with non-relatives in one's home was not common, according to most of my informants. One person argued that this might be because families had so little in the way of furniture or special food to share with one another. Socializing took place on sidewalks, across backyard fences, in taverns, and at churches. However, children knew no such prohibitions and were often in the homes of their friends. Few life events were kept secret from them, and they knew what went on in the families in their neighborhoods. They knew who spoke what language, what was eaten, how spouses got along, and what neighbors drank—what and how much. Even at times of crisis, children crossed their neighbors' thresholds.

I remember when people used to die. They would have them in the homes. They would have the wreathes on the outside of the house. They would have a big wreath. And we would be walking, "There's wreath, let's go in." And we would go in...Whether we knew the person or not. We thought it

was neat. [the body was] Right in the living room. All the time. That's the
way it used to be. Nobody ever had the casket in the funeral home.

My informants were changing from children and youth to adults in
this time period. Not surprisingly, some of the strongest memories and
most formative experiences have to do with family life. Some of these
memories are positive. My informants spoke of rich family times, centered
around food, fishing trips, or card games. They spoke of warm acceptance.
Many described healthy, loving interaction between their parents.

Others remembered more negative experiences with their families. For
example, one of the accepted parenting styles for men of this time period
was that of the stern task master. One man carried the scars of this in the
form of reduced hearing in one ear. This was caused by repeated slaps on
the side of his head given by his father when he thought he was moving
too slow or not listening closely enough.

> I had to do what he [my dad] told me...otherwise I got hit in the head. He
> never bothered about hitting me in the hind end where that cushion is
> made for spanking. He always knocked my glasses [off]...I had to go hunt-
> ing for glasses after he hit me because he always knocked them off. My dad
> was a bull headed, stubborn Frenchman....he said you can always try to
> prove me wrong, but there was no way you could ever do that. Even when
> I was grown up and married...he was never wrong. [when] We was little
> he would say something and if you didn't jump he would hit [you] across
> the head and knock you across the room or something. I don't know why
> I didn't lose my brains from that. This was the old [way]. I knew a lot of
> Polish people in Northeast. Their fathers were like that too. They were all
> like that....You would just be seen and be quiet. My dad was the boss.

Ethnicity continued to shape interaction and friendship. Indeed, Northeast was often described as a collection of ethnic villages. The majority of
the adult population in Northeast was foreign born. One man recalled
that all the homeowners in his neighborhood were born in Europe.

Ethnic patterns in Northeast Minneapolis were not locked in place. As
some ethnic groups prospered and moved out and up to more prestigious
neighborhoods they were succeeded by those who were not as successful.
The first settlers in Beltrami Park (then known as Maple Hill) included
many Swedes. They found work, achieved relative success, and moved north
to Windom Park with its newer homes and more prestige. Italian Americans moved in to replace them. Beltrami Park soon became known as an
Italian neighborhood.

In Northeast Minneapolis Italian railroad workers settled in the district known as Maple Hill or Dogtown. In 1905 the neighborhood was still composed largely of Swedes, Germans, and Poles, with only eighteen Italians. Over the next two decades, the latter increased to a peak of about 150 families. By 1920 about forty percent of the 766 Italians in Minneapolis were concentrated in this small area bounded by Hennepin on the south, Fillmore on the west, Johnson on the east, and Broadway on the north. As they did in St. Paul, Italians lived in small detached houses, which they usually owned. The neighborhood was noted for its flourishing gardens and its variety of barnyard animals—important sources of food. With the exception of those few who established grocery stores or saloons, the Italians for the most part worked in the section gangs or shops of the Soo Line Railroad. In time a considerable number secured sought-after jobs in Pillsbury flour mills. As in Swede Hollow, the Italians of Maple Hill comprised a mix of regional groups from the messogiorno. Certain towns of Calabria and the Abruzzi were strongly represented. Maple Hill (which in 1948 was renamed Beltrami) remained a coherent Italian community until well after World War II. (Vecoli 1981, 454)

One man recalled that in his neighborhood of Windom Park around ninety percent of the residents were Swedish-Americans. Rice confirms this in his survey of Scandinavians in Minnesota.

Another large Scandinavian settlement grew up in Northeast Minneapolis, where a concentration of flour mills, breweries, foundries, railroad repair shops, and small industries led to the development of a distinctive blue-collar community. In the early 20th century the boundary between the area's Scandinavian and Polish and Ukrainian people followed 5th Street, with the Scandinavians living to the east and the Slavs to the west. As late as 1930 Swedes were the largest single foreign-born group in Ward 9, the larger of the two Northeast wards. They dominated the Maple Hill-Columbia region, stretching from Broadway on the south to Columbia Park on the north, and the small Dogtown neighborhood south of Broadway. A stretch of Pierce Street was referred to as 'Swede Alley.' But even then they were beginning to move to South Minneapolis... Today in Northeast, Scandinavian neighborhoods are confined largely to an area east of Fillmore and north of 18th Avenue. They have been replaced west of Central mainly by the eastward-moving Slavs; in Dogtown they have been supplanted by the Italians. (1981, 263–264)

Ethnicity was expressed in the use of mother tongues. Informants reported growing up speaking or hearing Russian, Polish, Rusyn, or Swedish. One man, who was born in 1921, recalled having to learn English when he entered the first grade at Holy Cross Parochial School in 1927. His family only spoke Polish at home. He had learned a little English from playing with other children in the neighborhood but was not fluent in English before he attended school. He did not think of this immersion approach to language learning as difficult or unusual.

Children with older brothers and sisters had an advantage in learning English. Older siblings had started to learn English earlier and often taught their younger brothers and sisters in an informal manner by including them in their play with other children where English was almost always used. In addition, if a child was active in park programs or in events and programs at Northeast Neighborhood House he or she had extensive exposure to English.

Even as late as the mid-1930s, thirty-one percent of the population of Northeast could speak Polish, and many churches continued to use a language other than English in worship services and other settings during this time period (*Sun Newspapers* 1976, 3). Yet the tide was turning and English was beginning to displace other languages in the classroom, church, neighborhood streets, and home.

> Before World War I in the Holy Cross School, Polish and English had been used equally in classes; by 1930 it was employed only in teaching religion, although thirty-one percent of all the families in Northeast Minneapolis still spoke the Polish language in the mid-1930s. Attendance in high schools and the integration of neighborhood public schools reinforced the trend to English. Despite some complaints about the quality and decline of Polish, the strong tendency in 1915–30 was toward the adoption of English as a second language in church services and as the sole language in second-generation organizations. By the third or fourth generations English became the normal mother tongue. (Renkiewicz 1981, 374)

Some neighborhoods showed strong concentrations of one particular ethnic group. For example, many persons with Russian ancestry were concentrated around St. Mary's. Other neighborhoods were more mixed. One man listed Slovakian, French, Irish, and Swedish neighbors in his neighborhood west of Central and south of Lowry. A woman spoke of a mix of Irish, German, French, Polish, and Italian east of Central and north of Broadway.

At times, ethnicity created differences that were difficult to negotiate for children and young persons growing up in these neighborhoods. They learned early on that there were some ethnic groups that were acceptable and others that were not. One man, whose parents came from Poland, said, "And my mother did not like the Swedes and Norwegians, but they were not Polish, I suppose."

In Northeast ethnicity crosscut with location and religion. One man recalled:

> I had to go through the place where there were Polish people. What their elders were talking about came down through the children. So you'd try to get somebody a little stronger than you were to help you get home. It wasn't bad, throwing snowballs at each other and things like that.

A woman remembered:

> We were the only Orthodox in a Catholic community. They talk about bias these days. Do you know bias? At that time our church was still on the old Julian Calendar. And our Christmas came later. Did you ever live with, "You were the only one in the world to celebrate Christmas on the wrong day?" We lived through a lot.

Even though ethnicity continued to be an important feature of Northeast life during this time period, its importance was beginning to wan. My informants gradually entered a multiethnic, Euro-American world. One doorway to this world was the public school, where they met other students who represented a wide range of ethnicity. As they met young people from other ethnic groups, ethnicity sometimes became a topic of conversation. This might mean a serious comparing of backgrounds. It might also lead to lighter times.

> When we got older and [would] go to house parties and gatherings of kids who were fourteen or fifteen years old, we would make fun of our parents because they spoke backwards…I remember one party when we were saying, "How do you say this in our language and how do you say this?" And we would laugh. And one of them would say, "How do you say peanuts in your language?" And we thought and thought and thought, and somebody said, "Peanatsa."

Many churches were still defined by ethnicity. For example Holy Cross was Polish, St. Mary's was Russian, Mt. Carmel and St. Anthony's were Italian, St. Boniface and St. Paul's were German, Elim and Salem were Swedish, Our Lady Lourdes was French Canadian, St. John's was Rusyn[3] and St. Cyrils was Slovakian. Language again played an important role. Services were held in German, Polish, Slovakian, Swedish, and Italian. As children or young people, many of the subjects spoke of going to church Sunday after Sunday and not understanding a word of what was being said.

During World War One, a rising tide of patriotism encouraged some of those active in the local churches to think that English should replace other languages. The actual replacement of the existing languages by English came slowly. In 1928, Swedish was still being used in sermons at Salem Covenant Church (then known as Salem Swedish Mission Church). The then-current pastor could not preach in English. One man, who was confirmed at Salem Covenant Church in 1926, recalled that confirmation classes were taught in Swedish. He had no problems with this since he grew up in a home where Swedish was used and he was fluent in Swedish. Other children, however, could not understand Swedish. We can only guess that they did not learn very much in confirmation.

Churches established schools. Some of these were full time, day schools. They taught a standard curriculum with added emphases on ethnic and religious traditions. Others were supplemental in nature. The "Russian School" was held at St. Mary's after the regular school hours and emphasized language and religion. Elim Baptist Church held religion classes in the afternoon after public schools let out. In the earlier part of this era, public schools let students go to "religious training" classes during school hours. These were held at neighborhood churches. My informants remembered walking double file to classes at local churches.

Religion can separate as well as bring people together. For these subjects this was a time of tension between Protestants, Roman Catholics, and Orthodox. One point of tension occurred at marriage. When someone married a person from other Christian traditions the result was often heavy criticism or outright rejection by the family. One man reported that when his Catholic sister married a Protestant man his father attended neither the ceremony nor the reception. Even though the newly married couple lived across the alley from the wife's parents, the father-in-law did not talk to or remain in the same room with his son-in-law from the wedding until after the birth of the first child.

There was suspicion between Protestants and Roman Catholics. One woman, while a student at St. Anthony High School in the 1920s, was asked to be a godparent to a child born to a Protestant couple. When she told her classmates and that she had attended the baptism of the child at a Lutheran church, she was ridiculed by her classmates. They called her a traitor and asked her if she had admitted this transgression when she went to confession.

Within specific Christian traditions there were more subtle differences and points of dispute. For example, among the Protestants, subjects spoke of "strict churches" and those that were not so "strict." Salem Swedish Covenant was one of the strict churches (according to persons from other churches). This meant that attendance at movies, dances, and use of alcohol were greatly discouraged. One person who was from this tradition jokingly defined a strict church as a church "Where its members didn't drink in front of each other."

Relative wealth affected the unity of specific congregations. One woman recalled that even though her family was active at Holy Cross, her mother did not feel accepted by other women in the church:

> My mother didn't monkey around too much [at church]. She felt they were real cliquey and she didn't belong. And she had too much to do at home. With four little kids....There are always some that are the doers, you know. And they try to control things, and they're the big shots. I think she felt left out or inadequate or something. I would say yes [they were people with more money]. They might have been. Like one of them was the grocery store person. They made more money...they lived in bigger houses and had more money. So, I guess we didn't quite fit in.

From the earliest ages, one's primary friends came from neighborhoods or churches. This often meant shared ethnicity. This began to change over time. High school was a key turning point for many as they encountered and learned about other ethnic and religious groups in Northeast. Differences based on religion or ethnicity began to be reduced. One woman who lived on the west side of Central recalled thinking that those who lived east of Central were all wealthy Swedes. At Edison she was struck by two things. First, she felt poor for the first time in her life. She saw that there were other students who did have more money, fancier clothes, and more options. Second, she found out that not all the people living east of Central were wealthy. Many were just as poor as she.

Differences along the lines of skin color were highly charged, however. Persons who were not Euro-Americans were almost totally missing by this time period. This is striking since Northeast, or St. Anthony, was the site of the first neighborhood clustering of African Americans in Minneapolis.

> It was the settlers of St. Anthony who formed the first formal Black religious organization in Minnesota. The village of St. Anthony, settled in 1849, was the earliest municipal unit in what later became the city of Minneapolis, with which it was consolidated in 1872. There sometime in 1857 eight families of free Blacks from Missouri, Arkansas, and Illinois are said to have settled near the Falls of St. Anthony. Because houses were in short supply, they stayed in the basement of a hotel known as the Winslow House and at Fort Snelling until shelter could be erected. It seems probable that

the founding members of St. James African Methodist Episcopal Church of St. Anthony were among this group…They continued to meet in various St. Anthony homes until 1863, by which time their numbers had doubtless been augmented by new arrivals. Two years later the combined Black population of St. Anthony and Minneapolis totaled seventy-eight persons, fifty of whom lived in St. Anthony. (Taylor 1981, 75–76)

Only a few of the subjects could recall persons of color living in Northeast. One woman told of an African American woman living south of Lowry and east of Central. This woman was a midwife and assisted the subject's mother with a number of births, including the informant's own. A man recalled that an African American family moved into his neighborhood east of Central and south of Lowry and took over a local store. They only stayed for one year. No one in the neighborhood would buy from them, even though this store was heavily used prior to their arrival. They were forced to give up the business and leave the area.

My informants reported very little, if any, interaction with persons of color. Indeed, as they described a cultural patterns that reflected the strictly divided and stratified world of ethnicity of America in this time period. More than one informant said that Blacks lived on the other side of the river in North Minneapolis and "would have to have had a passport to cross the bridge into Northeast." As a further indication of the time, one woman reported that in the 1920s "Negro" skits with white students acting in black face were popular at Edison High School.

There was latent, and sometimes active, hostility toward Blacks. One man said, "Years ago you never found a Black in Northeast. Never." His wife agreed, "They weren't allowed to come." Another woman said, "The Blacks wouldn't dare come here. Cause the Northeast fellows were tough and they didn't want them. They let it be known they didn't want them on this side of the river."

Northeast Minneapolis was a blue collar neighborhood. The Soo Line was a major employer, and the whistle at the Soo Line railyards regulated the lives of those living nearby. A morning whistle signaled the start of school. There were whistles for lunch and dinner. At 9:00 p.m., a whistle signaled the start of curfew.

As Northeast developed, it took on a defined role within the city of Minneapolis. It was seen by outsiders as an industrial area with ethnic populations. Some of my informants report that they recognized that who lived in South and Southwest Minneapolis held negative stereotypes of Northeast and its people. In an interview with one woman, this topic came up as we discussed the use of the term "Nordeast" to refer to the area.

I don't recall hearing it when I was a youngster. Perhaps I wasn't sensitive to that.... [I] never, never [used it]. And my family, my brothers and sisters never used it either. And I don't recall any of my friends, who are all from Northeast and we still get together, they never used it. And I don't recall anyone in the neighborhood ever using it. I feel it is degrading. Referring to Northeast as the immigrant, the uneducated community...Crude. I never liked that term and I never used it. As I said, I don't remember anyone around the neighborhood ever using it. It's the outsiders that started that. That's my feeling. Maybe to irritate someone.

Although blue collar workers made up the majority of the working population of Northeast Minneapolis, there was a mixture of white collar workers and business persons in the area. There were no neighborhoods that were completely homogenous in terms of class. Business persons, mill-workers, and office workers lived as neighbors. What they held in common was a set of values about how one should live. Hard work and fiscal conservatism were highly valued, according to my informants. One man spoke of how his father had saved enough from his work at Ford Motor Company to buy a house with cash. This pattern of avoiding credit persisted throughout his entire life except for one instance. His father borrowed money to install a furnace in his new house. This created much anxiety, and the loan was quickly retired with sacrificial payments.

Long-term residents described Northeast Minneapolis as a good place to grow up. One man asserted, "Northeast was the greatest place there was. All working people, friendly, generous, tough going." A woman agreed, but she cautioned me not to make this too perfect of a picture, "...[community life] was so close and good. Everybody, they argued and fought. They weren't so peachy holy. But when it was over they would all go have a beer together."

Hard times and helping

What happened when people went through hard times? An enduring characteristic of Northeast is the insistence upon self-reliance. Individuals and families were expected to take care of their own problems. Accordingly, most help came from families and relatives. In this time period, many families experienced severe financial challenges due to loss of employment during the Depression. An immediate challenge for many was finding a place to live once income either stopped or was greatly reduced. An essential asset that could be made available to family members or other relatives was a place to live when resources were tight. One man recalls that his father converted his house to a duplex when a relative came upon hard financial times. After that time, different relatives lived with them off and on for some period of time. This pattern of modifying homes to provide more living units was common in Northeast.

The death of a parent was a crisis faced by some of my informants. For example, one woman lost her father when she was seven and her mother when she was sixteen. When her father died, her two brothers picked up work. No material help came from the government or the church. When her mother died, she was invited into her aunt's home. Her aunt cared for her until she finished high school. Later, after she had begun to work, she repaid her aunt for the expenses she had incurred.

Another type of crisis was divorce. As is found today, divorce often left a mother and in her children in severe financial straits. One man reported that his father and mother separated and divorced in 1936. My informant's mother was left with a nineteen year old son, an eighteen year old daughter, and my fourteen year old informant. His mother had never worked and did not seek work at this time. Instead, the two sons found jobs to support the family. My informant worked eight hours a night at a filling station. He lied about his age so he could start working before it was legal. He was still in school and described how he managed to carried this load.

> In them days there wasn't such things as alimony or child support or welfare or anything like that. So my brother and I, we both had to support my sister and mother. I was big for my age. He [the owner] figured I was old enough. So then I just had time…in the morning I had to take two transfers from Chicago and lake to 3rd Avenue and Central in Northeast here where I lived. And changed clothes, washed up, got something to eat to go to school. So then I fell asleep half the time in school, So that messed up my education. There wasn't an awful lot of time for sports or anything else.

In this time period, Northeast Minneapolis was an area seen as having a concentration of families and individuals in need. There were organized sources of help for persons in need. Some of these were backed with governmental funding and some were private. The Northeast Neighborhood House and Margaret Barry House were examples of attempts to meet various needs in the community. Other sources of need were "…branches of the Family Welfare and Visiting Nurses' Association, two homes for unwed mothers (the Lutheran Girl's Home at 1918 19th Ave. NE, and the Scandinavian Home of Shelter, 1020 19th Ave. NE), and two homes for the age; the Scandinavian Union Relief Home, 1507 Lowry Ave. NE and Little

Sisters of the Poor at Broadway and 2nd St." (Ashmore 1997, 15). Private charitable agencies were preferred as sources of relief, as opposed to governmental programs, when informal sources of help were overwhelmed or did not exist. In the 1930s, however, private agencies were besieged with need and the City of Minneapolis issued bonds to finance direct relief for those in need (Ashmore 1997). In either case, whether it be private charitable agencies or government relief, the long-term residents that I interviewed remembered strong resistance among most of the population of Northeast to this form of help. Private, individual instances of charity were more easily accepted, especially if given in the context of an existing relationship.

> I remember too as a kid, my dad getting rheumatism. And he was out of work for six weeks. That was kind of a traumatic deal as far as our family was concerned. To have the breadwinner laid up for six weeks. No sick leave. Back in those days you didn't even get vacation. I remember three or four fellows from his work coming over and visiting him one night after work. These guys came over and when they left, I still see him throwing an envelope on the bed. Full of cash. I don't know but there might have been $150 or something. That was a lot of money back then. They did it.

A form of help already mentioned was credit at neighborhood stores. Many of the subjects could remember their families relying on credit. One man, whose family owned a store, recalled:

> The people charged. We trusted everybody.…[when people didn't or couldn't pay] Just forgot about them. It happened often…[once] My dad figured up these charge accounts that people owed him. It was over $10,000 or $15,000 [his wife disputed this]. He threw the books away. He said, "How can these people pay? When they aren't working? And things are just too rough for them. They can not pay."

One woman remembered the generosity of grocers:

> O. F. Bergman owned a large grocery store on 30th and Johnson. The building is still there. He was a bachelor immigrant who really cared for people. One could have a bill there as high as $100 which was a very large amount during the Depression time. People who did seasonal work had to charge their groceries during the winter when there was no work. Most all the merchants on both Central Avenue and on Johnson Street ran charge accounts. Most of the people in Northeast would have been ashamed to go on relief and take "charity."

Pensions and social security had not come into play yet. Older persons continued to live in their own homes. Older persons who could no longer work because of failing health or financial stress and could not live independently moved in with their adult children. This was common to the experiences of many of my informants. One woman recalled that her paternal grandmother lived with them for a short while until her death around 1924. Her maternal grandfather lived with them later. She remembered him as a strict disciplinarian from "the old country."

The feasibility of this depended, to some extent, on the specific situation of the adult child. Fortunate was the aging parent who had a number of children who were willing to work together to ensure that their parent was well supported. One woman recalled that, after her mother died, her grandmother moved in with her father, brother, and her. This woman's brother lost his hearing one year after that and soon moved to Fairbault to attend a school for the deaf. Her grandmother continued to live with her and her father until they noticed that she was becoming forgetful and using the gas stove in an unsafe manner. Neither her dad or my informant were able to be with the grandmother during the day to supervise her use of the stove, so she was moved to the home of a second son where someone was available to be with her throughout the day.

Of course, not everyone had family or relatives to whom she or he could turn. They either might not exist, if a person never married or had no children, might have moved away, or might have been separated due to a difficult relationship. In recognition of this, the Union Home was established in 1906 by the Women's Relief Society as the Scandinavian Relief House for the indigent older person.

These were the formative years for long time residents of Northeast. It was a time when core values were transmitted and internalized. These include the value of hard work and the need for education. It was a time when primary friendships were made. It was a time when the first steps on the occupational path had she been taken. It was a time when beliefs and attitudes about community and helping and receiving help were formed. This included self-sufficiency, strong emphases on family, and a rather truncated role for the church. It was a time when the definition of who was a legitimate resident of Northeast and who was not was established.

Chapter 4

Adulthood in a Post-War World

The next time period begins in 1941, with America's step into World War Two, and ends in 1970. These long-term residents of Northeast Minneapolis were adults by the start of World War Two. Some of the oldest were raising children or working full time. The youngest had just graduated from high school. This was a time of great change for Northeast Minneapolis. Many men, and some women, experienced the war directly as soldiers and sailors in the armed forces. Others remained in Northeast Minneapolis, worked, and began families. New ideas and encounters with a broader range of persons and cultures changed the outlook of many living in Northeast. Economic, social, and cultural changes in the United States drastically altered the shape of American cities. This was the age of the automobile and a time when suburbanization was proceeding at a rapid pace. Meanwhile these long-term residents, all of whom but one remained in Northeast Minneapolis throughout this time period, were busy raising families, buying homes, building careers, and, eventually, moving into retirement.

World War Two was a defining moment and a turning point for Northeast. It was an immensely well-supported war in Northeast Minneapolis, and large numbers of young men entered the service. Most of the men I interviewed volunteered for military duty, rather than waiting to be drafted. They argued that this was a point of pride. Two of them hid physical problems during physical examinations so they would be accepted for duty. One man who wanted to join the Air Force actually used subterfuge twice.

They had a big sign [at the recruiting office], applications for air force mechanics, airplane mechanics. So, I walked in there and told them I worked for Wynn Stevens Buick. And that was an in right there. I didn't tell them I was not a mechanic. So then, when we got over to Fort Snelling [for a physical examination]…My left eye is never been any good. Even with my glasses on I can't really make your face out. It's always been that way. So, then the eye doctor checked me out. Checked my right eye. And then he got called away. And he come back and he asked, "What side did we check out now." I said, "You checked my left one." He said, "Oh, okay." So he checked my right one and he said, "Boy they are both the same. You are just fine." So, I lied to get into the service…I wanted to do my share.

Women were also caught up in the patriotic fervor. One woman enlisted in the WAVES along with her sister. As it turned out, they went through training together and were then stationed at the same naval base in San Diego upon completion of training. Their parents were thrilled to have daughters in the military. Their sons were ineligible for duty because of physical problems. With their daughters in the military they could join many other families in Northeast Minneapolis who displayed stars in their front windows to indicate they had children in the military.

Those who entered the armed services saw new places, tried out new jobs, and sometimes saw unspeakable horrors. They also met young men and women from other parts of the United States, some of whom spoke English with southern drawls, Brooklynese, and many other regional dialects of the United States. The persons they met came from all walks of life and a variety of ethnic backgrounds. Given that this was America in the early 1940s it is no surprise to hear that even though some of the men with whom I spoke were stationed in areas of the country where there were large concentrations of African Americans, none of them could report extensive interaction with them. If they did have contact with African Americans, it was with maids or others who were in subservient roles to them.

For those men who did not go into the service, World War Two was a time of opportunity as jobs opened up both in Northeast and elsewhere. New businesses and industries were starting in Northeast Minneapolis. Existing businesses expanded their operations. Many went back to work after long periods of unemployment. Some relocated to other parts of the country in search of higher paying work. As one man recalled, "During the war my brother went to California and worked there on the shipyards. He had bad hearing. He was 4F. My mother took that departure very hard."

Large numbers of young men left Northeast Minneapolis to enter the armed services. This affected the lives of the young women remaining as the men they were dating or had married were entering the service and leaving the area. At times, this led to an acceleration of wedding plans. Some women married men as they were ready to enter the service. Others married men who were able to return to Northeast Minneapolis while on furlough from the military. As one informant recalled, "[My sister's husband] was in the service at the time. He was at Pearl Harbor at the time of the bombing. They were not married then. When he came home they married, while he was on leave."

Many women and children were left behind by men who went to war, and young women received a crash course in self-sufficiency. They began raising children by themselves and learned how to balance jobs and motherhood. Some of them moved in with their parents, or other relatives, who helped with the children and provided many types of help.

World War Two also opened up opportunities for women in Northeast. Large numbers of women entered the work force for the first time.

> Women had worked during the war. So many women. In our normal type of life it was strictly the men was the breadwinner, that we had been raised with. Although my mother worked fifty-two years in the store. Some women worked but it was always in family businesses. Not outside the home as much.

Some of the many restrictions on women's work in these years were relaxed during the war. For example, although many businesses expected women to quit work if they married, wartime labor shortages encouraged businesses to relax this rule. Pregnancy continued to be a reason for automatic dismissal, however. One woman was hired at Pillsbury Flour Mills before the war broke out. She married in 1941 when her husband was home on furlough. She continued to work until she became pregnant. At that time, she was told to leave.

After the war, many men and women came back to Northeast Minneapolis. They found Northeast to be much the same but discovered that they had changed.

> During the war [as far as] I could see, nothing was ever changed... Everything was the same as when I left except for wear and tear on the paint and stuff on the houses. Over on Monroe were the butcher shop, and the grocery store, and the shoe maker. All that stuff was still there. It's all gone now, of course. I felt very grown up, coming home. When you go in the military, or any war or something like this, you either grow up or you don't. When I come out of there I was physically better. When I went in there I had young man's fat. I was a fat person, but I was kind of soft. Oh, I didn't

feel like I left. I just felt like it was part of me. Well, I went right back to
Stevens. I took the week off before I went back.

Northeast Minneapolis was ready for them and enthusiastic about their
return. They remembered "lots of parties" and warm welcomes by complete strangers when they walked down the streets of Northeast after their
return. Northeast looked just the same as it had before they left. They felt
they fit in easily. One man stated, "Oh, I didn't feel like I left. I just felt like
it was part of me." Furthermore, they were ready to get back on track. This
included employment and, for many, marriage.

World War II woke up the country from the Depression. Jobs were
created. When the GI's returned there was a tremendous demand for housing and services of all kind. For some of the these long-term residents this
meant that they were able to build successful and rewarding careers and
businesses. Howard is a man who was born before World War Two into a
family that owned a business on Central Avenue. Prior to the war he had
intended to enter business as an accountant. The war changed that. He
was out of Northeast for a number of years, learned new skills in management and leadership, and discovered some things about himself that led
to his return to Northeast Minneapolis and the family business:

Howard's Story

Howard was born to live in post-World War Two Northeast Minneapolis. He became a vital part of the Northeast community and helped shape
the community after the war through his business, civic, and church activities. To understand this, we have to start in the period between two world
wars to see how he came to embody the strengths and values of the pre-
World War Two community in which he was born. This formed the basis of
who he was and how he was able to move into leadership in later years.

Howard was one of the few long-term residents in this study who was
born in a hospital under the watch of modern medical care. He was born
on October 7, 1919, to parents who were leaders in the business and community life of Northeast Minneapolis.

His father was born in 1885 in a house on Central Avenue and moved
to a farm near Elk River. Howard's father returned to Northeast Minneapolis as a young man to live with his sister on Buchannan Street just
north of Lowry and build his future in the richer economic environment
of the city. After first working in a factory in Minneapolis, he was hired by

a jeweler in downtown Minneapolis and learned to be a clock repairman. He learned the jewelry business and opened his own store on Central Avenue in Northeast Minneapolis on July 8, 1911. The first day's activity consisted of selling a watch chain for fifty cents and doing a repair job for seventy-five cents.

Howard's mother was born in 1892 in Northeast Minneapolis. She lived in the neighborhood to which Howard's father had moved as a young man. She attended neighborhood schools and was one of the few women of her day to attend and graduate from college. She received her degree in teaching from the University of Minnesota in 1914.

Howard's mother and father were neighbors. Acquaintance turned to deeper interest, and they decided to marry. One problem they had to solve was where to attend church. Howard's father, and all of his many relatives who lived in Northeast, attended Salem Covenant Church. Howard's mother, on the other hand, attended Trinity Methodist Church. This problem was resolved when they decided on Trinity.

After they were married, Howard's mother taught school. In 1916, she quit teaching school and began working in the store. She continued working in the jewelry store until the age of seventy-six when she retired in 1968.

Howard's parents were community leaders. They were active members and took many leadership roles at Trinity United Methodist Church. Howard's father was highly involved in the business life of Northeast Minneapolis. In 1918 he and two other men put up $250 each to start a bank on Central Avenue. This became Fidelity Bank and Trust Company. Later, his father served as one of the vice-presidents of the bank.

An indication of his parents' business acumen was their decision to build a duplex in the Swedish area of Northeast just south of Lowry on Taylor in 1925. This was a substantial brick and stucco home, with three bedrooms on each of the two floors. This was Howard's home from the age of five until he married. The second unit in the duplex was always rented out and provided a useful source of income for the family.

Childhood years were centered on church, school, and play. Howard's playmates were neighborhood children and the many cousins living in the area. Howard's neighborhood was known for being a place where many of the men worked for Soo Line Railroad. This Soo Line connection continued at the family jewelry store where railroad Line workers came in once a month to check their watches.

Howard's formative years were ones where core values were clearly transmitted. As he states it, "People had an appreciation of the value of work. The liberty of having a job. There were a lot of people out of work. Times were very, very lean. Most everyone I knew, all kids, had to work to bring in a little something. We had paper routes."

He attended Prescott Elementary School, where his mother had also gone. After Prescott he attended Edison High School. High school was a busy time. Along with school, Howard was active in YMCA programs. He competed in their basketball league and was an active member of the Hi Y club for boys. Howard graduated from Edison High School in 1937. This was the year that Edison won the state basketball championship. He went on to attend the University of Minnesota and graduated in 1941.

Starting in high school and continuing on through college, Howard worked part time in the family store. He did not plan to make the family store his career. He studied business and accounting at the University and wanted to become a CPA.

Howard's future wife was also from Northeast Minneapolis. They attended Edison High school and the University of Minnesota together. In the spring of 1941, they both graduated from the university. World War Two interrupted the unbroken career path that Howard had been following. In July 1941, he entered the Army Air Corps and spent the first part of his military service in training, including Officer Candidate School, from which he graduated in June, 1942.

Howard married on July 2, 1942, and moved with his new bride to Duncan Kelly Air Force Base in San Antonio, Texas, where he went to depot supply officer's school. In September, the couple moved to Alexandria, Louisiana, where Howard was the depot supply officer at Esler Field. They remained there until June, 1943. Howard parted from his wife when he received orders for overseas duty. Soon he boarded a troop train in San Antonio, Texas, to travel to Fort Dix, New Jersey. It was a miserable ride. Troop trains had no air conditioning, and July was a hot, humid month. The troops wore woolen uniforms. The only source of air and the change of a breeze was through open windows. This was gained at the expense of soot from steam locomotives that covered the men with grime.

At Fort Dix they were processed and boarded the Queen Mary on July 20, 1945. The Queen Mary was originally designed for 2,000 people as a luxury liner. During the war, the troops were tripled bunked. A stateroom for two people bunked six to eight men. Thousands of GIs were onboard. Each man was assigned eight hours per day to sleep in a bunk. Other men would use the bunk for the two other eight hour shifts. Crossing the Atlantic was tense because of German submarines. One day during an antisubmarine drill Howard looked off toward the horizon and saw a big hulk he thought had to be a submarine. To his great relief, a spot of water shot up, and he knew this signaled a whale. The Queen Mary berthed in England on July 25, 1942.

Howard was assigned as chief supply officer at Burtonwood Repair Depot. The operations were immense, and Howard still marvels at the level of responsibility he was assigned as a relatively inexperienced twenty-three year old officer. The war ended in 1945 just before Howard was to be transferred to a unit that was to be involved in the Pacific theater. He was not able to return home right away. Others were ahead of him on the priority list for being returned home. Finally, in December 1945, he received orders to return to the United States and civilian life.

Howard boarded a troop ship called the H.M.S. Begum, which was a light aircraft carrier and carried 2,000 men. As the ship approached the Azores, it ran into an Atlantic winter storm with huge waves twenty to ninety feet high and winds of eighty to one hundred miles an hour. The ship was blown 1,000 miles off course into the North Atlantic. The storm was so bad that a sister ship sank. Howard's ship suffered severe damage. Under the flight deck two five inch thick and two foot wide I-beams sheared off. This allowed the flight deck to flop up and down as the ship pitched and rolled in the storm. Fortunately, the ship held together, allowing Howard and the rest of the men to make it safely to port.

Following his discharge, Howard returned to Northeast Minneapolis. His dreams of becoming a CPA were temporarily set aside. He found that his parents were exhausted after having struggled with the jewelry store during the difficult years of World War Two. Howard's older brother had also worked in the family business before serving in the United States Navy during World War Two. The two began work at the family business after they came back to Northeast Minneapolis. Howard only planned to work for a short time period to give his parents a break.

Although Howard wanted to be a CPA, he stuck with the family business. Looking back, he counts this as fortunate because he built a career in the jewelry business which he enjoyed and in which he excelled. In March, 1946, Howard, his brother, and his father established the jewelry store as a three way partnership. This continued until the death of his father in 1958. Howard, his father, and his brother worked together for many years. This was a successful partnership. It was helpful to have three people when making business decisions. That way it was easy to break a tie. Eventually, both he and his brother became certified gemologists. The family store was one of only two in the state that had two certified gemologists on staff.

When he returned to Northeast Minneapolis, Howard picked up where he left off. He lived in the same neighborhood, attended the same church, and worked in the family business. He also continued his friendship with a group of men he had originally met in the YMCA. By this time many in the group were active community leaders. Howard recalls that they either headed or were involved in almost every community project that came along. For example, one of them was the head of the Community Chest (comparable to the United Fund) for all of Northeast.

Like his father and mother, Howard and his wife bought a duplex in his old Northeast Minneapolis neighborhood. Howard's family lived in one unit and rented out the other. A daughter was born in 1948. A second daughter was born in 1955. In 1957, Howard bought a home in the newly developing St. Anthony Village. This was an area to which many successful businesspersons from Northeast were moving.

After World War Two, Howard's life revolved around his business, community activities, and the church. He served two years as the chairperson of his church. He also served twenty-six years on the finance committee, seventeen years as a trustee, as treasurer many times, and as president of the men's club. He was also active in the merchant's association, the Kiwanis, and the Masons.

His contributions to Northeast Minneapolis extended past the family store and church. Some of Northeast's key businesses have connections to Howard. For example, Marino's Restaurant, a tradition on Central Avenue, got its start in space rented from Howard in 1969. As another example, the hugely successful Medtronics was begun by men from Northeast Minneapolis with good ideas and entrepreneurial spirits. When they began to develop the pacemaker they needed a space to work and capital to fund their venture. Howard was one of the early supporters and helped provide some of the initial seed money that allowed the firm to develop.

This was a busy time. There were many weeks when he had five evening meetings. As he thought back, he remembered a ten year period when he was going to meetings almost every night. Now he regrets the time he spent away from his daughters as they were growing up. Yet, as he states it, "When you are in business on the avenue then you have almost a moral obligation to serve on the Community Chest and on the YMCA, in addition to your church activities."

Howard argued that one accepted a responsibility as a business owner to help build or improve the community. For Howard, this meant supporting the YMCA, being active in church, joining organizations like the

Kiwanis and Masons, and participating in the merchants' associations. Good fortunate required one to give something back.

Howard was proud of Northeast for its work ethic. Northeast had one of the largest commercial areas in Minneapolis, with many businesses and commercially zoned properties. Northeast was also a place with strong core values. Howard said that, "As long as you thought positively and you could eat and get clothing and realize the value of the family being able to be together and operate together. And then be able to be an education. That was the whole guiding force in life. And, of course, the churches molded and helped people too."

The 1950s was a time of change for Northeast Minneapolis. Many more women were entering the work force, a trend that Howard thinks began in World War Two. Some families were moving to St. Anthony or the newly forming suburbs of New Brighton and Fridley. Automobiles became more common, and streetcars disappeared around 1952 or 1953.

Business conditions changed more slowly. Central Avenue was still a vital shopping area. The best season was Christmas. Howard would extend store hours until 9:00 P.M. during the busy shopping season, which started three weeks before Christmas. There would often be customers waiting three to four deep in the jewelry store. Extra help had to be hired. Toward the end of the 1950s and into the 1960s retail stores began to disappear from the avenue. Shoppers drove their private automobiles to the brand new Apache Plaza Shopping Mall or to the many large grocery stores supermarket chains newly opened in the Twin Cities. Pedestrians began to disappear from the avenue. Dentists, doctors, and other professionals, who had rented office space above Central Avenue businesses, also left. People did not want to walk up to a second floor office anymore. Howard found that he could not rent his second floor spaces to professionals as before. Banks were some of the few professional services that remained on Central Avenue.

Conditions in Northeast today are very different. The work ethic and sense of responsibility that Howard thought characterized Northeast has dwindled. He does not think churches are as influential today as they were in his youth. He blames what he sees as general deterioration in the community on the failure of churches to continue to attract people and inculcate values.

Businesses have gotten bigger and more impersonal. Howard lays some of blame for this on labor. Labor pushed companies to get bigger in order to deal with strong unions. As a result, companies have lost the personal touch and much of their sense of community responsibility.

As business grew bigger and more impersonal, employees no longer had a sense of responsibility to the company or the community. A generation of people has been raised who see no need to join community associations or take part of community activities. Howard points to the decline in membership and impact of organizations like the Arcana Masonic Lodge on Central Avenue. He argued that it was a good influence in the community. In 1962 and 1963 it had 1,500 members. Now it has dwindled to about two hundred or three hundred. It is very difficult to attract younger people. Churches face the same challenges.

Howard and his wife now live in a condominium established for older adults just across the northern limits of Northeast Minneapolis. The family business has been sold. He continues his active involvement in friendship circles, church, voluntary organizations, and family activities. His life continues to be defined by involvement and commitment. He has been a community builder, yet he sees that the community he helped build is changing. He is fearful it may no longer exist as a strong, vital place to live.

Howard's life clearly shows the transition from pre-World War Two to post-World War Two life. The period after the war saw a full expression of key elements of a Northeast ethos and way of working developed in the crucial period between two world wars. His life, however, also shows how changes began to affect Northeast Minneapolis after the war. These started out slow but continued through this time period up until around 1970, after which they accelerated and began to take entirely new directions.

Northeast is changing

As long-term residents look back to the time after World War Two, they remember a time of prosperity and growth. There was tremendous pent-up demand for housing and consumer goods. Industry was in full throttle, and jobs were being created. There was a sense of optimism and purposefulness in Northeast Minneapolis.

The general shape of Northeast Minneapolis was in place at the start of this time period. Building and development was taking place in suburban areas, far from the center of the city. For many in Northeast, the newly developing Village of St. Anthony was the place to live. It tended to attract those who were more successful and desired newer, larger homes in this prestigious new area. It was initially built without a school, indicating its dependence upon Northeast Minneapolis as it was expected that the children of the Village of St. Anthony would attend schools there. Suburbs blossomed even further out as increasing prosperity brought a high demand for housing. Houses in Northeast Minneapolis were in short supply and many were neither modern nor large enough to meet expectations. In this time period, new homes were built in the Village of St. Anthony, Columbia Heights, Fridley, New Brighton, and areas further north.

The Twin Cities was expanding with the building of suburbs, the development of freeways, and establishment of shopping malls. These all affected Northeast Minneapolis. Subjects remembered a general pattern of decline toward the end of this time period. One woman described the changes:

> Only going down changes. Our meat store went. The dress store, the millinery store, is gone. Edith Larson went. O. E. Larson is still there. It seemed to go down. I was kind of glad I was out of that part of Minneapolis.

Northeast Minneapolis was coming to be seen as a place where urban decline had begun. Community perceptions did not always match those of city officials and urban planners.

> In 1958 Northeast was listed as a medium priority for urban redevelopment. The portion nearest the river was slated for clearance and future industrial cohesion. The rest showed signs of social cohesion and was to be stabilized through spot clearance and rehabilitation...In 1962 St. Anthony West was seen as a renewal area. At first the HRA proposed a standard program of clearance and rebuilding. The community was outraged. They asked the HRA to meet at a local church. 1,000 residents showed up and booed the renewal plan. A result was a modification of the renewal plan. The project [as revised] stressed rehabilitation, not clearance. (Martin and Goddard 1989, 96, 111–112)

Northeast did not win all of the redevelopment battles. In 1969, the construction of a major freeway, I-35W, began and cut a path two blocks wide through the east side of Beltrami neighborhood. Many homes were razed to make way for this. Some who live in Beltrami point to this as the start of a decline in the vitality of this area.

Some of the changes in Northeast can be linked to population shifts and movement. The expansion of the metropolitan area drew the children of these residents to other areas in the Twin Cities. One woman remembered that:

> A lot of the younger generation moved out. Then, of course, because the families became smaller they started renting out their apartments and get-

ting an influx of strangers. The young people that were my sister's age married and left the neighborhood... Then there were more renters coming in. More strangers in the neighborhood. The parents stayed... The older people stayed but it's the younger people that got out.

These changes affected the nature of life in Northeast. This same woman recalled that:

I think it wasn't as close as a community as it used to be. Because my sister and brother had their group of friends here in the neighborhood. And, of course, when they married they left. I don't think so [that new people fit into the neighborhood]. You would probably say hello but that was about it.

The character of life in Northeast neighborhoods was starting to change. One man talked about this:

Instead of owner-occupied homes we had an awful lot of rental units. Then again, the community wasn't stable. Oh, that must have been after the war. Maybe 1955. I think Lower Northeast, it happened a little faster than the other. A lot of folk wanted to move up to the other side of Johnson Street. And then into St. Anthony. St. Anthony developed. All home ownership. No rental properties in there. We built up there in 1950. Around 1950 was when we had the onslaught in there.

Much like today, changes affected some areas of Northeast more than others:

Our block was pretty stable. I think on the other side of Central, this block by the library, that kind of deteriorated. Kind of all of a sudden. I never did know who owned it. But there are a bunch of duplexes there. All of a sudden it got kind of raunchy. I don't know if that was a beginning of some of the bad spots of Northeast. The other side [of Central] was old too. But somehow that didn't go down as quickly.

I asked one woman if there were different parts of Northeast in this time period. She said, "There were tougher people there. Below Broadway. By the river. North was really bad." Changes were occurring in Northeast in this time period that were decreasing the economic vitality and quality of life. It is important to note that this was only true for parts of Northeast. Generally, those residential areas adjacent to Central Avenue and those areas in the more southern parts of Northeast were the first to see decline.

Key institutions

There continued to be changes in the major institutions of Northeast Minneapolis. Waite Park was developed in this era. This completed the park system for Northeast.

Northeast Neighborhood House found that the population it had been serving was aging. In addition, new persons, with very different backgrounds and a different set of needs, were moving into Northeast. The Americanization programs were no longer needed since second, third, and fourth generation descendants of the original European immigrants had become fully "American." The Margaret Berry House merged with Northeast Neighborhood House in 1963. In 1973, it closed due to lack of demand for its services. By the 1960s, both the Margaret Berry House and Northeast Neighborhood House had lost much of its clientele for their youth programs. Programs changed to include more efforts at community organizing and development and a broader range of services for seniors.

This was a time when fraternal organizations were heavily involved in the community. The first meetings of the Kiwanis were held in Northeast Minneapolis in 1952. This was also the heyday of the Masonic organization. The Arcana Lodge is presently located at Central Avenue and Lowry. The first lodge burnt on November 27, 1957. The new lodge was rebuilt on the same site with the same size and height and opened on June 6, 1959 (Olson 1996, 11). In 1962 and 1963, it had fifteen hundred members, according to one of its former officers. He estimated that in 1995 its membership had dwindled to two or three hundred.

Only one new church, Holy Trinity Lutheran Church, was established in this time period. It began in 1964. Meanwhile, other churches were considering whether to stay in or leave Northeast Minneapolis.

By 1960, Salem Covenant Church was finding problems with its location at 18 ½ and Central. many of its members were living outside of Northeast. As few as five percent of the congregation was living in the neighborhood. New persons that had no connection with the church were moving into the area. The church responded by trying various forms of outreach. Members went door-to-door to invite new neighbors to their homes. They found this unsuccessful as many of the new neighbor were leery about accepting these invitations. Children from the area came to Sunday School, but follow-up was difficult since the church found that when it would attempt to visit the families of the children, the families often had moved. One man who was a congregational leader during that time period described this time:

They [the church leadership] thought there was quite an economic barrier, because the community was comprised more and more of people
that were maybe on relief, and just the economic barrier, I think, was a
difficult one, especially in trying to bring those people into our homes,
because they felt uncomfortable and felt suspicious about what our mo-
tives were. So it became more and more apparent that we just were not
serving that community.

Eventually, Salem's leadership decided that it needed to find a new location. In 1971, the church moved to its present location in the suburb of
New Brighton.

In 1960, the Aaron Carlson home, which was the original location of
Bethany Covenant Nursing Home, was demolished. In its place a new facility was built to house the nursing home (Wiberg 1996, 40). Meanwhile,
just across Windom park, the Scandinavian Relief Home changed its name
to the Union Home for the Aged in 1961. The Central Nursing Home was
begun at 18 ½ and Central Avenue in 1961. It was remodeled and renamed
as Central Hospital. Now it is called Central Care.

Commercial and business life

In this time period Northeast Minneapolis began to see a decline
of manufacturing. In the two decades prior to 1980, there was a thirty-
four percent drop in blue collar jobs. Northeast saw relative gain of white
collar jobs in the time period (Kaszuba 1985, 1A).

At the start of this time period neighborhood stores were thriving, but
by the end of the time period they began to disappear. Central Avenue
continued to be a main commercial area and was described by a long-
term merchant:

> We actually had a lot of foot traffic up Central. Up until 1955 and 1960. The
> open night for most merchants was Friday night. It was 9:00 to 6:00 every-
> day. People would walk up and down the Avenue....Some of these people
> would go window shopping. During the Christmas season, it was triple or
> quadruple the normal monthly volume. They would shop all along Central.

Street cars continued to run up Central into the early '50s and provided easy access to its stores. Stores were open to 9:00 on Fridays. Foot
traffic was heavy. Jewelry, clothing, hardware, furniture, grocery, and drug
stores could all be found. Doctors and dentists had offices along Central.
Restaurants were kept busy. Banks were the center of commercial life.

People still would go to Central Avenue to shop or just to socialize.

It was still clannish, nice. We still had Central Avenue, the main drag, that was still very vibrant. They had lots of grocery stores. One, two, three drug stores. The one we were closest to was right on 20th. They had a fountain with stools. You could go and get a malt or whatever.

A strong business association worked to create a vibrant commercial and retail atmosphere. A long-term leader in this said:

There was a unified effort by people [referring specifically to merchants] within the community to be active with so many things. We have always had a very strong relationship with the YMCA. United Fund programs. Kitty Carnival every year. So many of the merchants were involved in so many things.

Another active businessman agreed:

We used to do things on the Avenue to keep interest. We had the Eastside Fair. We sold tent spaces. It ran about three days. It was in about 1953 or 1954.

Indeed, public festivals and events were heavily supported by merchants. One long-term merchant said:

The Central Avenue Parade has always drawn about the most traffic of any event. The reason they like it is because of the wide street. They can really perform. The Shrine loves it because [of] the horsemen, the motorcycles and their patrols. They can really maneuver.

One person said:

All of us [Central Avenue businessmen] were involved in the YMCA for several years. Every drive that would come along. I admire Jim Higgins. He would get a job of being head of the Community Chest, now it is United Fund, for all of Northeast....He was ingenious in organizing. Would set up individual block workers. Think how you get to know a community when working with campaigns.

Central Avenue was impacted greatly by metro wide changes that were happening in this time period. This included building suburban neighborhoods and the construction of shopping malls. One long-term businessman recalled:

Well, it was after that when they started. After the war it started changing. On Central Avenue they tried to get a large supermarket or large department store or something of that nature. There just was no way…[businesspersons] could see the handwriting on the wall. Then again too, when the shopping centers came in, why that kind of took away a lot of the local merchants. And then too, new developments were springing up. St. Anthony was built. They expanded into Columbia Heights. And so on and so forth… Professional people seemed to leave the Avenue. People got more spoiled. They didn't want to walk up to a second floor. We used to have a lot of dentists and doctors on Central Avenue. Lowry and Central. 23rd and Central. Like Dr. Arlander and Olson. As landlords, you couldn't rent to professional people anymore. They couldn't have their people climbing stairs all the time. So professionals left the Avenue for that reason.

It cut the foot traffic for sure. Gradually, the street traffic declined steadily. Once they built Apache. I think they built Apache about 1962. They tried to get us to move up there. I went through the ropes checking to see if it was worthwhile for us or not. Once they opened and these professional people started leaving. You had a thinning out of the variety of services. Services started to dwindle. And now with Central the banks are everything. It would be dead without the banks. You could just see the shriveling. Along with that comes the drying up of the property. If you can't rent it and get good tenants the valuation of the building goes down. You are only good as a healthy tenant, as far as value.

Along with the decline of Central Avenue there was also a weakening of regional identification of businesses with Northeast itself. This was especially true for banks and other businesses that became part of large corporate chains. One man talked about his experience in this regard:

I had the opportunity to be on the board of directors down at the Central Bank on Central. It was a small bank and a neighborhood bank. Norwest, the big company, acquired them back in the '30s. I was on the board for about twenty years. They had a mandatory sixty-eight requirement. I got off about five years ago. I am seventy-two…it has lost the friendly neighborhood touch. You know it happens when you go big. The big bank owned the bank and they called the shots. But it lost the local flavor. Because they don't have the long-term neighborhood people that used to be involved in the bank.

A weakness of neighborhood identification and commitment on the part of merchants shows up in this time period and continues into the next time period.

Daily life in Northeast Minneapolis

My informants argued that in this time period Northeast Minneapolis was still a hard working, blue collar neighborhood. The persons with whom I spoke were building careers, taking active roles in churches and community organizations, and raising families. It was a busy time for them.

They were also in a phase of life where they saw many changes in their family lives. Most of their children were born in the late forties and fifties. Thus, their children were attending school, involved in many activities, and graduating from high school at the end of this time period. Some of them entered the 1970s as "empty nesters." Their parents were aging and dying. Fifteen of the twenty-one persons with whom I spoke lost parents during this time period. For two, their parents died before this time period, and the remaining three have had their parents die since 1970.

This was a time of general prosperity. Many enjoyed upward mobility. Some were very successful in business. Others utilized the GI Bill to attend business schools or colleges or universities.

Ethnicity began to lose some of its power in shaping day-to-day life. English was spoken by almost everyone. Churches used English almost universally, although there continued to be some use of other languages in special or alternative services. For example, Salem Covenant Church switched to English by 1940. Some older persons in the church demanded Swedish services. The pastor compromised by holding two services, a Swedish service in the basement and an English service in the main floor sanctuary.

Social interaction reached past neighborhood and ethnicity to include persons from other traditions and heritages. One man who attended Salem Covenant Church reported that this is when he noticed that Swedes started to be marry non-Swedes. Friendships also reached across ethnic boundaries. They were based on common interests and membership in neighborhoods, churches, clubs, and associations. The persons with whom I spoke argued that this was a continuation of the breakdown of ethnicity begun in high school at Edison where students interacted with persons from other neighborhoods in Northeast or at Vocational High School, located in South Minneapolis, where students from all over the city interacted. Their social worlds expanded past Northeast to include things like dancing at the Marigold Ballroom in South Minneapolis. They were becoming all-American.

For those persons who had been in the armed services during World War Two, there had been many opportunities to interact with a wide variety of persons from many areas of the United States. Northeast Minneapolis became more of an all-American town and less a set of ethnic villages.

There was a limit in the willingness to cross ethnicity boundaries and interact with persons who were different. Northeast was still almost totally made up by persons of European descent. People of color were rarely seen in Northeast. In particular, few African Americans lived in Northeast (see FIGURE 4.1). As late as 1965, Northeast, along with the Lake Calhoun area, had the lowest percent of African Americans in its population of any area in Minneapolis (Minneapolis City Planning Council and City Commission 1965, 81). It was in this time period that North Minneapolis, with its large African American population, took on the image of urban decay in the minds of many in Northeast. It was increasingly seen as dangerous and a place to be avoided. Informants argued that North Minneapolis was the possible future of Northeast Minneapolis "if things went wrong."

My informants described the unwelcoming nature of Northeast with regards to African Americans. Violence or the threat of violence kept whites and African Americans apart. "No. They [African Americans] didn't dare come over here. Pollock boys were tough," explained one woman.

This was a time of nearly absolute separation of whites and African Americans. My informants had little if any experience interacting with African Americans. One woman recalled that this did not prepare her well for working in a setting with African Americans as co-workers: "Even at Vocational I don't recall any Black students. It was very awkward, not having any exposure to Blacks."

Some of my informants looked back at this time with nostalgia.

> Now the Blacks they had their area [in old days]. And we'd go over there because they had the best barbecue ribs and stuff. We'd go over there one

FIGURE 4.1: *Ethnicity in Northeast Minneapolis*
(Minneapolis City Planning Commission and City Council 1965, 81;
Urban Coalition 1996, 3)

	Percent of Whites in the population of Northeast	Percent of African-Americans in the population of Northeast
1960	99.6	NA
1980	97.4	0.2
1990	93.1	2.0

or two o'clock in the morning. Never get bothered. [It was] north [Minne-apolis]. And there were some over south but mostly over north. I'll never forget behind the Pine Tavern, it's called the Legend down there on East Hennepin, there was Joe Hopper's Garage. This colored guy, Louie was his first name. He had a filling station right over on Washington. Right off where the freeway is now. In fact there's a liquor store or market there now. He had a Standard Oil filling station. He'd bring his client's car down to Joe Hopper's Garage for front end alignment. He was a big colored guy. Hell of a nice guy. We were going to go over to Pine Tavern right next door and have a drink. We said, "Come on Louie." He said, "No, I better get back over to my own side of town before dark." We got a guy at work [who was African American]…some years back. He was going to buy a new car. He was going to get a black one. My friend Houie said, "Earl, you get a black car nobody'll see you inside that car." He laughed and laughed and he bought a white car.

This same informant contrasted these "good old days" with today.

See, now we got these Blacks from Indiana, Detroit, and Chicago. And our home town Blacks… You watch the papers and you read they're always from out of town. Most of them. Yeah. We got people from India now. Vietnamese. Other parts of the world. And you go down Central Avenue. We used to have so many good cafes down there. Now they're all Vietnam-ese joints, or Egyptian or Palestinian joints or some damn thing. I don't even go in them. I have no desire to go in them. I don't like that kind of food, anyway. I was raised with English cooking, more or less. Beef and mashed potatoes and gravy. Pasty pies and stuff like that. I go to Little Jax for a steak or something.

All of my informants pointed out that today there are African Ameri-cans in Northeast whereas in the past there were none. One man explained why this was.

They called Northeast the last frontier. Because there was the least bur-glaries, the least everything. I found out why. There was a young fellow that had a gang in Northeast. There was twenty-one or twenty-two guys in the gang. Nobody dared break in Northeast because then they had to deal with him. Him and his bunch went every place but they never bothered Northeast. And at one time there was a big stink in North Minneapolis. Black young people in North Minneapolis were going to come to North-east and show him who is boss. Because they knew of this. They met in the middle of the Lowry Avenue Bridge. This guy and his gang. The Northeast police knew about this too. They were over off of Marshall, just sitting around. They didn't even bother. The police didn't stick their nose in. The

Blacks turned around and went back. Oh, this was quite a while ago....had to be in the late 1970s. So then this guy got bored. He was twenty-one-years-old when he was leader of this bunch. He got bored. So he went over to Rogers one Sunday afternoon. Walked into the grocery store. He was going to hold the grocery store up. And the sheriff walked in for a pack of cigarettes while the guy was doing this. So he ended up in Stillwater right now. So the gang broke up. Then Northeast was wide open. But it still less problems over here than north and south.

At the end of this time period changes accelerated, and Northeast Minneapolis became more diverse. Northeast Minneapolis changed from a place where strangers were rarely seen to a place where this was much more common. One of the factors that encouraged this was the departure of many of the children of the long-term residents with whom I spoke and others who were in their generation. This meant that housing became available and much of this was converted from owner occupied to rentals by the end of this period. I asked one woman to describe what changes she observed when there began to be more renters. She replied, "I think it wasn't as close as a community as it used to be. I don't think [renters fit into the neighborhood]. You would probably say hello, but that was about it."

Northeast retained the values associated with its hard working, blue collar history. My informants spoke of this era as a good and stable time.

> I bought a new '53 Ford. Dumb thing. I didn't need it. But I got in the show room and smelled it. So anyway, them's good years. We didn't have much, but we didn't need much. It was a good time. And things were stabilized. You know you could walk the streets anytime. No sweat or nothing...It was known as the hell of a good neighborhood in them days...You could go to the bars...We would often talk about how great it was. We had Catholics and Irishmen and Pollocks and Lutherans and whatever. We all got along. We had great times.

Schools continued to play key roles in Northeast neighborhoods.

> So, we lived there. And my kids went to Pillsbury. Wooden school, you know. But they had some good teachers...Mrs. McCaughlin, she lives right there still. Still alive down there, as far as I know. Wonderful, what you call a real old time teachers. She comes walking up sometimes the evening and tell us how the kids are doing... A wonderful school that them dumb jerks tore down. In fact, there is an article in the Northeaster about it about two weeks ago. How clean a school it was and everything. The kids could walk to school. They come home at noon and heat some soup up. Everything

was safe. What a wonderful deal, and the dummies go and there that school down. Who knows [why they tore it down]? The stupid jerks. Well, I…it was just nuts. We knew the teachers. We go to PTA meetings over there. And, the teachers knew us, and we knew their kids. And they'd report on how our kids were doing. And the neighbors went there.

As referred to above, demographic shifts meant there were fewer school aged children. This led to changes in school policy. In this time period schools that were deemed to be outmoded were demolished. Others were closed and used for other purposes.

Other changes occurred that affected the general ethos in Northeast. in earlier times, loyalty was expected and given between employers and employees. Before 1970, one businessman told me that much business was done on the basis of verbal contracts. Trust was assumed. His business did not even use the services of a lawyer. Subjects report this started to change at the end of this period. One man said the first owner of the plant at which he worked had started on the floor as a sweeper. He and the engineers at the plant used to walk on the floor and talk with the workers. They would ask them for ideas. Later, the plant was sold. The new boss and management no longer talked with the workers: "They didn't come to us. Like we didn't know a damn thing or something."

As this time period began, Northeast Minneapolis was getting back to work after World War Two. My informants spoke of a continuation of values and ways of life that they had known as children and young persons. But changes were occurring.

Hard times and helping

Patterns of care giving and receiving that we saw in the previous time period continued to be the expectations for most who lived in Northeast Minneapolis in this third time period. Self-reliance was valued. When people went through hard times, the family continued to be a mainstay. Churches, neighbors, and friends offered important, but more limited, forms of support.

A major change began to take place in the 1960s. Governmental programs designed to help older persons were developed and offered to older persons in Northeast Minneapolis. These greatly improved the conditions in which older persons lived. Programs designed to lift individuals, families, and neighborhoods out of poverty were being designed. This trend accelerates and expands in the next time period.

The third era was a time of adulthood for my informants. They were involved in family life, work life, community life, and the church. In many ways, they were living out the values and patterns imparted to them in the first period. There continued to be strong, localized neighborhoods. Northeast had clearly become an all-American town, but it retained its ethnic roots. This continues into the next time period.

Chapter 5

Today's world is very different
for these persons

The fourth and last time period began in 1970 and continues to the present. At the start of this time period, the oldest of my informants was seventy-one and the youngest was forty-two. In 1995, when I conducted life history interviews, their ages ranged from ninety-six to seventy-two. In this era, long-term residents moved into retirement, saw their parents, siblings, and friends die, and began to experience age related physical slowdowns and illnesses. In addition, they have seen substantial change in Northeast Minneapolis in terms of population characteristics and social and business conditions. Northeast Minneapolis has become smaller in terms of population, poorer relative to the rest of Minneapolis, less blue collar, and older (see Figure 5.1).

Demographic changes have greatly affected Northeast Minneapolis (see Figure 5.2). The population age profile has become bipolar. The percentage of older persons in the population has increased as its long-term residents have aged in place. Meanwhile, many of their children have moved out of Northeast, often to suburban areas of the Twin Cities. The middle-aged range of the population has decreased. Northeast has been attracting younger individuals and families which has increased the percentage of younger adults and children in the community.

FIGURE 5.1: *Conditions of life in Northeast Minneapolis, 1960–1980*
(Kazuba 1985, 1A, 8A)

	1960	1970	1980	% CHANGE
Population				
Northeast	52,691	46,289	37,912	– 28.00
Minneapolis	482,872	434,400	370,951	– 23.20
Median Family Income				
Northeast	$21,154	$25,147	$24,900	18.10
Minneapolis	$15,342	$24,969	$25,356	65.30
White Collar Jobs				
Northeast	2,789	3,158	4,034	44.60
Minneapolis	43,084	45,145	58,638	36.10
Blue Collar Jobs				
Northeast	9,442	8,625	6,227	– 34.00
Minneapolis	63,517	59,070	44,150	– 30.50
Retirement Age				
Northeast	11.10%	NA	21.00%	9.95
Minneapolis	13.40%	NA	18.00%	4.60

FIGURE 5.2: *Northeast Minneapolis population by age, 1980–1990*
(The Urban Coalition 1996, 1–2)

Age Groups		UNDER 20	20–24	25–44	45–64	OVER 65	Total
EAST OF CENTRAL							
1980	Age Groups	4,706	2,071	5,257	4,313	3,498	19,845
	Percentage	23.71	10.44	26.49	21.73	17.63	
1990	Age Groups	4,108	1,470	7,177	3,021	3,363	19,139
	Percentage	21.46	7.68	37.50	15.78	17.57	
Change 1980–1990		– 598	– 601	1,920	– 1,292	– 135	– 706
WEST OF CENTRAL							
1980	Age Groups	4,487	2,151	4,678	4,003	2,824	18,143
	Percentage	24.73	11.86	25.78	22.06	15.57	
1990	Age Groups	3,969	1,459	6,233	2,889	2,924	17,474
	Percentage	22.71	8.35	35.67	16.53	16.73	
Change 1980–1990		– 518	– 692	1555	– 1114	100	– 869
NE MINNEAPOLIS							
1980	Age Groups	9,193	4,222	9,935	8,316	6,322	37,988
1990	Age Groups	8,077	2,929	13,410	5,910	6,287	36,613
Change 1980–1990		– 1116	– 1293	3475	– 2406	– 35	– 1375

Many of the new residents who have moved into Northeast Minneapolis are ethnically different than those persons who have lived Northeast for a long period of time (see Figure 5.3). Northeast Minneapolis was
known for ethnic diversity and its variety of Euro-American neighborhoods. It is developing a new form of diversity in terms of color and non-
Euro-American nationality. In 1980, there were only 951 residents of color
among the 37,988 residents of Northeast, or just 2.5 percent of the population. In 1990, this had changed so that there were 2,484 residents of color,
or 6.8 percent of the population. Northeast still had the second smallest
population of color among the eleven planning communities of Minneapolis, both in terms of absolute number and in percentage of the total
population (The Urban Coalition 1996, 3).

New arrivals often differed from long-term residents in terms of lifestyle.
Renting became more common, and home ownership declined somewhat
(see Figure 5.4). Long-term residents pointed to the decline in
homeownership as either a sign or cause of a perceived decline in quality
of life in Northeast. They point, specifically, to a low degree of commitment to the area on the part of renters and a high degree of residential
mobility among present day residents in Northeast (see Figure 5.5).

FIGURE 5.3: *Ethnic makeup of Northeast Minneapolis, 1990*
(The Urban Coalition 1996, 3)

	AFRICAN AMERICAN	AMERICAN INDIAN	ASIAN	WHITE	HISPANIC	OTHER	TOTAL
East of Central	253	420	325	17,990	271	119	19,378
Percentage	1.31	2.17	1.68	92.84	1.40	0.61	
West of Central	274	582	349	16,041	346	162	17,754
Percentage	1.54	3.28	1.97	90.35	1.95	0.91	
NE Minneapolis	527	1,002	674	34,031	617	281	37,132
Percentage	1.42	2.70	1.82	91.65	1.66	0.76	

FIGURE 5.4: *Homeowners in Northeast Minneapolis, 1980–1990*
(The Urban Coalition 1996, 24)

	Home Owners, 1980	Home Owners, 1990	Change, 1980–90
East of Central	5612	5548	– 64
West of Central	3757	3732	– 25
NE Minneapolis	9369	9280	– 89
% of Residents	57.30	56.90	– 0.40

FIGURE 5.5: *Long-term residents in Northeast Minneapolis, 1980–1990*
(The Urban Coalition 1996, 8)

	Over 5 Years, 1980	Over 5 Years, 1990	Change, 1980–1990
East of Central	11,471	9,825	– 1,646
Percent of Residents	57.80	51.33	– 6.47
West of Central	9,571	7,474	– 2,097
Percent of Residents	52.75	42.77	– 9.98
Northeast Total	21,042	17,299	– 3,743
Percent of Residents	55.39	47.25	–8.14

Not only was the population more ethnically diverse, more likely to be renters, and less likely to be long-term residents but, even though there has been some reduction recently, it also continued to have a substantial percentage of persons in poverty (see Figure 5.6).

As the long-term residents with whom I spoke talked about current conditions in Northeast Minneapolis they noted these changes. They often stated that there was a new way of life emerging in Northeast among more recent arrivals. The were many characteristics of this new way of life, as understood by these long-term residents. They argued that persons newly arriving in Northeast are more mobile today than they were in the past. Schools, one of the key institutions that defined neighborhoods in Northeast, are no longer neighborhood schools.[1] My informants argued that the result of this was that school-aged children do not know the other children in their neighborhoods. They also pointed out that Northeast has moved from being an area of the city with a high degree of home ownership to one where there is a high percentage of absentee landlords. They felt that neighborliness is on the decline and that there is greater separation between and less concern for others than there was in the past. They argued that these changes work together to challenge older persons living in the area in that they make it difficult for older persons to find ways to contribute to the community. Many older persons feel that it is hard to trust their neighbors and others living in Northeast today and that there is a general sense of increased danger in the area. All these changes help to explain the fact that many expressed a greater fear of crime today than they remembered in the past.

Northeast has long been a center of industrial activity and offered a large number of blue collar jobs. This changed in this last time period. New manufacturing processes demanded physical plants which were more spread out

FIGURE 5.6: *Persons in poverty in Northeast Minneapolis, 1980–1990* (The Urban Coalition 1996, 10–11)

	Persons in poverty, 1980	Persons in poverty, 1990	Change, 1980–1990
East of Central	1,619	1,583	– 36
Percent poor	8.16	8.27	0.11
West of Central	3,357	2,270	– 1,087
Percent poor	18.50	12.99	– 5.51
Northeast Total	4,976	3,853	– 1,123
Percent poor	13.10	10.52	– 2.58

and required more room. A greater reliance upon trucking at the expense of railroads meant that freeway access was paramount. As a result, industries moved out of Northeast Minneapolis for more suburban locations.

Meanwhile, Central Avenue continued to fade as a commercial street and neighborhood stores were almost totally gone from Northeast Minneapolis. Shopping centers further proliferated around the Twin Cities. One of the first was Apache Plaza Shopping Center in St. Anthony. Soon newer, larger, and more modern shopping centers were built in the surrounding suburbs of the Twin Cities. In addition, large supermarket and drug store chains found the Twin Cities attractive and built extensively in the area. These forces combined with the automobile and an extensive freeway system to change the nature of shopping in the Twin Cities. Commercial avenues were replaced by malls, and neighborhood stores were replaced by supermarkets. The effects on Northeast were dramatic. Sales, in 1985 dollars, in Northeast declined from 152.2 million in 1977 to 120.5 million in 1982. This is a decline of twenty-one percent in five years (Kaszuba 1985, 1A, 8A).

These long-term residents have lived through many changes in Northeast Minneapolis. For some, their commitment and loyalty to neighborhood is deep. Kathryn is such a person:

Kathryn's Story

Not many of us have eaten most of our breakfasts within five steps of the exact location of our birth. Kathryn and I were sitting at her kitchen table when I asked where she was born. She pointed to a door over my left shoulder and said, "There, behind that door, in that room." In that small room, now used as a pantry, Kathryn and her brother and sister were born.

Kathryn's mother and father came from neighboring villages in Lithuania. They knew each other from having met at many weddings and were rumored to be great dance partners. It was after they had separately migrated to Northeast Minneapolis around 1913 that they met again and began to court. Soon, they were married and moved into the house in which Kathryn was born and in which she has lived all of her life.

Kathryn was born in 1927 as the third of three children. It was just about the time that the streets were paved, but there was still a rural flavor to the Holland neighborhood with large gardens, cowsheds, and chicken coops in the backyards of many of the homes.

The neighborhood was mostly Polish, and Kathryn's family was the only Lithuanian family in the area. From the time when Kathryn was a young girl through her young adult years, Lithuanians in the Twin Cities would meet to socialize. They rented a hall, and there would be dancing. In the summer there were large picnics. It was a close community in those days. Gradually, through deaths and marriages with non-Lithuanians, the sense of community dwindled and the gatherings stopped.

Her father could build almost anything without a pattern or instructions. He could sew and do plumbing and electrical work. The only thing he claimed he could not do was ironing clothes. He was a caring husband who gave primary care for Kathryn's mother over sixteen years as she struggled with complications from diabetes. Kathryn remembers that her parents were close and affectionate and worked together as a team. Her father stood out in the neighborhood for the gentleness and respect he showed his wife. Her father helped her mother, and if he needed help, she was there to help him. When he dug out the basement for the house she was there with shovel and wheelbarrow until it was finished. There were few firm lines between men and women's work in Kathryn's parents' house.

When she was young, the neighborhood contained almost all that was needed. During the summer a man would come door-to-door selling vegetables that were grown in fields near by. Another man came by with his horse-drawn wagon to buy rags and other useful junk.

The neighborhood was close. Families who lived in the neighborhood stayed for long periods of time. There were few moved in or moved out. Childhood was a time of a great deal of freedom. The streets were used for "kick the can" or "crack the whip." Softball was played on open lots between the houses and railroad tracks that ran through the area. In the winter the neighborhood children would sled at Columbia Park. Of course, since Northeast was an area with many industries there were always more exciting places to play. There was a large pole yard near Columbia Park.

Kathryn remembers riding the poles with her girl friends. Poles were offloaded from train cars by rolling them down a wooden ramp made up of strong timers running from the platform to a lower level. The girls would roll a pole to the edge of the top edge of the ramp, and then one girl would wrap her legs and arms around it. The other girls would push it to get it rolling, and the pole and rider would roll and roll down to the end of the ramp.

Parks were important to young girls in Holland neighborhood. Marshall Terrace Park was heavily used. In the winter the children would skate there. Kathryn remembers the warming house with a huge barrel stove.

Northeast Neighborhood House also provided much for neighborhood children. Kathryn loved the library and took cooking and sewing classes. She also played basketball. Since there were no sports leagues for girls at that time, Kathryn played on teams formed for in-house games. A special time was Halloween. The hallways were darkened and scary things confronted the children as they walked through spooky corridors. Eventually, all ended up in the auditorium for treats.

Kathryn's family was Catholic and attended St. Hedwigs, but the church was not as central a part of their life as it was for many in the neighborhood. This did not necessarily reflect a less vibrant spiritual life. Instead, the explanation lies with the fact that the local churches, Holy Cross and St. Hedwigs, were Polish-Catholic churches. Lithuanians just did not belong. Kathryn remembers participating in bazaars and other celebrations, but she did not attend church on a regular basis and never attended catechism. Lithuanian ethnicity, at times, meant exclusion, but it was most often a point of pride for Kathryn.

Kathryn's family was unique in that it had a car when she was a child. It was a touring car and used for trips in the area. The family would drive to St. Paul for get-togethers with the Lithuanian community and other friends. Sometimes they would drive to Lake Minnetonka for a picnic. On many Sundays, they would take the car north to Coon Rapids where the family would fish. There was a farmer who allowed parties to fish and picnic on his land for twenty five cents admission. Kathryn's father would attach a hook to a line, weight it with a bolt, and tie it to a stick. Then he would throw the line out into the water, place the stick in the sand, and wait for a fish to bite. The rudimentary equipment did not seem to keep her father from bringing home fish for supper.

Kathryn attended Schiller School through the ninth grade. After completing ninth grade at Schiller, Kathryn attended the vocational high school in Minneapolis, where she studied sewing. The school was physically divided into a girls' side and a boys' side. Girls and boys met only in history and English classes. There was not a rich social life at vocational. School dances were held, but they were not well attended. The school had a football team, but, since there was no home field, there not much interest in it. Kathryn thinks that the fact that students came from all over the city made it difficult to socialize. They just lived too far away from each other to get together very easily.

Kathryn was around ten years old when her mother was diagnosed with diabetes. It was frightening for Kathryn. She thought her mother was dying on many occasions. However, with care and good luck, she lived until the year after Kathryn's father retired. Kathryn's mother died at the age of sixty-one in 1954. Kathryn regrets that she died before she was able to meet the man Kathryn married. The only contact he had with Kathryn's mother was through a touching letter he had written to her before she died.

World War Two was also a frightening time. Kathryn's older sister was married at the time to a man who was serving in the military near Pearl Harbor. Kathryn's sister and two children had moved in with Kathryn and her parents. The news of the attack on Pearl Harbor was terrifying for the family as they feared for her sister's husband. Throughout the war there was deep concern for him and his welfare.

She graduated in 1944 from vocational high school where she received her high school diploma and a trade certificate. She had learned to hand sew and use various machines. Upon graduation she went to work full time at garment factories. Over the next few years she worked at three different factories. They were always going out of business. The first one was Ladies Leader where she worked for about three years. Then she worked for Jean Lang for about three months. Finally, she worked at Perry Brown for about two years.

These factories made fine clothes. Patterns were transferred to stacks of fabric about eight inches high. These were laid on the cutting table where the pieces were cut out, bundled, and distributed to the power machine operators. The entire operation was located on one floor of a large warehouse where cutting, sewing and pressing all took place. An inspector checked the garments before they were boxed. Most of the workers were women. Men pressed and cut the garments, did the maintenance, and worked in the shipping department.

Meanwhile Kathryn lived at home with her mother and father. Both her sister and brother had married and moved into homes of their own. Kathryn's social life continued as before. She went dancing with her friends at ballrooms like the Marigold in South Minneapolis. Many of her friends still lived in the neighborhood. They were also working and unmarried in those first years after World War Two. The first of Kathryn's friends married three years after high school.

Many young persons moved away. Other persons moved into Northeast, and it became more common to see strangers on the streets and in the stores of Northeast Minneapolis. Most of the newer persons rented. Next door to Kathryn was a house that had been occupied by a large family. When the children married they left the area. Then the parents rented part of the house. The new renters did not fit into the neighborhood. The neighborhood lost some of its sense of community. Many of the renters stayed a long time, but Kathryn recalls that she never developed more of a relationship than exchanging greetings when meeting on the sidewalk.

After working at garment factories for five years, Kathryn was hired by the Veteran's Administration in 1949. She had taken a civil service exam and was hired to work in the director's office at Fort Snelling. She did clerical work and took care of the credit union accounts. It was a good change, and she enjoyed it.

She remembers parties and dances for the employees. One dance stands out in her memory. It was Christmas. As she thought about attending, she wondered what would happen if one of the African American men who worked in the VA would ask her to dance. She did not know how to respond. She could not even remember any African American students at vocational. Her parents had never talked about African Americans. Kathryn's awkwardness came from a lack of contact or knowledge. No African American men asked her to dance, but it strikes her that this was the first time she had ever had contact with any African Americans. She had never seen an African American in Northeast.

An order came for cutbacks at the Veteran's Administration, and Kathryn was laid off. This was a shock. She had enjoyed her work and the responsibility given her. She then applied at the Honeywell plant near Sunset Cemetery, just outside the boundaries of Northeast Minneapolis. She was hired as an inventory clerk. She kept a running record of all the cables and wires.

Three years after beginning work at Honeywell, she began to teach evening sewing courses at vocational. She taught one to four classes a week, depending upon enrollment. She enjoyed teaching and taught for over twenty-five years. Some classes were at the vocational high school, and others were at Henry High School in North Minneapolis, the North Minneapolis YMCA, and at a YWCA in South Minneapolis.

Around 1952, Kathryn met her future husband who was home on leave from the Navy. They corresponded during the time he was in the service. Kathryn's mother was very sick during this time, and Kathryn was heavily involved in her care. Kathryn's mother then began to fail due to complications with diabetes. She died at home in 1954. Unfortunately, she died before Kathryn's future husband could return to Minnesota so they never met one another.

On June 4, 1955, Kathryn married. Her husband was a Lutheran. Even though he converted to Catholicism, they were not allowed to marry at St. Hedwigs Catholic Church. They were married in the parish office.

She and her husband moved into Kathryn's home. Her husband was a student at the University of Minnesota. Kathryn's father continued to live there. Kathryn worked until she was pregnant. At that time she quit. She did not want to use day care for her children and felt that she would be torn between her responsibility to her children and her responsibility to her employer. Her son was born just after her husband graduated from college in 1959. Kathryn's second child, a daughter, was born a few years later.

In 1973, her husband bought season tickets to the Guthrie Theater. They began to attend performances. The first production was *Straw Hat*. Kathryn was deeply impressed by the costumes. The next day her husband called the public relations director at the Guthrie Theater, whom he knew through his work, to tell her of Kathryn's reaction. She suggested that Kathryn join the stage hands as a volunteer costume builder. Kathryn did and volunteered for two years. In 1975 she was asked to join the staff and has worked there since.

Kathryn builds costumes. She enjoys it immensely because of the exotic materials that are used and various techniques that are employed. At first she was shocked by the atmosphere. It was the first time that she had personally encountered homosexuals. She found she liked them. She remembered going into the costume office and finding a young man struggling into a beautiful gown. Some of the men liked to cross-dress. She enjoyed working with young, creative people, both straight and gay.

As Kathryn and her husband were raising their children they talked with them about their futures and emphasized that college was a good opportunity. They also sought good high schools for their children. Both of them attended private schools in the Twin Cities. They also went on to college and successful careers.

In 1971, Kathryn's father died. He had had some problems with his heart and then suffered a major stroke.

Today, Kathryn still meets with neighborhood friends. None of her friends live in the neighborhood, but some live in the Twin Cities. Kathryn counts it lucky that the husbands get along well. New Year's Eve is usually reserved for getting together. In earlier years they would go dancing. Now they chat and play card games. Other friends live farther away. One lives in California, and another lives in New Mexico. Kathryn stays in touch by mail and telephone. She also has been able to visit them in their homes. Additionally, she also sees them when they return to Northeast Minneapolis to visit family. These long-term friends are important to Kathryn. She also has made new friends through her church and work at the Guthrie.

The neighborhood is still important to Kathryn, but her community now focuses on St. Hedwigs. She and her husband have become active members of the parish. Much of this can explained by the arrival of Father Ted Guminga around 1980. Kathryn and her family have developed a close relationship with him.

The neighborhood differs today in that there are fewer young couples with families. When older persons die, quite often the homes are sold to absentee landlords. This has brought a decided change in the neighborhood.

Some of these changes began in the 1970s. The first thing Kathryn noted was that renters stayed shorter periods of time before moving on. She also pointed to a change in appearance and behavior. Some had strange haircuts and an unkempt, grungy look. One couple who lived across the street had huge, noisy parties. There was more garbage, such as paper and cans, thrown into the streets than there used to be.

There was another man who lived across the street whom Kathryn suspects was dealing drugs. At night people would come out carrying brown paper bags. There was constant stopping and going at all hours. Police cars often come into the neighborhood to check things out. Windows have been broken out of vehicles. Kathryn said that they have never had this before.

Kathryn has always enjoyed taking evening walks. Now her husband opposes this. She was attacked in the backyard in the summer. She went out to the garage to get something and was jumped. She recalls being angry and scared. She screamed and told her assailant she was going to kill him. He put his hand on her mouth, but she kept screaming and struggling. Perhaps because she did not act scared, he jumped the fence and ran off. She saw him on a bicycle going round the corner. Kathryn insists she would still walk, but she would look and be careful. Still, her husband demanded that she not take walks.

Her biggest concern was who they are going to get as next door neighbors. An absentee landlord owns the house. He has around ten other houses in Northeast and is known to rent to families on AFDC. She is worried about what will happen.

Kathryn is a good example of someone who has lived through many changes in her neighborhood and is attempting to adapt to these changes. Yet it is clear that some of these are easier than others. Kathryn was worried that some of these changes might force her to think about leaving the neighborhood. She felt out of control.

Retirement is the defining event

By 1995, all of my informants have retired or are soon planning to retire. For some, retirement has meant moving into a new era with many possibilities for growth and continued or expanding involvement in family, community, or church activities. For others, it has meant pulling back from involvement and interaction. All agreed that retirement is much better for them than it was for older persons they knew when they were young. One woman compared her life with older persons she knew when she was younger.

> More help [is available]. You have to pay for a lot of it. Now at Eldercare don't they have a place where you can come in and let you have the day off [referring to caregiver respite services]? It think that's wonderful. So, we don't know how lucky we are. I can go out. I can still drive…See the kids. Help them out a little bit when they need some help. It's [retirement] good for us. We're retired. We have no financial problems. We have pretty good health. We still have a lot of good friends.…they [older persons she knew as a younger person] didn't have it that good. Today you go by anyplace you see seniors waiting for buses to go gamble. We don't gamble. Once in awhile. We are not gamblers. Seniors got money. I went over to Franks today to get a few things. She said, "Are you a senior? Why do you get ten percent off?" I said, "Thank you." You go over to Town and County on Tuesdays, and they give the seniors five percent off. You go into any restaurant. McDonalds, you can always go get a free cup of coffee. Your main thing when you get older is your health. And your kids. But we have a lot to be thankful for.…I don't want the 1930s. That was rough. It is better now. We have inflation but still we manage some way. We are lucky we are living in America.

A woman who had raised her children alone after a divorce in the early 1950s talked about her parents and their retirement.

> When my folks got too old to work people didn't retire. They just quit working when they couldn't work anymore. Then my brother supported them....There were no pensions. I guess my ma got some social security.

Another woman remembered that when she was young older persons were left in precarious financial straits when they stopped working. She said that the only persons when she remembered as having pensions were those who had worked with the railroad. Many older persons turned to their children for help when they stopped working. She remembered that some widows found live-in housekeeping jobs if they were not able to move in with children.

Retirement has not been equally generous. Some of these long-term residents were quite successful financially. Others earned generous pensions. Yet some worked in companies with no pensions or suffered a series of financial hardships that made it difficult to save money for retirement. For them, social security is their primary means of support and retirement has been a lean time.

> When I retired I had a company shirt on. I said, "I got to wear this shirt home because I don't have one of my own." He [his supervisor] said, "After working here forty years you deserve to have that shirt." That's all. There was no bonus or nothing. The guys in the shop made a collection. I got my union pension. They had a little party. The shop stopped working. And they had lunch and everything like that. Gave a little speech about all the years I worked for him.

For many, retirement has not meant inactivity or lack of involvement. Many of the informants started whole new endeavors after retirement. One man is working almost full time as a volunteer at a local medical center, recovering a long buried love of science. Another man is an active volunteer with Meals on Wheels. A third man became active in a national professional organization and continues to be involved in business deals of many types. A woman changed churches and was baptized at the age of 82. A man who is deaf became active in national associations that focus on the needs and concerns of the deaf, held national offices, and traveled internationally to attend and participate in conferences. Another woman took her skills as a seamstress, which were honed in garment factories, and now designs costumes for a theatrical company, expanding her social world greatly to include types of people with whom she never previously had contact. Another woman has developed expertise in telling the history of Northeast and gives walking tours of the area where she visits thirteen churches, gives a history of each church, and links this to the ethnic group that started the church.

One woman described what her retirement has been like.

> I worked all my life. From the time [my son] was two until retirement I worked. I have had all the work I want. When I first retired for about four years I did tutoring at the school. It drove me crazy when I first retired. My son was gone. My daughter was gone. I didn't have that camaraderie you have in the office. I was home all alone. I started cleaning. Spring cleaning. I already belonged to the hiking club. And I have friends. We always do something. And I belong to another hiking club from the Neighborhood House. We hike on Tuesday mornings. Then I belong to another group called Camp Natch. It was sort of a nature, bird watching and nature group. I was real active with them. Took a lot of trips. I have done a lot of traveling. When my kids started growing up, every vacation I would take one grandchild on vacation. That was fun. It took the oldest granddaughter to Hawaii. And I took a couple of the kids to California. One to Florida. So each had a big trip with me. They liked it.

Many are grandparents. Some report an active role in the lives of their grandchildren. Many men have been able to develop different kinds of relationships with their grandchildren than they had with their own children. They can talk more easily with their grandchildren than they could with their own children. They can be friends. One man compared the role of a modern father with that of his own father in the 1920s by saying, "Nowadays, the male is part of the family. He helps take care of the kids and he plays with them and all this other stuff. All that vicious stuff is gone."

As these persons reflected on their lives in Northeast, they pointed to a general sense of satisfaction with their own situations but an unease about changes in Northeast Minneapolis itself.

Key institutions

The three pillars of Northeast Minneapolis neighborhoods are parks, schools, and churches. As these long-term residents thought about changes in their neighborhoods, many of them spoke of the way that current residents of Northeast use public parks.

> There are more playgrounds and wading pools [today]. But that's for the very young. The older ones in high school have seemed to have disappeared from all those places. There used to be football games and everything else at Bottineau Park. They still have the skating and hockey rinks.

But I see very few kids. In the summer time they have a baseball field there. They have about three softball fields. This year I haven't seen anyone playing softball down there. They have tennis courts but I don't know how often they are used. There are no band concerts there. They used to have that. And they were well attended.

Schools have been greatly affected by public policy. In the 1960s and 1970s there was pressure to modernize schools. Some long-existing schools were hopelessly outdated and it was decided the best solution would be to tear them down. One man talked about the effects of this on his neighborhood:

So, when we moved here they went to Thomas Lowry School, was right over here. That was a wonderful school. We talked about this at a Audubon Park meeting, that we have every month down here in the park about the neighborhood. And this one lady says, "Everything started to go to hell when they tore that school down." And it did. It did.

In an effort to desegregate Minneapolis schools, students began to be bussed to other neighborhoods to achieve racial balance. These forces resulted in the closing of some schools and the inclusion of children from outside of Northeast Minneapolis in local schools. It also resulted in Northeast children being bused to schools outside Northeast Minneapolis (see Figure 5.7).

The fact that students were often in schools in neighborhoods other than those in which their families live was often pointed to as a cause of neighborhood deterioration. One man expanded on this by linking it to a wide range of things he considered to be societal problems:

That was the biggest thing that was ever pulled with the education system. You live in this home, whether you are you black or white, if you got a home here you go to that school. Quit this crapping bussing all over and getting the kids away from your neighborhood. And kids will act up when they're away from home....And then, like I say, kids are kids. When they're away from home they will do things they wouldn't do around home. Because the neighbors know them and they will tell on them.

It is clear that the concern with today's schools and their students is not just with the fact that children go to school in neighborhoods different than where they live. It also has to do with culture and ethnicity. Indeed, Edison High School was often pointed to as an example of undesired change. A large percent of the Edison student population is made up by students of color. In addition, there is a large number of students at Edison

Community and Caring

FIGURE 5.7: *Where students in Northeast Schools live and where*
Northeast children go to school (Anderson 1995, 1)

	Where children in Northeast go to school	Where students in Northeast schools live
Northeast	66%	38%
North	18%	51%
South	16%	11%
Total	100%	100%

FIGURE 5.8: *Ethnic identity of school aged children* (Anderson 1995, 1)

	Northeast	Camden (North of Lowry)	Near North (South of Lowry)
Native American	274 (8%)	191 (5%)	286 (3%)
African American	318 (9%)	1,258 (32%)	5,459 (62%)
Asian American	229 (7%)	288 (7%)	1,945 (22%)
Hispanic	140 (4%)	72 (2%)	122 (1%)
White	2,472 (72%)	2,119 (54%)	945 (11%)
Total	3,433 (100%)	3,928 (100%)	8,757 (100%)

who are immigrants. It was expected that over one third of the student population in the school year 1997–1998 would speak little or no English (Anderson 1997c, 27:3). Not only are there ethnic and cultural differences that challenge many of the long-term residents' ability to understand the current student population in Northeast schools, but class also plays a strong role in this. The majority of students in Northeast Minneapolis schools are poor (see Figure 5.9). This is striking when comparing Northeast schools with two neighboring areas, Columbia Heights and St. Anthony.

My qualitative methods class carried out surveys in 1996 in the Logan Park neighborhood of Northeast. We found out that there was a general fear of youth on the part of many adults. Youth were seen as carrying out most of the crime and vandalism in the area, and were often assumed to be people of color. There is little contact between many expressing these opinions and young persons in Northeast. Clearly, much of what is known comes from stereotypes. Discomfort with ethnic and cultural differences combines with a general fear of youth to create a great deal of apprehension and mistrust of schools and students on the part of many older adults in Northeast Minneapolis.

FIGURE 5.9: *Percentage of students living in poverty in Northeast Minneapolis, Columbia Heights, and St. Anthony Village public schools* (Anderson 1997D, 16)

School	Percent of Students in Poverty	Total School Population
NORTHEAST MINNEAPOLIS		
Northeast Middle School	80	914
Edison High School	62	1383
Webster Open Elementary	78	771
Sheridan Elementary	74	709
Holland Elementary	79	386
Waite Park Elementary	75	458
Pillsbury Elementary	57	652
Putnam Elementary	77	315
Bottineau	67	150
COLUMBIA HEIGHTS		
Highland	42	456
Central Middle	36	630
Senior High	25	903
Valley View	32	474
North Park	30	486
ST. ANTHONY		
Wilshire Park	10	624
Middle School	10	292
Senior High	6	402

Churches are still a vital part of Northeast. However, my informants argued that there is less commitment to and involvement in churches on the part of younger persons who have moved into Northeast Minneapolis. In focus groups with pastors and priests, it was argued that younger persons are not as loyal or committed to churches as older persons. Furthermore, those that are church attendees often have little interaction with older persons.

Northeast Neighborhood House had long since been transformed into a social service agency serving a range of needs in Northeast Minneapolis. Its sister organization, the Margaret Barry House, closed in 1973.

In this time period support for fraternal organizations faded even faster than in the previous years. One woman who was active in the Polish White Eagle Association described how the leadership had tried to recruit younger people. This has been unsuccessful. The Polish White Eagle Association has dropped earlier restriction to serving only persons of Polish descent or belonging to the Roman Catholic Church. It now accepts "all Christians" (Polish White Eagle Association 1981, 11). Even this expansion of ethnicity has not brought in many new members.

Commercial and business life

Many spoke of changes in Northeast's business and commercial life. They used to know the persons who owned the businesses and stores in Northeast Minneapolis. Now they do not. Stores are larger and more impersonal.

> All the stores now are big affairs. The smaller stores now will be the hardware stores. The one on Central has been there for sometime. The one on 13th Avenue over here, that's folded just two years ago. It just couldn't compete. Most all the grocery stores went out. Meat market, things of that sort. There still are two banks on Central Avenue. Of course, they are part of big chains. Norwest and 1st National. The small shops like the shops where I used to buy my clothes over there. That's gone now. They were on Central. Central was a busy place then.

There is less a sense of loyalty to Northeast businesses on the part of residents. There is also less loyalty to Northeast on the part of businesspersons, many of whom no longer live in Northeast: One man who had been in business for over fifty years spoke about this.

> I think that back when I first started. Everybody in Northeast stuck pretty close in Northeast. Even business-wise. I don't think people ventured out to doing business in another area. They stayed pretty close to our area. Now it's all over.

Central Avenue has long been the primary commercial avenue in Northeast Minneapolis. Yet many of my informants spoke of changes along Central. One man who has been a long time leader in the business life of Northeast said:

> Particularly during that time frame [the 1960s] and even now either side of Central there is deterioration. There is a physical change in homes and the way they were maintained. I could start to see it there. At one time that

area was in pretty good shape. The area that I would see as getting bad was around University. Now that area [around University] is cleaning up. And either side of Central Avenue is at its worst right now.

These comments are fairly general among merchants who own businesses along Central Avenue. In a 1995 survey of businesspersons who operate on Central Avenue it was found that:

Merchants along Central are concerned about the adjoining residential neighborhoods that have taken a strong turn for the worse...[the merchants argue that] most of the adjoining residences are not owner occupied, creating a large number of residents that don't have the pride of home ownership. The merchants feel absentee landlords neglect their rental properties and accordingly this has pushed market rents down creating a housing environment that is inferior and therefore temporary...Another result of this unfortunate situation is crime. Today, according to the merchants, the community has turned its back on drug abuse. It lacks the willingness to work actively with local authorities to bring it under control. Vandalism, prostitution, domestic disputes, thefts are some of the major discouraging events taking place in the immediate neighborhood...Many merchants see the busing of children from different neighborhoods as problem [sic] for Northeast. They see several students regularly spending time loitering through residential and commercial streets creating a nuisance for the neighborhood residents and businesses. Shoplifting has become a major problem for retail merchants. It is their feelings that some of these students lack a sense of pride, responsibility, and discipline that they might otherwise have in their own [neighborhoods]. (Aaron 1995, 8–9)

Besides the social changes, businesspersons often point to larger changes in other parts of the Twin Cities that have affected Central Avenue.

A lot of it [reason for change] was the supermarkets. Central used to be the shopping hub. On Fridays and Saturdays Central Avenue was really buzzing down there with grocery stores and meat markets and that type of service situation. And then after St. Anthony Village and Apache were developed, this killed the local merchants. There are no grocery stores on Central. Maybe there are one or two little ones. That might have had a contributing factor. And then lower Northeast down on University a Rainbow store came in. That affected neighborhood type of stores. Also business and professional people moved to St. Anthony Village.

These businesspersons often spoke of a decreasing sense of loyalty to Northeast on the part of many of the residents and complained bitterly about residents of Northeast who drove out of the area to shop. They felt they should shop where they live, yet the 1995 survey cited above found that less half (seven out of sixteen) of the merchants queried saw their perceived trade area to be the local neighborhood, Northeast Minneapolis, or Northeast Minneapolis and the northern suburbs. Most argued that their trade area was the entire metro area. Furthermore, only two of the merchants resided in Northeast Minneapolis, and only five shopped with any regularity in the area (Aaron 1995, 3–7).

Neighborhood stores were affected even more quickly than those along Central Avenue. The building of large grocery stores, with their own meat counters, signaled the end for them. One woman spoke of her experience as owner and operator of a small neighborhood store:

> They started building the supermarkets. Our first supermarket was Red Owl in St. Anthony Village. God, that was a gorgeous store. When that opened up, oh my gosh. Today that store is still there but it is little compared to the big new one. That's a Sentryz. They got the Town and Country. Sure [it took our customers away. We started to see our store hurt in the] Late 1950s. We sold it in 1988. We closed the doors. Where I ran the grocery at one time we threw all the groceries out and put in wines. Wine cellar. That was good.

Although they first began to feel the impact of supermarkets in the 1950s, she was able to continue to keep the store open by changing strategies. In the 1970s, the store changed from a grocery store to a wine and liquor store.

Daily life in Northeast Minneapolis

Many of my informants have encountered health problems in this last time period. Some of these are changes common with increased age, such as arthritis and vision changes. A few of these residents have encountered more severe problems that have meant restrictions on their level of activity and mobility. All, however, live independently.

In this last time period family life has changed dramatically for some of my informants. Losses are inevitable in aging, and these long-term residents are in the stage of life where loss through the death of family and friends becomes more common. Parents have died. A number of them have lost brothers or sisters during this time period. For a few, children have died. For others, spouses have passed away. Often these persons were involved in an extended period of care-giving to a parent or spouse. One man talked about the deaths of his brother and sister:

Oh, it was rough! Shook me up pretty bad. Well, it did everybody. That was the last of the older ones that remembered things. My sister had died before. My older one. And she had a mind that could remember everything. And I am sorry that I did not ask more questions of them. And there is nobody to turn to…I don't even remember my grandmother and grandfather's names. Their first names, I mean. Never seen them. Different things.

Of those who were widowed, only one man had remarried. It is generally easier for men to remarry than women. He had had no children with his first wife and acquired a large network of kin, including children and grandchildren, with his second marriage. The marriage entailed a move from his home to that of his wife's. It opened a brand new chapter in his life.

It's a whole different life. And I am very happy about it. Because there is a lot of different things I didn't know about. I am really a greenhorn. In a lot of ways, compared to what my new wife is. Because she had all this business of raising kids. And just last Saturday the youngest baby was baptized and we had to be there…There is still birthdays. You got to go to all the birthday parties and all the wedding anniversaries…I love that [being called grandpa]. Two little kids they run up, across the road, and call me "grandpa."

Relationships with siblings were important to many of my informants. The quality of these relationships is conditioned by the amount and type of interaction over the previous years. One man described how perceived favoritism toward his older brother drew his sister and him together:

Because my sister and I were told a lot of times that we wasn't wanted. Wish you weren't even born because you're just in the way. My brother was the love baby. So her and I got closer together this way. And we're still very close. I see her a lot cause her legs are bad and she is overweight. She lives in this high rise down on 314 Hennepin. I doing something for her all the time. I enjoy helping. Of course, while I am over there she pulls out her brandy bottle and we have a little sniff or two.

On the other hand, another man talked about the relationship he had with his sister who is his only living sibling and living in California. Their relationship was remarkably cool. He attributed it to their childhood. At that time, his sister would often take on a role of limiting his behavior, and an antagonistic relationship developed.

My sister who is the one alive in California was always after me to, "Keep you mouth shut because you are going to get in trouble with Dad." I was the little maverick about bringing up subjects like whether I should be a

Catholic or whether I should be a Protestant or join Demolay and all these
crazy things…Now it is taking dope and wearing the cap on backwards.
But I got into a lot of trouble with Father because of my negative attitude.
She still talks about sitting at the dinner table and Dad and I would start
talking about something and she would kick me under the table, which
meant shut up. And she still talks about it.

Thus, family and extended kin were still important and vital parts of
the lives of my informants. Churches and voluntary associations were also
important. Many of these persons have been active in churches throughout their lives. One man had been a key participant and leader in his local
Catholic parish. He had been involved in sodalities and was a long time
usher. He is not longer involved and said that the church did not want
him any longer because he was too old.

One of the changes that was mentioned by all the informants was in
the ethnic and racial composition of Northeast Minneapolis. At the start
of this time period, in 1970, the ethnic makeup of Northeast Minneapolis
neighborhoods was little changed from previous eras. This gradually
started to change.

Some of the ethnic groups that have made up Northeast saw much
change. For example, in 1985 only thirty-eight of Beltrami's 1000 residents
were single ancestor Italians (Kaszuba 1985, 1A). Those ethnic populations
that more easily blended into the Anglo-dominated majority culture, such
as Scandinavians and Germans, have not disappeared in terms of representa-
tives, but they have become less visible in terms of identifiable communities.

Persons who are ethnically Eastern European continue to be visible
and strongly focused on their ethnic heritage. In part, this is due to the
presence of strong churches.

And, if anything, the biggest pocket resisting change is Northeast's ethnic
identity. At Holy Cross, the largest of three Polish Catholic churches, the
congregation in eight years has jumped twenty-three percent to 1,300 households. A second Polish-language mass, largely for the benefit of those who
live in the suburbs, has been added Sundays. Thirty families that have fled
Poland since 1981 have joined the church. Of the ten neighborhoods in
Minneapolis with the largest single-ancestry Polish populations, eight are
in Northeast and largely within walking distance of Holy Cross. Every Sunday at 7:00 a.m., the pillars of Holy Cross—the people who were baptized
there during World War I and will have their funeral mass there—climb
the steps of the church for the sunrise Polish-language mass. Invariably,
they settle into the same seats. The Edward Rajtar family, whose ailing

patriarch lives half a block from Holy Cross, sits on the right near the front. Sophie Jadlowski typically sits in the third row on the left. Stan Muskala, the brother of the former pastor, sits behind the Rajtars. Frances Siwek, whose husband owned Siwek Lumber and Millwork Inc. on NE Marshall St., sings in the choir. John Rajtar, the lector at the 7:00 a.m. mass, has missed one Sunday since January 1956. "That," said Rajtar, a Polish immigrant with a thick accent, "was due to the alarm clock wasn't wound or we didn't hear it go off." (Kaszuba 1985, 8a)

A more challenging change for these long-term residents is an increase in the percentage of non-Euro-Americans who are living in Northeast. One woman described this:

> It [her neighborhood] was fairly stable for many years. But it has changed a lot now. The houses have gotten old now…Edison changed a lot when they started busing in the Black children from North. As they were here and went around the neighborhood, they found out it was a reasonable place to live….We never had Blacks before. And I don't know if we had anything against [them]. They were more centralized in North Minneapolis and the part of South Minneapolis that is not too far out. Now they've gone way out….Well we never had any [Blacks] in our area, as long as we lived there. They would just be here and there, not centralized. In fact, they are still that way. But we're getting a lot of Vietnamese. You will see that most of the stores on Central are either Vietnamese or Indian, like that.

Many spoke of a change in the ethos of Northeast. There was a general agreement that Northeast's tradition of self-sufficiency had eroded.

> But I think if anything drove Northeast, it was accumulation of ethnic groups that wanted to make good. Wanted to provide a better future and a better education for their kids to enable them to rise a little more…[now] all we hear about…the fatherless families, you know all the AFDC stuff and the irresponsible tenants.

One man explained the changes by saying that:

> Now when I think of deterioration a large part of it is the lack of appreciation and lack of Christian teachings. The lack of ambition. The deterioration of the churches in a good percentage of the population that now just has no interest. You are raising a generation of people that have no religious affiliation and don't get any of the teaching of a Sunday School. And you are getting an awful lot of people that have moved in with really poor moral judgment. That is the biggest impact in the declining impact of the

churches in Northeast. As far as compounding our problems with housing, welfare, and AFDC and vandalism. And then going into criminal activity and gang activity. And drugs.

One woman described this succinctly as, "Nowadays, people have kids
and wait for somebody to support them." Another woman compared immigrants in recent years with immigration in the earlier part of the 1900s
when her ancestors arrived.

Now I know they [recent immigrants] need help. They're coming into the
U.S. and taking jobs from the people who live here. That's not how it was
years ago. Now they mentioned on 60 Minutes, I think it was last Sunday,
about several thousand Iraqi refugees, and we were fighting the Iraqis in
the war for all those oil wells and all that. And they settled them here…but
they can't talk English, which is understandable, but they have to work
hard to climatize them with the United States.…They come with a different
attitude. They [immigrants in the early 1900s] didn't need sponsors, but
they worked hard. At that time there were more jobs to get, see. So you see
that's the difference. Now there are a lot of Americans out of work. And I
think they should draw the line…I feel sorry for the ones…but you
wonder…If they come here with the idea that they are going to make something for themselves, you see now we have Asians that have formed gangs,
they have buy guns. So you see that…but of course our own people are
buying guns left and right too.

My informants often noted that there was more distance between
employers and employees. There was less loyalty of either toward the other.
From the perspective of the employer this means a lack of loyalty on the
part of employees.

There was more loyalty [in the past], I will start with the employees first. I
was [at my place of business for] fifty-three years. We had other employees
that had been thirty, thirty-five, forty years. Where today, that isn't so.

I think loyalty to employers and employers loyalty to the employee has
changed. I don't know if the union movement has brought that about or
not. If you have a employee that has gone out on strike. Maybe they have a
right. But I think that takes something away from the feeling that the employee and employer had…But years ago I think the employer looked out
for the employee a little more. Help through hard times. I still did that
when someone hit hard times at work. In that last ten or fifteen years I
even loaned money personally to the employee rather than through the
company. If someone come to me and said they needed $500 or $200, I
would give it to them personally and never charge them any interest…I

know of two times when [the owner of the business] loaned money so employees so could build a house.

This was further explained by the same man:

Loyalty that the employees have to their employer and also that the employer has to the employees has certainly changed in the last fifty years. Everyone seems to be more for themselves. The individual is more for themselves and the company is more for themselves. It is tougher to accept for the small business person than it is for the corporate type of person. Because the personal relationship that one develops with the employees…I recall a discussion that I had twenty years ago. Where a young man whom I was discussing this loyalty problem with said, "They don't teach loyalty at the University anymore. You got to look out for yourself, period." It was a disappointment.

From the perspective of an employee this looks different:

But the old man, senior, every day he walked through the shop. He knew everybody by their first name and asked you "How's it going? Need anything? Is there something you need?" Then if you needed new drill bits you got it right now. Now, the junior, Stevens number two, he owned one of the big buildings out at the race track. He was a great horse racer. Of course, the old man, senior, he was born poor and he worked his way into this business with nickels and pennies. Now junior he was born into money. He had no idea the value of a dollar.

    The old man now, there was a few guys that stayed with through World War Two, stayed in the shop. Where they could have went to a defense plant and make bigger money. And then when they got older they wasn't capable of producing. Making their guarantee. But he kept them on until they was retired age. Because they stayed with him. Now, junior, it is black and white. If you're in the red and you can't get out of the red then you're not working there anymore. Strictly a business. The old man was a friend of everybody.

Another man spoke of this from his perspective:

But them days the office guys mingled with the shop guys. We had picnics together. Somebody got married, he worked in the office, he'd invite the guys from the shop. Not all of them, but his friends. And we got along…That started changing when the old man that owned it, C. P. Doherty. He was born right end of the block up there. And he started there at fourteen years old as a sweeper. He ended up owning the thing…And then the engineers would come out in the shop and talk with us guys. "What do you think about building that this way? Is it going to work or not?" We'd say, "Well, we tried that once and it didn't work." And we worked together. And later on the new management took over after Doherty sold it. They didn't come to us. Like we didn't know a damn thing or something. It changed....Nowadays its worse yet. Some guys are retiring before their time. As soon as they can get out of there.

For long-term residents, this last era is frightening. Their understandings of who should live in Northeast, what the rules of interpersonal conduct should be, and what values are important have all been challenged. They are increasingly living around persons who are very different than they. These differences are making it difficult for neighbors to respond to each other when needs arise.

Hard times and helping

What happens when people go through hard times? In our conversations, it was common to hear that although long-term residents still knew how to act responsibly and take care of themselves new residents did not.

Family is still important as a source of help. If they existed and there was a good relationship with them, my informants relied upon their siblings, children, or more extended kin. Long-term friends are very important. It was common to hear of close contact with childhood friends. One woman meets regularly with two other women who are her age. They have moved out of the neighborhood and live in nearby areas of the city. She also has visited and keeps in phone contact with other neighborhood friends who have moved farther away. Another person said that friends are, "the greatest thing when you get older. The best friends are your old friends. You can do whatever you want. Move to a different neighborhood....I call as many as I can that live in the city."

Where do they find these friends? First, they maintain long-term friendships. It was common to hear an informant talk of a friendship of fifty to sixty years' duration. Second, they also find friends among neighbors and through continued involvement in organizations like church and Kiwanis.

Increasingly, these persons turn to various types of programs for help. Pensions and services for seniors have greatly expanded since 1970. These are heavily used. Yet the people with whom I talked spoke of a reluctance to accept help that seemed like charity or welfare (they strongly distanced themselves from AFDC and spoke of paying for meals if they used any of the congregate dining services). Many are quite enthusiastic over the current political talk about cutting or eliminating welfare.

The church was not mentioned very often when they spoke of where they turned for help. When I asked about this they said that it would be inappropriate to accept help of a material kind from the church. They did acknowledge the importance of friendships and spiritual or social support through the church.

For many of these long-term residents, looking at Northeast Minneapolis and the changes that characterize it in this fourth period of their lives was troubling. They argued that long standing values and ways of doing things are being lost. In a word, they fear lost of a Northeast ethos.

Many argue that neighborliness has declined. Some complained that busing destroyed Northeast neighborhoods. Others argued that people are less interested in being neighborly today. Some blamed this on the different lifestyles of the persons who have moved in. One man referred to a more general social shift:

> I don't think that the neighborhoods are neighborhoods any more. They are just places where people stay. In other words, very few people know anybody except those in apartment houses they are in. And what they do know of each other is only bad stuff instead of good stuff.

This involves numerous, small scale changes that eventually add up to redefine the neighborhood. One man talked about the neighborhood he lived in for over eighty years:

> The one [building] on our side of the street over there…has changed drastically. I don't know how many apartments have been made up there. The people that live there are not people that we would normally be with. I am sure at some time or other there must of been some drugs there. And also across from the street from there was the worse one yet. A long time ago we never saw the police. Things change and then you saw the police cars more often.

Northeast Minneapolis has changed in the minds of these residents. It no longer feels the same. One woman spoke about this:

> For me, I hardly know people anymore. When I drive up and down the streets I have no idea who lives where anymore. There was a time I could honestly say I think I knew everybody who lived on this side of Central. I knew the house and I knew who lived there. But not anymore. I don't get out much anymore…I think maybe people are more within themselves. As I think back, it was so wonderful. We used to have community sings at night. Everybody would come blocks and blocks around. And you would see each other and get acquainted.

Many of my informants pointed to a more general change in the nature of public and business life in Northeast. In particular, they spoke of a decrease in a sense of responsibility on the part of many in business. One man, who was a long time businessman, explained:

> You had a corollary responsibility when you had a business and you were trying to help build or improve the community. These other things were working toward that goal. Supporting the YMCA. And helping the poor. You feel you are so lucky you want to give something back. Well, helping the poor through good programs. YMCA, fatherless boys programs and things like that. As business has gotten bigger and more impersonal people went to work in boxes, like the Honeywell employees. Well, we have raised generations of people that don't want to join anything. Don't feel the responsibility like a merchant does. Another big impact was our Masonic Lodges on Central…all of us were Shriners. And we all belonged to Arcana Lodge…The Lodge was a good influence and did a lot of good community service work, too. We had 1500 in the Arcana Lodge members when I was auditing records in 1962 and 1963. Now it's dwindled to about two hundred or three hundred. It is very difficult to get younger people. Same as in the churches.

For many there is a diffuse and gnawing fear. This was sometimes spoken of as more crime and less safety. They spoke of neighborhood deterioration. In many ways, this is a fear of urban decay. This leads to a reluctance to continue to be active in the neighborhood. One woman explained, "Even around here with all that we have, I think this is a good neighborhood. Nothing is good anymore. I don't go out much at night."

One of the primary concerns is a lack of safety due to a perceived increase in the rate of crime. One woman talked about the changes that have taken place in the high rise development in which she lives:

> I think it is very different [than when I first moved in]. When we came here we were almost all older people. So everybody was acquainted and worked together. Now there is kind of an animosity between people. We have a guard come on in the evening. Because we have rough people sometimes. Then he has to patrol the parking lot because they've been stealing cars. Damaging cars. It is outside probably [those who are doing the damage to cars]. We have to have people evicted because they bring in drugs.

Another man who has been in business on Central Avenue for many years spoke about this:

> Well, myself I feel we don't have the freedom that we had before. We are always concerned. One thing that bothers me is this is the first time, and I

have never worked off of Central Avenue in all my life, this is the first time that we have to have security on our front and our back door. In the office. A person comes up to the front door or the back door. They got to ring a button. And our secretary answers it. If it is okay she will press a button and you can come in. We never had that before. It's a big change…We had problems across the street and we had problems here when we were re-building. We had graffiti on the walls. We had break-ins. They had set a fire in the back of the building here…We never had that when we went to school. Now it's changed. Even up there at the school at 29th and Johnson. The merchants up there. They had to close sometimes, two hours after school is out. The junior high. Because the kids were floating around there. They would come in and they were shop lifting and so on and so forth. They just had to close. Now it is a little different. They do have police security on all this. Edison has one full-time police officer with a squad car. And they have two plainclothesmen. At the school all day long.

Only one person had had a personal encounter with crime. She was assaulted in her backyard. Others had had suffered property damage. One woman spoke of numerous small cases of vandalism and theft that she had experienced:

I got that evergreen out there. Then I had some [ceramic] ducks that were about this big…One day I came home and thought gee that looks bare. Then, I liked those so well my niece had two of those made for me for Christmas. Then I found at a sale that they had three little ducks. So it looked like a mother and a father and three little ducks. I come home and those three little ducks were stolen. Then I bought one of those windsocks that was an American flag. I hung it on my clothes post. Bought it on Monday. Hung it on Tuesday. On Wednesday it was already gone. From the backyard.…A year ago Christmas I used to have candy canes I would save and put on my Christmas tree. I don't know how many years I had them but they were all in the cellophane. So she made me some plastic poinsettias that I hung on my tree. And I thought those canes would be cute. I don't want to eat them. So I took yarn and hung them all over the tree. It really looked pretty. I had one this big left after Christmas. They kept stealing them.

These incidents created a sense of unease. This was heightened by an-other experience she had:

One time they had someone that moved in there [a building across the alley from her house]. Evidently she was a prostitute. A policeman came and he told me to watch. I said, "Watch, I can't sit there and watch. First of all the fence is here. And what they do over there, that's their business. And if it bothers me, then it's my business." Anyway he told me to watch because she used to have men coming in. She lived on the basement level. I guess she would take the screen off of the window and they would go in and out that way. Well, they finally got her out of there.

My informants argued that absentee landlords were responsible for much of this negative change. Closely intertwined with the criticism of absentee landlords was a range of criticism leveled against new arrivals in Northeast. It was assumed that most of these were renters.. There was a distinct fear of new people who were moving into Northeast. It was presumed that they were persons of color, on "AFDC," living outside of a traditional family form, rarely gainfully employed, and living some sort of aberrant lifestyle.

New types of people are challenging for those who grew up in neighborhoods where there were no strangers. Now, these long-term residents are surrounded by strangers. A woman talked about this as she described changes in her neighborhood:

Almost all the houses around here are different people. The kids we grew with next door. They are all gone. Some of them are dead. The house next to that. She's died. There is a young woman living in there now. Then in the next house some young fellow bought it. I don't even know what his name is. There are people moving here I don't even know who they are. They are younger. They work. And I am here. And we have no reason to interchange.... It is just that we have different interests. They have their own friends.

Often, the new arrivals are seen as a source of trouble. One woman illustrated this:

But you know the neighborhood has got so run down. I walked to the store the other day...You know a couple years ago that second house on the corner, we had some young kids that moved in there. And I don't know if it was drugs, whatever. It was party every night and music until all hours. And then we would call and report them and junk here and there. And they would drive up this driveway [north of house] like they are going right to Chicago. And then they would back out. You didn't know if somebody was going to get hit or something. And then one night they had fight there. There was shooting and windows were broken out. So I called 911 and they wanted to know all the information and I said, "I'm scared to death. I am not going outside." A lot of the kids were running in this yard. They're trying to get away from the shooting, you know. Well, then six police cars came. The policemen said there was a standoff between one gang and another gang.

My informants often complained about the increased amount of renting in Northeast. Those who rent are seen as more unstable and less committed to the neighborhood than those who buy.

> East of Central they have had problems. Cause there was a lot of rentals. And rental property is hard because the people don't care... Not all of them. But I bet the majority of those people. If you have heard of anybody that has rental property, they're constantly fixing something up that the renters damaged.

It is ironic that renters are seen as sources of trouble since there was a good deal of renting in Northeast when these residents were young. One difference, however, is that renting often took the form of subdividing existing housing and renting out a portion of one's house. In addition, it was common to rent to relatives. Last, these residents remembered that those who rented stayed in place for years.

Race is, and has long been, an issue in Northeast Minneapolis. A major difference today is that people of color are living in Northeast. It is more likely that there will be face-to-face encounters between whites and people of color. At times, this is starkly negative. One woman recounted two occasions where she saw this in Northeast:

> We used to have a colored girl working for us [at the telephone company]. Real nice girl. She has retired. I told her I would like to take you out to celebrate your retirement. I was retired. She drove here and picked me up. Then we up to a restaurant. Everybody that knew me didn't say anything. She took me home. The next time I went there, boy was I criticized by the different ones that were there. Even the help. When I was still working at the telephone company I used to wait for the bus [in her neighborhood in Northeast Minneapolis]. There was colored man that waited there. One time somebody said, "quit flirting with that man." I said he's a married man. We were just talking. They said I shouldn't be talking. One day he came out and said, "Lauretta we are moving." He said his kids are being harassed. My wife is being harassed.

At one level, racial differences are just that, differences. As such, they present newness and ask for adaptation in response. Yet for those who have never had extensive first hand contact with persons who are racially different this can be challenging.

> This is quite a stable neighborhood. I wouldn't say there are many drastic changes. Except in the last two or three years there have been Blacks moving into this neighborhood which we never had before. I would say there is

a little prejudice. But I never have heard of any problems that they caused. But it is different than what it used to be. They get off the bus, walk by the house, go their way that direction [east on 15th], but I wouldn't know where they live or who they are. No acquaintance whatsoever with the Blacks.

A businessperson who has been active on Central Avenue for a long time explained:

The people walking up and down the street [are different today]. I'd just as soon not mention the way. It isn't the way. It's the appearance. Entirely different. Never had them before. Northeast Minneapolis never had them before.…I would say 26th and Central, without going into detail, that has not helped our image in Northeast [these are Middle Eastern delis and grocery stores].

What this man was talking about was race. The people to whom he was referring were people of color. In this case they were persons of Middle Eastern heritage. In the conversation, he referred to them and other persons of color who worked along Central Avenue as African Americans.

There's all kinds of African Americans down there on 19th and Central. [They sell] African imports. So on and so forth. All food. As a matter of fact they got about three stores.…They're just different. They are not interested. They got their own kind. They got their own following. We had an opportunity. I suppose we're clannish or something like that. But we had the opportunity of renting to them. But we have turned them down. Because of the fact, first of all with that type of food coming in it is hard to keep your building clean. And too at the same time, a lot of bugs.…

There was a close association between crime and race in the minds of my informants. One person was talking about crime in Northeast. I asked him if he had heard of any gang activity. He replied:

Not lately. But prior to a year or so back. But there are gangs. And its not too far to come across the river either. Lot of times the gangs have a tendency to be a little jealous too. And if a community is doing a little better than some other community then naturally there is a jealousy there. At least that's what I feel. There is jealousy and they will come in. They will think the grass is always greener on the other side of the street and the other side of the river, too.

"Other side of the river" refers to North Minneapolis. North Minneapolis has a large concentration of African Americans. A dominant theme when my informants were talking about people of color was that of "coming in" or "invasion." People of color were often pointed out as examples of bad elements that have moved into neighborhoods and caused deterioration. One woman argued:

> Like I said, we have a lot of the Blacks that came in. They don't keep up their homes…We even have a lot of Indians. Right across the street. We had a family for about a year. One family moved in and before you knew there were five families living there. This is how they come in. The house is condemned now. Then there was an Indian family living next door. She was a real severe alcoholic. She drank a lot. Don't work. She was always there to give the welfare check to the landlord. And they sit there and drink all the time. It was woman with a lot of male friends…Then, of course, when the Indians were here there was a lot of damage on garages and stuff. I just had all my flowers pulled out. The Indian girl did it. I caught her at it. She was twelve. She was bored.

Race and concerns about race seem to be the subject of widespread worry in Northeast Minneapolis. Although most persons are too sophisticated to speak of their fears, stereotypes, and prejudices out loud, these murmurs do surface occasionally. When it does, it is stark. For example, at a March 1997 meeting of the Columbia Heights City Planning Commission, plans for expansion of a gas station on the corner of 37th and Central Avenue were discussed. Some residents opposed this, arguing that this would attract troublemakers who are sometimes housed by Hennepin County in the Hi-Lo Motel located across the street from the gas station. One man went further and was much more explicit in his accusations:

> Heights residents made it clear they fear that crime, which they say is moving into their suburb from Minneapolis, could increase if the gas station at 37th and Central expands…But one resident said the restaurant, that gas station owners plan to add, would attract a bad crowd, which he identified as minorities, some from the Hi-Lo Motel, across 37th Avenue in Minneapolis. "You're going to have a problem," he said at the city hall hearing. "You know what I mean—of the race that's in there. You got to stop it, from Minneapolis"…[later, the chair of the commission, Marlaine Szurek said] that some Columbia Heights residents perceive a link between crime and minority persons because many Sheffield neighborhood residents were black, and that police often were called to the neighborhood before the city purchased and replaced many rental properties there]. (Anderson 1997b, 7)

Often all this works together to create a sense of being under siege, as expressed by one woman:

Northeast is not what it used to be. On 2217 2nd street they're peddling drugs. The cops are trying so far to catch them. They walk in and out all night. It is a dump. I see they put an orange sign out, "Condemned." And the owner of that house lives in South Dakota. We have a lot of Indians living in Northeast. A lot of them. I would prefer the Blacks to Indians. Indians get mean. They drink and they get mean…And now we got drugs peddling in the neighborhood. That's terrible. All hours of the night. They're going to catch them but you got to be right there. There was a shooting there not long ago. The same house…I don't know. I just think that it is not as good as it used to be. The other day I was going down 2nd street. There were these three Black kids, about twelve years old. They stood in the middle of the street. They wouldn't let me by. I honked the horn. They wouldn't move. They had nice bicycles. They were dressed nice. So finally I popped my head out and said, "Come on you guys. Get the hell out of the way." They kids said, "Fuck you." I thought, "What am I doing? Why didn't I just turn off and get out of the way." What they'll do is they will shoot you.

So, many agreed that Northeast Minneapolis had deteriorated in this period. They blamed this on a host of causes. One man summed up his feelings about why he thought the area had deteriorated:

Well naturally, because the older guardian passed on [and their children sold their homes.…You got a lot of absentee landlords now. And they rent to AFDC's and all this crap. So far, we are not too bad but it's coming up from the Central and Polk Street and that is terrible. Oh, I wouldn't even go down there…We were talking about that down at the meeting the other night. This lady lives on 29-something Polk Street. And she's got a beautiful old home, a duplex with beautiful hardwood flooring in it and everything. And she said that her backyard across there and around there there's all these AFDCs and they're fighting and screaming and drunk. And there's no way she can sell her property. And her property, she's got to give it away properly…Nah, they're trash. Pick out any nationality you want. We won't say one nationality or nothing. Just trash. People that don't give a shit about anybody else and throw their garbage…Cops are down there all the time…Next door the absentee landlord don't mow his lawn or nothing. He had a bad couple in there. Finally got rid of them…

Change was very much on the minds of these long-term residents. Yet they still live in Northeast and are paradoxically proud of that. They would often argue in the midst of these descriptions that there is still a distinct sense of life in Northeast.

I still think on the whole that it is that way [a strong neighborhood]. Here is an example of a young woman at the theater that bought a house between Broadway and East Hennepin. It's between 2nd Street and Monroe, something like that. She bought this house and she loves Northeast. She married and they're still there. She said, "People are so friendly." ...Yes. I can recall even bus riders used to always say there's such a big difference with the people in Northeast. They're friendly.

And my children when they come back they look up all there friends and they love it. It is really a close neighborhood. It is unfortunate that we have these uncaring people coming in...There is just too much transition. It is changing too much. I am not comfortable with it...I think we are seeing more and more minorities moving into from the downtown area. Through the Bottineau area and into our area. I don't know if these are working minorities or non-working minorities. We just don't know...I don't mind the neighborhood changing. I just don't want it to be just one problem with crime after another...We were very upset when this house here [next door] was finally sold. We had hoped it would be torn down. The guy who was working on it was trying very hard to upgrade it. But it is going to [be rented as] section eight. And it's going to be low income, single mothers. Just don't know what it's going to bring.

Yet there is also a recognition that some of the newcomers are real residents of Northeast.

I don't know. It seems pretty much the same to me. People are still hard working. They probably earn more but everything costs more. The younger people had better education and training. They didn't have to do just menial jobs. Like my parents, the immigrants, they are no different than the immigrants coming in now from Mexico, the Hmongs and Viet Nam. You have to start at the bottom. If you are starving you will take anything. Just so you can work. It is not as ethnic as it was. Now you don't know what people are when they move in. I don't know what nationality the people next door are and the ones next to that. Before we knew every house, this was Polish, that was Russian, that was Polish, that was Czech. Now nobody asks. We are just all Americans. What difference does it make?

Long term residents of Northeast Minneapolis have seen much change in the last time period. Much of this change frightens them. Yet they also maintain that there is much of "old Northeast" that still works. The next chapter looks at care giving and receiving. It describes a Northeast pattern of care giving and receiving, and how this is changing.

Chapter 6

Crisis and caring in Northeast Minneapolis

Long-term residents have gone through and continue to go through much change. They were born and raised in strikingly different social, cultural, and technological settings from those in which they now live. They have learned how to cope with challenges brought on by crises such as deaths of friends or family members, job losses, illnesses, or divorces. Part of this coping has entailed providing or receiving support from members of their effective communities. Yet these communities have in turn been affected by the many changes through which these persons have lived.

Older persons who are long-term residents of Northeast Minneapolis spent their childhood and youth between two world wars and in the midst of the Great Depression. The oldest subjects were profoundly affected by economic hard times. This was a time when they, or their spouses, were beginning to work and establish families. Lack of steady employment and difficulty in finding affordable housing created severe challenges. The younger subjects reported that they were aware of the Great Depression but that they were not directly affected since they were still in school and not yet intending to work. For all, this was a formative time when roads were being paved, electricity was coming in, and Northeast residents lived in small, well bounded, face-to-face neighborhoods. These were neighborhoods where few strangers were seen, the population was Euro-American, and many people still spoke Russian, Polish, Swedish, Slovakian, Italian, or German. The core values of hard work, thrift, and community identity were transmitted and internalized by the people whom I interviewed.

World War Two was a key event for these long-term residents. Those men and women who went into the armed services experienced things that changed them profoundly. For those who stayed behind, World War Two was a time of relative prosperity and opportunity. After World War Two, Northeast Minneapolis went to work, and my informants were busy at their places of employment and in their families, neighborhoods, and churches. At first, there was economic growth, but in the 1960s and into the 1970s economic growth slowed and Northeast began to see a general decline. As these persons approached retirement, changes began to occur in Northeast that worried them. Their own children were finishing school, going on to college or work, and, for many, moving out of Northeast seeking larger, more modern homes in the suburbs. The population in Northeast was graying. The persons with whom I spoke felt that people were not as friendly and outgoing. Loyalty and trust were breaking down. Fewer business owners seemed to live in the neighborhood, and life, in general, seemed less familiar and less personal.

Now, these people are retired. Personally, they find it to be a good time of life—much better than it was for their parents and grandparents. But Northeast continues to change. Familiar neighborhood schools like Pillsbury and Thomas Lowry have closed. Children from Northeast, which is still predominantly white, are going to schools in South and North Minneapolis, which have large populations of people of color. Children from South and North are going to schools in Northeast. For some of these long-term residents, there is a nostalgic twinge of pain as they think about the closing or changing of schools in Northeast. For others, the presence of unfamiliar young people, many of whom are children of color from outside the neighborhood, is frightening.

There is an increasing fear of crime and insecurity among the long-term residents with whom I spoke. I was told that it is not safe to take walks in the neighborhood and that it is important to keep doors locked. Recently, there have been highly publicized murders and rapes in Northeast. This has been terrifying to the people of Northeast Minneapolis. Rumors of even more problems circulate. Only one person with whom I talked has actually been a victim of violent crime, yet all expressed feelings of victimization. Lastly, Northeast Minneapolis, the "all-American" neighborhood where the population was Euro-American and strangers were rare, is now full of new, unknown people. Those who are walking the streets, moving into neighborhoods, and operating stores look and act differently. Sometimes this is a difference of unfamiliarity. Sometimes it is a difference of lifestyle or public behavior. More frequently in present day Northeast it is a difference of skin color or nationality.

Over the course of his or her life, each of my informants have learned how to give and receive care in times of need. Indeed, they have each faced and survived many crises. As their neighborhoods have changed around them these persons have found different constellations of resources upon which to draw. Some, such as Alice, whose story is told below, struggle to find ways to give or seek care in present-day Northeast.

Alice's Story

Alice's father was born in a small village in a part of Austria-Hungary that is now located in Slovakia. There were too many people and too little land. America held out the promise of a future so he left his village and emigrated to the United States in 1906 when he was nineteen years old. Alice's father joined his brother and other young men from his village who had settled in Northeast Minneapolis. Like many other young men in his situation, he found a job working for the Soo Line Railroad in the air brake shop. He could not speak English when he arrived so he began to attend evening English classes at Holland Elementary School. These were offered by Minneapolis Public Schools. He was successful in learning English and also took classes in subjects such as math.

Alice's maternal grandparents also emigrated from Austria Hungary, first settling in Pennsylvania. Soon after Alice's mother was born, they moved to Northeast Minneapolis. Almost twenty years later, Alice's parents met in activities at St. Mary's and were married in 1912.

Alice was born in 1920. She was the only one of the four children to be born in a hospital. All the other three were born at home with a midwife.

Alice's family lived south of Lowry and just west of University in an area called "Lower Northeast," directly across the street from Schiller Elementary School. It was a neighborhood of homeowners.

They were the only members of the Russian Orthodox Church living in the neighborhood. Most of their neighbors were Polish Catholics. Alice remembers the feeling of being a minority during the Christmas season. At that time St. Mary's was still on the Julian Calendar and celebrated Christmas later than others in the neighborhood. Alice asked, "Did you ever live with being told you were the only one in the world to celebrate Christmas on the wrong day?" There was a positive side to this, however.

When the Polish Catholics threw their Christmas trees away Alice's family would choose the best one for their Christmas.

Alice and her siblings spoke English. Her parents would sometimes speak Russian with each other if they did not want the children to know what they were talking about, but they did not encourage their children to learn Russian. Alice's father wanted the family to be one hundred percent American, which did not mean totally rejecting one's heritage.

St. Mary's Russian Orthodox Cathedral, as it is now known, was a central focus point for her family. In particular, music was important, and Alice's mother and all the children joined the choirs of St. Mary's.

Alice's father was also active at St. Mary's and belonged to church lodges in some of which he was either chairman or president. He was also president of the church on numerous occasions.

Alice went to "Russian School" at St. Mary's. This was held from 4:00 to 6:00 on Monday through Friday. There the students learned what they needed to know to be able to participate in church. The curriculum included "Church Slavonic," the prayers, and the Russian alphabet. When Alice was a child, only Slavonic was used in church.

She remembered that neighborhood life, was rich and full. Alice stressed that this was not a peaceful, earthly Eden, however: "Everybody argued and fought. They weren't so peachy holy. But when it was over they would all go have a beer together. You know, that kind of thing. There was never any 'fighting' fighting. Or bitterness. Oh, we would yell at the Pollocks, as we called them. We were Russian. They were Polish. 'Oh you Pollocks, this and that.' I call it kid stuff."

It was a good life. There were many children in the neighborhood, and playmates were easy to find. Alice and her friends found their own fun. Alice played jacks by the hours. The front sidewalk was perfect for hopscotch and jump rope. These did not cost anything. Immediately behind her house was a large open area where nightly baseball or softball games were held. Everything was within shouting distance. Marshall Terrace Park was two blocks away and was the place to go ice skating or play larger, more organized ball games. When five o'clock came, whistles or shouts of parents brought the children in for supper. After supper the children came back out of their homes and played until the corner lights came on. Then it was time to go home.

Groceries and everyday items were bought in neighborhood stores. On Saturdays, Alice and her family, and later Alice and her friends, would walk to Central Avenue to shop. There were nice stores, such as the Miss

Johnson's Department Store and Lohmar Men's Wear. When she was in high school she and her friends would stop at the offices at Argus Publishing to catch the latest news and gossip. Later they would buy malted milks for a nickel at a popular malt shop.

Alice was active in the many programs at the Northeast Neighborhood House, or the "Nut House," as Alice and her friends called it. A highlight was the yearly Halloween party. The facility's basement would be converted to a haunted house where scary, spooky things lined the halls. Hundreds of children would file through the darkened halls, ready to be terrified at any moment.

As Alice looked back, she realized that most of the families in the neighborhood were poor. Yet she does not remember thinking that she lacked anything. The neighborhood offered the riches of people who knew one another and cared for one another. Yet, neighbors were not expected to help one another to a great extent. There were enough children to take up the work when extra needs arose. Self-reliance was expected and valued. Northeast was a hardworking neighborhood and people were expected to take care of themselves. For example, Alice's mother struggled with various health challenges for over ten years, starting from the time of Alice's birth. She kept this as a secret known only inside the family. After a particularly difficult time, she would be back on her feet as soon as possible so no one knew she had been sick.

Alice attended Schiller Elementary School from kindergarten through eighth grade. Mary Martin was the principal. Alice said she was a wonderful human being, but as kids, they thought she was "the meanest thing that ever walked on two feet." Alice said she was teeny at five feet high and maybe five feet wide, but her word was law. Schiller had some big, tough Polish boys, but Ms. Martin was not awed by them. She never hit anyone, but she would stand with her hands on hips, look a misbehaving student in the eyes, and say, "No." That was it. It was over. She demanded and received obedience and respect.

For the children, neighborhoods were defined by the schools they attended. The "Holland kids" went to Holland Elementary School. The "Schiller Kids" went to Schiller Elementary School. These lines were blurred when Alice went to the Russian School at St. Mary's, for children from a variety of public schools attended there. Alice noticed that there were never children from the neighborhoods east of Central, such as Windom Park. Swedes or Norwegians lived there, and Alice thought of them as being rich and different than the children in her neighborhood.

Alice attended Edison High School after Schiller. No one else from her family was attending at the time. She was on her own for the first time in her life. She had heard so much about Edison that she arrived very excited about being there. The only challenge she recalls is remembering which stairway to use since you only went up the up stairwell and down the down stairwell.

Once at Edison she found there was a clique that came from "Norwegian Hill," around 29th and Johnson. They were not mean, but they knew each other and stayed in their own group. Alice wanted to break into it. Even though she now knows they were also poor, she thought of them as wealthy.

Alice wanted to go to college and become a nurse. By the tenth grade it was obvious she would not have the money for college, so she switched into the subjects (such as stenography, typing, and office training) that would prepare her for office work. This was and continues to be a disappointment.

She graduated from Edison in June, 1937. She remembered her graduation as being gorgeous. The boys wore suits. The girls in her class wore long, pastel-colored gowns. They were fluffy things in which the girls swooped down the aisle. It felt very fancy and high class.

After high school Alice often went dancing with friends. A popular dance hall was the Calhoun on Lake Street in South Minneapolis. Four or five young women would take the street car from Northeast to South Minneapolis. There was never a question of "fooling around" on these occasions. Alice and her friends were constantly warned by their parents not to be "bad girls." The penalties for losing one's reputation were heavy.

After high school, Alice's first job was with the *Minneapolis Star*. She worked in the circulation department in a large office with many other young women. They folded fliers that would be sent out with the newspapers. These contained information for the carriers and would often announce contests to encourage the carriers to build up their subscription lists. If a carrier signed up five new subscribers he won a prize or received points toward a prize, such as a free trip to the State Fair. Alice was able to meet young women from all over town. They were all in the same stage of life and would talk about common interests, like boyfriends, dating, or fashions. Alice started at ten dollars a week. After paying her parents five dollars a week for room and board, there was still enough to buy what she needed and start a savings account. She had a regular income and new friends. It was a great time of life.

Alice worked for the Minneapolis Star from 1937 to 1942. She was promoted two or three times and moved from the circulation department to the want ads department.

World War Two broke out, and in 1942, the armed services started recruiting women. Alice thought that looked exciting. In January, 1943, Alice enlisted in the Navy and joined the WAVES. Her sister joined a week later. Alice's family, along with most of Northeast Minneapolis, was very patriotic. Many residents put signs in their yards reading, "Help the Boys in the Service." Alice's two brothers both were 4F. Her mother was excited to have two children involved in the war effort and put two big stars in the front window.

Alice and her sister rode a troop train to New York where they attended basic training at Hunter College which had been put under the control of the Navy. They were there for three months and met young women from all over the country. Alice loved it and thought of her days in the Navy as the best days of her life. It was her "college experience." She enjoyed meeting young women from around the United States. There were differences, such as the various accents, but they had much in common. Alice remembered many conversations about boy friends.

After boot camp, Alice and her sister were sent to Norman, Oklahoma, where they took Yeoman training for six weeks. They then received permanent assignments. Alice and her sister were both assigned to San Diego, and were thrilled. Years earlier they had visited an aunt who lived there and thought it was "heaven on earth." The two sisters were stationed at the Naval Training Center where 33,000 sailors were being trained.

In 1943 or 1944, with all of the children gone, Alice's mother decided it was time to move. She wanted a brick house on the east side of Central Avenue and found one set up as a duplex, south of Lowry and just a block east of Central. Alice's parents sold their old house to Alice's brother, moved into the lower unit of the duplex, and rented out the upper unit.

While living in San Diego, Alice had been corresponding with a young man from Sioux City, Iowa, whom she would eventually marry. They had met earlier in September, 1941. He had been studying in Iowa City at the University of Iowa and decided to transfer to the University of Minnesota. He had heard of her through a mutual friend and was standing at the base of the church steps as Alice was leaving the service at St. Mary's. He looked at her and said, "Oh, are you Alice? My friend told me to look for the prettiest girl in church and that would be you."

Then the war came, and each joined the military. He was in the Army Air Corps and served in China, Burma, and India. A few years later, he future husband wrote Alice a letter from Burma. He was going on some kind of mission where they would fly behind the enemy lines to pick up the wounded. He told her that he figured that this mission might be his last and that he might not come back.

Of course, he survived and eventually returned to the United States where he was stationed in Texas. In late 1944, he sent telegrams to Alice every day for a week saying, "It's Tuesday (or Wednesday, Thursday, etc.) and I think I'm in love with you." Eventually he wrote, "Why don't you come and visit me?"

So Alice took a trip from San Diego to visit him. After being together four or five days he said, "Why don't we just get married?" Alice thought that made sense. They were married at the base chapel on February 6, 1945.

Alice was discharged in April. She moved to be with her husband at Muskogee, Oklahoma, where he was then stationed. In October, 1945, he was discharged, and they moved to Sioux City, Iowa, where his mother was widowed and lived alone. Her husband thought they would be doing his mother a favor if they lived with her. It turned out that it was hard for Alice to live with her mother-in-law, so her husband suggested they try living in Minneapolis. They moved in with Alice's family for a short time. Shortly after that they moved into the lower unit of the duplex that her parents owned. Renters were already in it, but they were supportive of returning veterans and volunteered to move out to let Alice and her husband have the place.

It was great to be back in Northeast Minneapolis. She had many friends and there were endless parties and dances. Her husband decided to use the GI Bill and return to the University of Minnesota. Alice went to work for the Smaller War Plants Corporation.

Her husband went to college for a year and half but he was bothered by not having enough money to live the lifestyle he wanted. So he quit college and he started doing manual labor in commercial construction projects. He loved his work and was soon promoted to foreman.

He worked for several companies before he ended up with a large construction company. He would often work out of town to places like Sleepy Eye and New Ulm, Minnesota. Alice decided to quit work and travel with him. They moved quite to follow jobs that would last three to four months. In between jobs, they returned to Northeast and lived in Alice's parents' duplex. It was a good time. They lived a "fast life" with many parties filling up their evenings.

When they were in Waterloo, Iowa, her husband met an architect with whom he became friends. The architect was designing a project to be built in Ankara, Turkey. He asked her husband if he wanted to supervise the construction. Her husband jumped at the chance for adventure. Alice agreed to go even though she hardly knew where Turkey was. Her husband left for the project, but when he got to New York the project fell through and he had to return. He was very disappointed.

Alice and her husband adopted a baby boy in 1956. They decided that they needed to stop traveling and settle into a permanent home. One Saturday in 1959, they spent the morning with an architect going over plans for a house. They had bought land in Northeast and were finally going to have their own home. To celebrate, they had a barbecue supper on Sunday with friends. After their friends went home and their son was in bed, her husband was lying on the couch. All of a sudden, he said, "Geez, I don't feel good. I don't feel good." Then he said, "Geez! I don't feel good at all." He was white and perspiring heavily. Alice called the doctor who told her to bring him in to the hospital right away. It was a massive heart attack. Her husband entered Eitel Hospital by Loring Park and died ten days later at the age of forty.

Alice stayed in the duplex with her parents living downstairs. Some money was raised at St. Mary's to help Alice and her son. Her husband had a life insurance policy from which Alice received additional funds. She also received some help from social security. The rent was cheap. Alice did not work until her son was in junior high school. He was three years old when her husband died and she wanted to be home with her son when he was growing up.

Alice did not date other men. She was too tired and busy. By then her parents were getting older, and Alice doing most of the housework. Also, she felt she had had a good marriage. She did not think she wanted to start over again. During this time the church was her lifeline. Her girl friends did not shut her out after her husband died. She continued to be active and involved at St. Mary's.

Northeast was a good place to live for Alice and her son. Central Avenue was still vibrant. Close to Alice's home was a drug store with a soda fountain, where Alice would take her son and buy malts or other fountain treats.

Her father and mother kept busy. Her father kept a detailed journal, continued to be active in church, and was on the church board. He also was a handy person and could paint, repair, or fix anything at church. Alice's mother worked at Anchor Laundry. She loved it and said that was her fun time, even though it was hard work and hot with no air conditioning. She continued working there until she was seventy.

Her father had a heart attack in 1969. Complications arose, and he contracted pneumonia. This led to his death. Alice's son was thirteen at the time. Alice and her son continued to live in the upper unit of her parents' duplex. Her mother lived downstairs.

When her son was thirteen he complained about a sore back. Alice took him to the doctor who decided the pain came from the acrobatics that her son was doing on his bicycles. It did not turn out to be so easy, and the pain got worse. Alice made contact with a doctor at the Washburn Clinic where children with psychiatric troubles were sent. The doctor investigated and sent her son to see a neurologist, who found a malignant tumor at the base of the spine. Doctors operated and removed as much as they could. Her son was given thirty radiation treatments (cobalt) over the next thirty days.

He was able to return home and continue with school. In a drafting class at junior high, he was supposed sit on a high stool while bending over a table to do his work. This created great strain and pain for her son's back. He could not stand it and would wander about. The teacher saw this as misbehavior and kicked him out of class many times. Alice talked to the teacher and counselor. They told her he was just acting up and would have to conform.

About a year later the cancer appeared in his chest and then, later, in his head. The doctor said that there was little they could do. Luckily, a doctor at Northwestern Hospital was trying out a new treatment. He began to treat Alice's son. The treatments worked. After six months he was clear of cancer, and he seemed to be fine.

When her son started junior high, a friend, who was working for the Board of Education, called her one day and asked if she would help out in the office with a large project. Alice went in and found she enjoyed working there. She met many new people and liked the interaction. She worked for about four or five weeks. A few weeks after the project was over, her friend called and told her that the curriculum department needed someone permanently. Alice applied and was hired. She worked there over fourteen years, eventually retiring in 1987.

After finishing high school, her son moved to California in 1978 or 1979. Then around 1982, her mother's health began to fail. After falling and breaking her hip. Alice's mother entered a nursing home. She quickly became confused after she moved there. Alice was alone in the family duplex. She did not want to be a landlord and the responsibility for renting out the second unit of the duplex. She and her brothers sold the house, and in 1983 Alice moved into an apartment back in the original neighborhood where she grew up. Her mother died that summer.

In 1985, she moved into the apartment in which she now lives. It is close to the area in which she grew up and to her church.

Meanwhile, her son had married and found work. Then he started to have problems with intestinal blockages and had numerous operations. While in the hospital he developed bed sores on his lower back which developed into serious ulcers. More operations followed. His wife sued for divorce during this time. Her son returned to Minneapolis in 1988 to move in with Alice and continues to live there. He is now weak and unable to work. So he stays in the apartment most the time. This makes it difficult for Alice to entertain and is a source of constant worry.

Meanwhile, Alice continues to be active with church and her friends. Northeast, however, is full of people she does not know. As she drives up and down the streets she has no idea who lives where. There was a time when she felt she knew everybody who lived west of Central. Her safe, familiar neighborhood has changed.

Alice's story is illustrative of the changes through which my informants have lived. These changes have challenged the patterns of care-giving and receiving learned early on in their lives. She was raised in an era where life was well defined and founded. Families and individuals were self-reliant. Church, friends, and neighbors provided limited support in times of crises. Now she is faced with the twin challenges of aging and caring for a disabled son. Her personal resources are limited. She feels "out of touch" with her neighbors. The church continues to be her lifeline.

Crises and caring in the formative years

Northeast Minneapolis was, and to some extent still is, an area of Minneapolis that is characterized by small, well-defined neighborhoods. In the first three periods of the lives of these long-term residents, neighborhood life was rich and highly interactive. They report that they knew who lived in their neighborhoods, saw relatively few strangers, and experienced high degrees of interactions between neighbors. These were formative years for them. They learned who they were and how to act in different situations. Most germane to this study, they learned how to give and receive help. This is most clearly seen in times of crisis. The most common types of crises experienced by those with whom I spoke were economic, marital, illness, and death.

These long-term residents lived through the challenge of the Great Depression, the defining experience of World War Two, and the growth and expansion of the postwar era. Many of them experienced numerous economic crises in their lives. For the older informants, unemployment was a real threat as they began their work years and established families in the worst years of the Great Depression. One woman's husband lost his job early in the Depression and remained unemployed until World War Two. She described how the family coped during this time:

> You know, we never even thought about going on welfare. Never thought about it. But we didn't order any magazines. Didn't smoke. We didn't go to the theaters. We didn't go out for dinner. We saved every bit. And then my husband being quite mechanical, he would work on somebody's car. Off and on. Whenever he could. Some of them he would work and get the parts for it. And then these guys couldn't pay him. So it was a rough time... [my parents] did help because we lived in the duplex. [my father] was, at that time, getting $25 a month rent. He rented to us for $15. If we couldn't pay he just kicked in. We just kept a record of it. So after [my husband] got working at Northern Ordinance then we paid my dad back every cent.

This illustrates two common ways of coping with a crisis. First, family was a first and most important source of help. Second, a family should find some way to "make do" by finding ways to reduce its need for income or seek informal forms of employment. Many of these persons reported that they or their parents had skills or knowledge that translated into income, such as doing mechanical work on the side. Another example was reported by a man who said that his father had developed a recipe for seasoning sausages. He used to make sausages and sell them to neighborhood stores. As still another example, one woman remembered that when there was no money to buy coal in the winter, her father and other men in the neighborhood would dig peat from an area near Stinson and 18th and burn it in the furnace.

For the time periods that this study is considering, marriage was expected for both men and women. Being single created a lifelong crisis. One never completely fit in. Four persons had never been married—three women and one man. In all four cases, they lived at home with their parents until their parents died. In two cases they continued to live with unmarried siblings after the death of their parents. A single person in Northeast Minneapolis was excluded from many areas of activity. One primary area was the church.

> If they [young adults] don't get married when they are in church, there isn't a place for them. Most of our groups are couple groups... When singles come in, it is difficult. We never really felt at home in the Mariner group [a

Sunday school class that has functioned as a long-term friendship group].
Because they were all couples.

Divorce was a second type of marital crisis that affected two of my
informants. One of the men I interviewed told me what happened when
he was fourteen and his father divorced his mother and then moved out
leaving him and his two siblings alone with his mother:

> My dad, he left. In them days, there wasn't such things as alimony or child
> support or care or anything like that. So my brother and I, we both had to
> support my sister and mother...For awhile there was no money coming in
> anywhere...my brother and I got a job working with the Tank Car [a ser-
> vice station]...

Divorce was looked at in strikingly negative terms during this time
period. A woman, who was divorced in the early 1950s , described what
happened:

> I was stigmatized. Especially in the Catholic Church. That was terrible. And
> whether it was my fault. You weren't supposed to get a divorce...The couples
> kind of dropped me. I hear that time and again from widows now. Friends
> that they have around. All of a sudden they are not friends anymore.

Being divorced and a single mom during this time period was even
more difficult. The woman speaking above went on to describe how her
family provided the primary source of help:

> I worked all day at work. And I would come home and I would wash clothes
> and I would help the kids with their homework. And I would read to them
> and I would put them to bed. And I would get up in the morning. Send
> them off to school. I would go to work. Come home. Clean the house. Do
> this. My daughter was taking accordion lessons. [My son] was taking gui-
> tar lessons. You know how busy you get with kids...And then my brother
> was still single. He was living downstairs. Even after my dad died. He was
> so good to the kids. He was the father to the kids...Well, my mother took
> care of the kids when they would come from school. She lived downstairs.
> So they would be down there until I come home. And then I would take
> over. She helped a lot.

Being a lifelong single person or experiencing divorce meant that vital
sources of help, such as the church or spouse, were not available for a
person. Furthermore, each of these added a social stigma that further challenged a person's ability to find support.

While only some of my informants experienced unemployment, life-long singlehood, or divorce, all faced the challenge of illness. For some, this was their own illnesses. For others, it was the illness of a spouse, parent, or sibling. In all cases, illness damaged the ability of a family to cope. In earlier years, there were few forms of help available. One man spoke of a time when he was in his late teens:

> Then my mother was sick. She had a goiter. She couldn't afford to have it taken care of. She almost died of that because she had it so long. She was so sick from that....she never got any assistance, but because we didn't have enough income or anything like that she got in on the relief end of General Hospital. Then they operated on the goiter. It was like an octopus, it was all over her neck.

The help given his mother was a form of public relief. This man clearly saw it as an exception to the normal forms of helping for Northeast Minneapolis. Even today, he remembers this as being somewhat disgraceful.

Other forms of charity were more acceptable. Help from friends or co-workers would occasionally be given and received.

> I remember too as a kid, my dad getting rheumatism. And he was out of work for six weeks. That was kind of a traumatic deal as far as our family was concerned. To have the breadwinner laid up for six weeks. No sick leave...I remember three or four fellows from his work coming over and visiting him one night after work. These guys came over and when they left, I still see them throwing an envelope on the bed. Full of cash. I don't know but there might have been $150 or something. That was a lot of money back then. They did it.

Some families had the means to hire help when needed. One woman's mother had a long battle with illness:

> My mother had a stroke. If she had lived until January she would have been sick ten years. She was bed ridden...[her sister] wasn't married and then she graduated from school and she stayed home and took care of my ma...And then when she got married we hired a lady to take care of her during the day...I would never trade her for a million dollars...It was in the years [that she helped]. Ran into years.

Illnesses challenged the ability of extended families to cope. Another challenge occurred when there was a death in the family.

The death of a family member was an occasion when neighbors were quick to help one another. This was in a fairly limited way. I asked one woman if her neighbors helped when her mother and father passed away. She replied, "If you were going to have the thing [wake] at your house, afterwards, then all the neighbors pitched in. And brought food and all that stuff."

If there were special circumstances, the types and duration of help might be extended. For example, one woman spoke of a fire that caused the tragic deaths of two young children in a neighbor's family:

> Well, everybody helped. The brought hot dishes over. He worked for the post office. They took up a collection. To help pay for the hospital expenses. And her father paid for the nurses round the clock. So it was tough for them.

Churches were often involved at times of death but only to a limited extent. For example, they would hold a funeral. Occasionally, some would offer more extended forms of help. One woman talked about how she and her son were able to cope after the death of her husband:

> Of course, we had family. The parents [hers] were right there.... Our custom at church is you give money when people die. You send a sympathy card but there is always money in it. So I did get quite a bit of money that way. But other than that I didn't get any big dole or anything like that...And of course, we lived with my parents, which was what I call dirt cheap. So we managed.

Although neighbors and churches offered support during at a time of death, most of the day-to-day help that families needed came mainly from the family itself. One woman spoke of who was involved in the care of her mother as she was dying in 1954, "My dad. My dad and I. He was very good. He was retired at that time. He was a very caring man....I don't think my mother would have wanted it any other way. It was just me and Dad."

Members of one's immediate family provided most of the care. A woman spoke of her experience when her father died:

> My brother was still living at home. My brother lived with my mother until she died. And after she died he got married. He was fifty-two when he got married for the first time. He looked after all of us, actually. He was just that kind of guy. He felt that was his responsibility. That was a big help to all of us. [Would the church help out?] I don't know. Maybe if you ask. But we never got any help. I don't think we needed help. We weren't hurting. We were doing all right. [After her father passed away]....Everything seemed to work pretty good.

More extended kin also helped out. Another woman described how her family coped after her father died:

I had two brothers at home yet at that time. My oldest brother kept the broom factory going after my dad died. There was one aunt who lived about two or three doors away from us. She loved to cook. And she would bring, when my grandmother lived with us, she would bring over home-made soup. A big kettle full. She enjoyed cooking. So she was making soup for Grandma.

There was a characteristic pattern when a death occurred. At first, help came freely from many sources, including neighbors and the church. This was in the form of food, comfort, assistance with coping with daily responsibilities, and, sometimes, money. This help began to subside shortly after the death. For those who continued on, once again self reliance and turning to one's family were the primary coping mechanisms. Indeed, in considering the response to these few types of crises a pattern emerges. These long-term residents consistently described a care-giving and receiving strategy that they learned in their long lives in Northeast.

A Northeast pattern of helping

When crises occurred in the lives of these informants, the first and most acceptable form of help came from families and relatives. For those who parents were still alive, parents were important sources of help when problems arose. Many of the informants lived for periods of time with their parents when they ran into economic difficulties, marital problems, or were just beginning their work lives. The types of help given by parents to children were wide ranging and extensive.

Siblings were potential sources of help. Whether or not this materialized depended in large part upon the quality and nature of the relationship in earlier stages of the person's life, proximity of the sibling, and the life circumstances of the sibling. Sometimes these factors were combined. I asked one woman who helped when her parents died:

Nobody. My sister was in Missouri. When she came out she said, "I didn't come here to work." I took care of my dad's place. After the funeral I closed down the place. Both my sisters-in-law, when they saw I was working alone, they got up and helped me. I had a very good relationship with my sisters-in-law.

Children were also important sources of help for their parents. A form of help could be providing a place to live and care when a parent could no longer live alone. Although it was relatively rare for a parent to move in with an adult son or daughter, it did occur in the lives of some of the informants, either when their own parents moved in with them or when they were young and their grandparents lived with their parents:

> I remember my grandfather staying there for quite a long period of time until he got tuberculosis...I can [also] remember on two or three different occasions where some of the [other] relatives were there for three, four, or five weeks... We had our visitors staying down in the living room. They had a daveno bed that unfolded.

Families were the primary line of defense in times of crisis. Friends and neighbors provided a backup source of help. However, there is a curious contradiction in the accounts of many of my informants. They spoke of rich interaction with neighbors and friends, but many of them said that neighbors did not visit each other in each other's homes very often and that help from friends was limited in nature or extent. Although many subjects spoke of strong communities in Northeast Minneapolis, this seems to contrast with a sense of self-reliance that was and continues to be a cultural value for the persons I interviewed.

> My mother was really the sickest of the neighborhood, but she was so perky. Once she was back on her feet you would never know she had been sick. Most of the other women were very strong women. Some of them worked cleaning offices in the evening...Then they had the old Nelson Paper Mill. A lot of the women worked there. It was manual labor. Immigrants could do it without any great education. They all worked. We really didn't help each other. Because everybody had enough kids to do it.

In general, Northeast was a place where people and families were expected to be self-reliant, yet individual acts of charity and help were given when persons went through times of struggle. One woman wrote of two examples:

> Individuals, too, were generous even when they had nothing. I remember once when the women in our block heard about a "poor" family and got together to take a basket of food to them. We had practically no food, but still they took some to a family they thought was worse off. There were no picky eaters those days. We were just glad to eat three meals. A neighbor who did day work (cleaning) sent her four children to our house with a quart of milk and a loaf of bread for their lunch. She did not pay Mom for watching her children. If she didn't work, they wouldn't have had the milk and bread. Two of the four children became professionals. Another very poor neighbor boy became a judge.

Another source of help was the local church. Yet this group of long-term residents claimed a fairly limited role for the church in times of crisis. When I asked one woman if families expected the church to help in times of need, she replied, "No. My folks could have gone, but they had a lot of pride. I think they would starve before they would ask for help. At least I know my folks would."

This does not mean that churches are unimportant in the lives of these people. Quite the contrary, the church was an important potential source of support, especially for those experiencing the death of a relative. The type of help given, however, seems to be largely limited to spiritual and emotional help. For example, one woman spoke of the response of the church when her mother passed away, "The church responded wonderfully. My mother was a wonderful person. Everybody loved her. She was a demonstrative person. Hugged everybody. The pastor wrote a thing for her funeral."

I asked my informants to expand on the appropriateness of receiving help from the church. They describe a limited range of types of help that they thought the church would or should provide. For example, one man spoke of his mother who was severely crippled with arthritis and needed much help. Although family members helped a lot, the church did not provide any help to her. This is surprising since this family was very active in the church and his parents had both been in leadership over many years. Again, the type of help that was appropriate was often described as spiritual.

A last form of support was the larger community or society. Few institutionalized forms of support existed in this time period compared to today. One form that was used by many of the eastern and southern European ethnic communities was the settlement house. In Northeast Minneapolis, the Northeast Neighborhood House provided language classes, various forms of lessons on how to cook "American food" and manage an "American style household," sports and recreational activities for children and youth, and some medical and social services, such as dental care. It was not necessarily, however, a source of help in times of crisis

When I asked my informants about the availability of institutional help in times of crisis they were uniform in their responses. A typical answer was:

> My parents were furiously independent. They were not going [on] relief
> or anything like that. So, we made it on our own. Everything was poverty
> stricken then. Nobody ever thought of going...we never heard of AFDC
> until the war or something. People just made it on their own. You survived
> or else. Nobody around was on relief. Nobody. And they were all hard

workers. The guy next door worked at the Soo Line. The guy next door there was a tailor. Sat and sewed all day.

This was often compared with what these long-term residents assumed to be true for more recent arrivals in Northeast Minneapolis. One woman said, "[My family] survived. I know they never went on relief. Nobody went on relief around here. That is what they called it then. Now it is AFDC and all that stuff."

One man spoke of his present situation and need for economic help and compared himself to what he thought would be the response of newcomers to the neighborhood:

> And of course I don't get that much social security. I missed a lot in the army and I was in and out of the Vet's Hospital. My social security ain't the biggest. So, we have a little tougher going. Oh I don't know. I always tried to donate but I never got no help from no organization and that. So, I don't know who gets the help, but I never had. I remember when I had my heart operation I was going to be laid up for some time. I didn't have no money. Somebody says go down and get food stamps. So, my boy took me down. It was on Glenwood. And here's these goddamned guys getting out of Cadillacs with a goddamned baby. "Let's go home," [I said]. My boy said, "No dad, you're entitled to it." I said, "Bullshit. We'll make it some way or another." I remember we were playing cards down at the shop one day. And we had this one guy he was pissed off because he couldn't get food stamps. One of my friends said, "God damn it. You'd seen what [my informant] went through. He didn't go asking for it." It made me feel pretty good. It made me feel wonderful.

These long-term residents are survivors. They have lived through many crises and challenges. They relied upon hard work and self-reliance. Yet all have seen times when they needed additional help or have been called upon to help others. They did this in a way that followed a Northeast pattern. The reality is that Northeast Minneapolis has been changing. Indeed, in the past three decades it has changed significantly.

Crisis and caring in a changing world

As we look at the first two eras of the lives of these long-term residents, we can see that help giving and receiving were well defined and clearly delimited. Self reliance was an expectation. Family was the first line of defense. Friends and neighbors extended more limited forms of help in times of need. Churches provided spiritual help and guidance but were not remembered for actively offering other forms of help in times of crisis. Formal services were rare, and it was considered somewhat disgraceful to accept them.

In the fourth, most recent period of these persons' lives there have been many changes. Some of these have affected the ability to give or receive help. As we look at help giving and receiving today we see that these residents continue to follow patterns they have learned over their lifetimes.

Family is still the first line of defense. For those persons who are married, spouses provide rich support. One man spoke of the importance of his wife, "Of course, [my wife] has been a support. And I would think that would be far above anything else I have been exposed to. Just been constant."

Another source of family support is one's siblings. This source of help seems to be limited by the quality of the existing relationship and its history. A woman talked about the deaths of her brother and sister. She was much closer to her sister.

> My younger brother died when he was fifty-nine of leukemia. He went on for several years. The never did call it leukemia. They called it pre-leukemia. [During that time that he was sick did you help?] Well, I would go and visit him. I would never help him. My other sister died last year. She had a liver disease. [Were you pretty involved with her care?] Oh yeah. She was right below me [in a high rise apartment building] and I never even took the elevator most the time. I'd run and down the steps. And took care of her and helped her.

Another man lived with his brother for a long period of time after his parents died. Neither were ever married. I asked him who helped when his brother was sick in the long period of time before he died. He replied, "My sister...all of them helped that were around here. I had taken care of my brother. Died of Parkinson's. He was crippled for many years. My sisters were around all the time."

Children can also be rich sources of support. One woman with two daughters and two sons reported, "My sons had been my salvation. I can confide in my sons. And it never, not even their wives know what we talk about. Very confidential....I am very fortunate, I enjoyed all my children."

Of course, children can also be a source of tension. One woman's son has had a long history of illness and bouts of depression. He is presently living with her and a source of great stress. For others, children live some distance away. They are often in frequent contact but unavailable for day to day help when needed.

Lastly, other relatives can be helpful. One woman who never had children spoke of who helps her now, "Well it would be this dear nephew and niece, Jenell and Scott. They are my closest. He does my year end book work for me. So he knows all about me. He knows if I got five cents or five million."

The persons with whom I talked argued that part of the long-standing character of Northeast was knowing one's neighbors. They argued that other parts of the city weren't like this. Furthermore, they argue that this is still a characteristic of Northeast for those persons who have lived there for a long period of time. I spoke with one man whose sister moved to a newer, more suburban area of the city:

> She lives out in Bloomington....Well, they got certain neighbors that are very good friends. They don't have the spectrum that I do. I know people here, here, here and here [indicating directions from his house]. They know more or less just in their block. Maybe part of another block. Some other people they happen to work with....I know people all around....Here you walk into a tavern or something and right away you get to know somebody. Right away they're all so friendly. And I have had other people say that too. Over here. It's a working class. And I don't know, we just get along....I got some neighbors here. My goodness sakes. They're just great.

The tradition of support from neighbors, family, and friends continues but is largely limited to those known over a long period of time.

> The greatest thing when you get older. The best friends are your old friends. You can do whatever you want. Move to a different neighborhood. Like my brother and his buddy Pee Wee. They were buddies all their lives. And now you get apart. I call as many as I can that live in the city.

Long-term friends and neighbors are important in the lives of these people. My informants argued, however, that this does not extend to newer neighbors:

> First of all, your old friends are your best friends. Friends you make now, they're acquaintances. Until the last few years we would get together once of twice a week. We do have a few things in common, the majority of time is sickness. You discuss an awful lot of your ails, aches and pains.

Churches continue to be strong presences in Northeast Minneapolis. Yet the persons with whom I spoke think that the help churches offer should be limited to sources of spiritual help. One woman complained that present day pastors are managers of social services, not spiritual leaders. This was born out in focus groups with pastors. They spoke of a cultural and generational divide. Newer, younger members of congregations not only accept help but they often demand it. Older members refuse help when offered. A priest spoke of a woman who left his parish when he sent someone from the parish over to see if they could help meet some of her financial needs.

On the other hand, publicly funded social services have expanded greatly and most of my informants accept a variety of types of help. Indeed, some argue that they have earned it. They see a huge difference between this, however, and those younger persons who take welfare. They argue that many persons living in Northeast today do not respond to needs as persons would have in the past. For example, one couple talked about differences at times of death. I asked what neighbors would do if there was a death in the family: "Visit. During the funeral. Plenty of food was brought in, for an army. It doesn't happen as much [today]. Many funerals, they get a caterer. Even among the people who have lived here a long time."

Many whom I interviewed blamed this change on a greater reliance upon governmental programs. One woman contrasted life in Northeast in the past with life today. She told me about a time in her life when a neighbor had lost her husband:

> She went to work. She worked, like my mother did, in restaurants. And she worked in people's homes, doing house cleaning and stuff. And they would give her clothes. She could bring leftover food home. And that is how she raised those two girls…They survived. I know they never went on relief. Nobody went on relief around here. That is what they called it then. Now it is AFDC and all that stuff.…Now-adays, people have kids and wait for somebody to support them. I shouldn't talk that way. There a lot of people that can't help it.

This woman argued that the Northeast pattern of helping that she had learned was not the pattern of care-giving and receiving that newer arrivals exhibited. She tried to be generous in her assessment, but she clearly thought that something was wrong with her new neighbors. She is not alone. In looking at care-giving and receiving in the present-day lives of these long-term residents it is clear that they continue to value and try to employ the Northeast pattern of care-giving and seeking learned earlier in their lives. This has worked effectively over most of their lives. Unfortunately for them, there are changes in Northeast that make it increasingly possible that this pattern will not work as well for them in the future. Neighbors have been an important component of their effective communities. Changes are occurring in Northeast Minneapolis that will make it likely that this component will be missing or play a very weak role for persons, such as the informants in this study, who are long-term residents of Northeast.

Urban change, effective communities, and the future

In their neighborhoods in Northeast Minneapolis, long-term residents are increasingly surrounded by those with whom they have little contact or knowledge and from whom they are often separated by their own deep-seated stereotypes and misconceptions. This often means that neighbors who played important roles in the lives of these persons in earlier years are missing as a source of informal care-giving and receiving. This is tragic and deeply ironic. These long-term residents survived the many crises with which they have been faced largely through their abilities to access support when it was needed. Knowledge of and interaction with neighbors was an important component and acted to establish a sense of identity and security. Long-term residents spoke frequently of the face-to-face nature of the neighborhoods in which they were raised, how common it was to know everyone in their neighborhoods, and the deep sense of safety they felt. Today in Northeast Minneapolis, this is no longer true. They are increasingly finding themselves in the roles of strangers in a world of strangers, and they find it to be a frightening and unsettling time.

For the persons with whom I talked, old ways of building community and interacting with neighbors are breaking down. These long-term residents lived much of their lives in relatively homogenous ethnic enclaves in well-defined neighborhoods. Community used to be defined in terms of ethnicity, residence, and religious affiliation. They also lived in the "all-American" town of Northeast Minneapolis, with its many Euro-American ethnic groups sharing a blue-collar ethic of hard work and self-reliance.

Care-giving and receiving built upon this form of community. Generally, a person in crisis tried to access layers of support and relief. This can be visualized as a number of concentric circles, with the person in need at the center, the inner-most circles being generally the most available and most frequently used sources of help, and the outer most circles being less available and less frequently used by the person in crisis. The width of the circles indicates the general importance of each source of help (see Figure 6.1). The pattern of care-giving and receiving into which these long-term residents were socialized (left-most pattern in Figure 6.1) shows that help from public institutions is located at the very margins.

FIGURE 6.1: *Northeast patterns of care giving and receiving—*
A comparison of early patterns with those of today

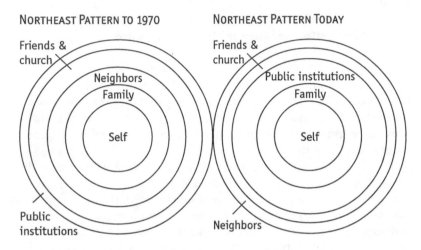

In looking at the present day pattern (right-most set of circles in Figure 6.1) it can be seen that there has been an expansion of role and importance for public institutions and governmentally financed forms of social support. Older persons presently living in Northeast Minneapolis have access to a much larger array of services provided by public institutions than do older persons who lived in Northeast in earlier years. These include social security benefits and services provided by agencies and institutions designed to work with older persons. There is little reluctance on the part of most of my informants to receive the services offered. Indeed, it was often argued that these services were well deserved and earned through a lifetime of work and contribution. These services were strongly contrasted with "welfare," which was often argued is used by those who attempt to take advantage of the "system" and show little interest in solving their own problems.

A second change depicted in these two sets of circles is the shift in position of the circles denoting neighbors. In the left-most set of circles, neighbors are seen as available, fairly important sources of help. They were persons who were similar to the person in need. In the right-most set of circles, neighbors are seen as scarcely available and largely unimportant. In the eyes of my informants, neighbors today are likely to be different from them in terms of color, values, and lifestyle. They are likely to be on welfare, or, in the words of my informants, they are "AFDCs." That is, these long-term residents assume that many of their new neighbors are described by a stereotype as an "AFDC," who is assumed to be irresponsible, short sighted, sexually out of control, prone to abuse of alcohol and drugs, and dangerous. This is an embodiment of the specter of urban blight and is clearly racialized as frequent references were made to "across the river," which referred to North Minneapolis with its large population of African Americans. It is these very people, the "AFDCs," welfare recipients, and persons of color, who are thought to be moving into Northeast Minneapolis. In other words, the dangerous stranger is now the neighbor. They are not seen as good neighbors. For many with whom I talked, they just do not belong in Northeast.

This creates a dilemma for older persons in Northeast Minneapolis. They are in a period of life when there is the danger of isolation just when they need strong, effective networks. Persons who are now living in close proximity to them are not thought to be "good neighbors." This assessment is clearly based upon stereotypes since my informants often said that they did not know those persons who had recently moved into their neighborhoods. On the other side, newer residents often complained of judgmental attitudes and lack of acceptance on the part of older persons who have lived in Northeast for long periods of time. Ironically, many of my informants noted that the new neighbors they have gotten to know seemed to be hard working and likely to fit into the working class ethos of Northeast Minneapolis. Unfortunately, these long-term residents have little contact with newer residents. Mutual stereotypes and lack of shared involvement in community institutions separate them. In considering Figure 6.1, it can be seen that those areas of the circle that provide the strongest forms of informal support, self, family, and friends, are the ones most likely to disappear in later older age. Reliance upon self becomes more difficult with declining health. Reliance upon family becomes more difficult as one moves into the oldest old category. Friends die off and disappear as important sources of help in the support networks of these persons. Older persons are left with the need to turn increasingly to public institutions for help. They often become competitors with younger persons for public dollars and services, which adds more tension between long-term residents and newer arrivals.

The result is a growing social rift between long-term residents and newer arrivals in Northeast Minneapolis. This rift makes it unlikely that there will be substantial interaction between the two groups. As such, they will continue to understand one another on the basis of stereotypes. For older persons, this means that the newer arrivals will be seen as dangerous and as persons to be avoided. New arrivals, many of which are much younger, often see older persons as unfriendly and biased against them. This would seem to indicate a negative future with a spiral downward into deeper and deeper levels of mistrust and animosity.

There is hope in that Northeast Minneapolis continues to have strong, functioning institutions, such as local churches and neighborhood associations, that have the possibility to rebuild community through well-planned and carefully executed programs of community education and community development. Long-term residents and newer arrivals could to engage one another in these settings, learn more about each other, and find mutual interests and goals toward which to work. Northeast Minneapolis has provided a strong and supportive environment for those long-term residents who are the subjects of this book. They have found a mixture of informal and formal sources of support that have enabled them to thrive. This can be the model for the future, but it will only be possible if the definition of whom is a legitimate resident of Northeast Minneapolis is brought up-to-date to include the diversity and strengths found in those who live in Northeast today.

Appendix 1: City of Minneapolis

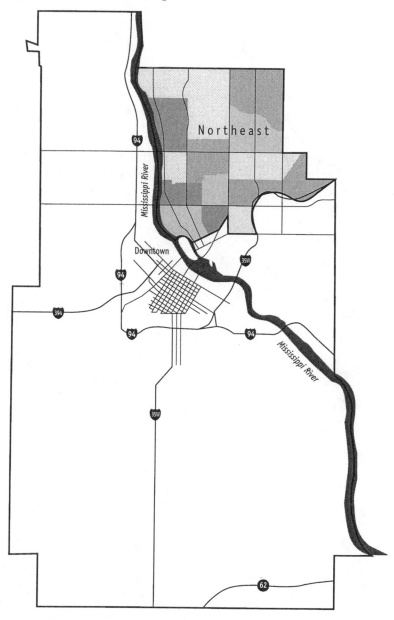

Appendix 2: Northeast Minneapolis

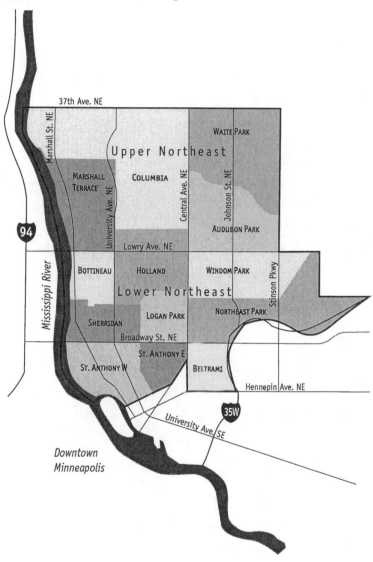

Notes

Chapter 1

[1] Phyllis and other names used in this book are pseudonyms. Details of her story have been slightly altered to protect her identity.

[2] The argument that extended families used to be the norm and that they provided rich care for their dependent members needs to be modified based upon the work of Laslett and other researchers. Based upon extensive work with historical records they have argued that extended families have never been the norm in Western society. Thus, there could be little likelihood that this was an universal solution to the needs of the elderly (Laslett 1985).

Chapter 2

[1] It is interesting that almost 150 years later there were plans to return to the early use of the falls. New modes of generating power had long since made the falls obsolete for many forms of manufacture. In 1995, Crown Hydro proposed to restore an old waterdriven turbine system under some presently unused flour mills. Originally, a canal diverted river water under the mills where it turned a turbine that drove milling equipment. Plans were to restore this and also provide a sightseeing and learning attraction in a proposed Mills Ruins Park. Estimations were that it could provide electrical power for 3000 homes (Anderson 1996, 8).

[2] "The two communities [St. Anthony and Minneapolis] had more in common than a waterfall. Their inhabitants, drawn heavily from New England and the Middle Atlantic states, developed a similar civic consciousness in which pride and a kind of inverted humility were mingled. Social and cultural institutions grew as luxuriantly as they had in the fertile ground 'back East,' and the local inhabitants watched with pleasure the evolution of a 'polished and refined society' at the falls. They were inordinately proud that the new towns were 'people from the colleges, court-rooms, pulpits, counting rooms and workshops of the East.' Affirming this identification, the Minnesota Republican [December, 1857] claimed: 'We are Yankees by birth and profession, by inclination, education, habits and twang.'" (Kane 1987, 39)

[3] A similar tension appeared one hundred years later. In 1994, a local artist, Susan Fiene, created a coloring book depicting ethnic motifs of groups found in Northeast Minneapolis. This was to be distributed through the Minneapolis public schools. The distribution of the coloring book was delayed until she deleted religious references and added more representation of then current minority populations. In the end, sixty percent of the drawings were of minorities. This incident is an indication of the battle over an identity for Northeast Minneapolis. In the early 1900s it was between two forms of Euro-American identity—Anglo and non-

Anglo. In 1994 it was between Euro-American and non-Euro-American identity (Simonson 1994).

⁴ St. Mary's Russian Orthodox Greek Catholic Church is a cathedral of the Orthodox Church in America.

⁵ Russian ethnicity, as referred to by the residents of the neighborhood, includes Russians, Rusins, and many other persons from East Slavic regions of Europe.

⁶ In 1997, there were again discussions about what parks should be like in Northeast Minneapolis. In the Logan Park area there was a move to build a fountain surrounded by a formal garden on the south end of the park on Broadway between Monroe and Jefferson. The supporters of the fountain argued that it would bring distinction to the area, help define it as a separate place, and welcome persons to the neighborhood. Opponents argued that to build the park would require that basketball courts be torn out. They argued that the courts are used by young men, many of whom are African-American, and provided a needed area for recreation. In many ways this struggle was a struggle for identity. The pro-fountain faction was behind a move to regentrify the area. The anti-fountain faction argued that the present character of Northeast included a wide range of class levels and ethnicity. They pointed out that regentrification would exclude some of the existing residents of the neighborhood.

⁷ This counters the argument made by many today who compare immigrants in the present with those from earlier times and find that those of earlier times did not need the governmental support that is demanded by those in the present. Clearly, a range of programs, governmental, church-based, and informal, existed and were used by immigrants in Northeast Minneapolis in the early 1900s.

° At least part of this conflict has to do with ethnicity. Bishop Ireland was opposed to parishes strongly focused on Old World identity. That is they were not "American" parishes. Of course, it is at least ironic that he was strongly supportive of the Irish American community. In 1997, a similar controversy arose. Holy Cross, established in 1886 by Polish immigrants, had been seeing a general decline of its membership throughout the 1970s and 1980s. In the mid-1980s new immigrants from Poland boosted the number of members and reinforced its Polish identity as Holy Cross played a similar role for them as it had one hundred years earlier for Polish immigrants at that time. Father Stanslaw Rakiej, an associate priest who spoke Polish, saw his role expanding as the proportion of persons who spoke only Polish grew to over twenty-five percent of the congregation. Tensions grew between those who were strongly affiliated with Polish identity and those who were not (Hawkins 1997, 7). At that time Archbishop Harry Flynn, the head of the Catholic Church in St. Paul and Minneapolis, removed Father Stanislaw Rakiej, a Polish-speaking priest at Holy Cross in Northeast Minneapolis. The reason given was there was disunity in the church due to conflict between those parishioners who spoke Polish and strongly focused on Polish nationality and those who might or might not speak Polish but thought that Holy Cross should diffuse its focus on Polish nationality. It was stated by the Most Revered Lawrence H. Welsh, an Auxiliary Bishop with the Bishop of the Minneapolis Vicariate, that "Father Stan's presence had become an occasion for division rather than unity….For the good things that Father Stan did, Archbishop Flynn and I are grateful. For the disunity that has sprung up around him in recent months, we express our deep regret. We ask you to work with us to repair this rich tapestry of faith, 'old' families and 'new,' English and Polish speaking, in union with your pastor, the Archbishop, our Holy Father John Paul II and the whole Church. We will keep you informed of opportunities to do so. Asking through the Blessed Virgin Mary, Queen of Poland, that God bless you all…" (Welsh 1997). Many members of who were more strongly focused on Polish identity were convinced that the decision reflected an anti-Polish bias (Anderson 1997a).

Chapter 2

[1] Ironically, fortunes have reversed over the past decades. Northeast has been relatively stable compared to areas in South Minneapolis which have seen difficult years in terms of economic and social conditions. Perhaps that explains why the term "Nordeast" is now used in a more familiar, nostalgic way by many who live in Northeast Minneapolis.

[2] The Hollywood Theater has been closed for some time. There have been recent efforts to restore the building and reopen it. Thus far, these are unsuccessful.

[3] The ethnic identity of St. John's Byzantine Catholic and St. Mary's Russian Orthodox Cathedral is complicated. Both draw from essentially the same community of persons from Eastern Slavic areas of Europe. St. Mary's was established first and affiliated with the Russian Orthodox Church largely because Archbishop Ireland would not approve the establishment of a Byzantine Catholic Church in Northeast Minneapolis. St. John's was established later with the sanction of Archbishop Ireland who wanted to counter the influence of St. Mary's.

Chapter 5

[1] The Minneapolis school system changed its twenty-year-old policy of busing school children to achieve racial parity for the 1996–97 school year. It allowed the redesignation of selected schools in Minneapolis as neighborhood schools, including some in Northeast Minneapolis.

Bibliography

Aaron, Joshua
1995   *Northeast Minneapolis Central Avenue commercial corridor: business survey report.* Minneapolis, MN: Center for Urban and Regional Affairs.

Alexander, Blaine B., Robert L. Rubinstein, Marcene Goodman, and Mark Luborsky
1992   A path not taken: A cultural analysis of regrets and childlessness in the lives of older women. *The Gerontologist* 32(5): 518–626.

Anderson, Mike
1995   Neighborhood schools won't necessarily end student busing. *Northeaster* (February 20): 1, 8–9.

1996   Private businessmen say they can save the city some money on proposed energy restoration on project near St. Anthony Waterfalls. *Northeaster* (February 12): 8.

1997a   Priest's removal rocks Holy Cross. *Northeaster* (January 27): 1, 4–5.

1997b   Race and crime fears surface at Conoco expansion hearing in Heights. *Northeaster* (March 10): 7.

1997c   Students who don't speak English pose a challenge for schools. *Northeaster* (April 21): 3–4.

1997d   Can parents spend school money better than the school board? *Northeaster* (December 15): 16–17.

Angel, Ronald J. and Jacqueline L. Angel
1997   *Who will care for us: Aging and long-term care in multicultural America.* New York: New York University Press.

Antonnuci, Toni C.
1985   Personal characteristics, social support, and social behavior. In *Handbook of aging and the social sciences*, ed. Robert H. Binstock and Ethel Shanas. New York: Van Nostrand Reinhold Company, 94–128.

Armstrong, M. Jocelyn
1990   Friendship adaptations in later life: A cross-ethnic perspective. Paper presented at the Strategies of Adaptation to Aging Session, Annual Meeting of the American Anthropological Association, New Orleans, LA.

Ashmore, Kerry
1990   YMCA's early foothold in Northeast took many forms, many attempts to establish. *Northeaster* (February 21): 12, 17–18.

1995 Look at Northeast 60 and 70 years age." *Northeaster* (October 23): 16, 20.

Ashmore, Margot
1997 NE community took care of its own, and will continue, with welfare reform. *Northeaster* (June 23): 15–16.

Baerwald, Thomas J.
1989 Forces at war in the landscape. In *Minnesota in a century of change: The state and its people since 1900,* ed. Clifford E. Clark, Jr. St. Paul, MN: Minnesota Historical Society Press, 19–54.

Bakke, Raymond J.
1987 *The urban Christian: Effective ministry in today's urban world.* Downer's Grove, IL: InterVarsity Press.

Bear, Mary
1990 Social network characteristics and the duration of primary relationships after entry into long-term care. *Journal of Gerontology: SOCIAL SCIENCES* 45(4): s156–162.

Bellah, Robert N. and Christopher Freeman Adams
1994 Strong institutions, good city. *Christian Century* (June 15–22): 604–607.

Berkman, Lisa
1983 The assessment of social networks and social support in the elderly. *Journal of the American Geriatrics Society* 31(12): 743–749.

Berkman, Lisa and Leonard Syme
1979 Social networks, host resistance, and mortality: A nine year follow-up study of Alameda County residents. *American Journal of Epidemiology* 109: 186–204.

Bolin, Winifred Wandersee
1976 Heating up the melting pot. *Minnesota History* (Summer): 58–69.

Calhoun, Craig
1991 Indirect relationships and imagined communities: Large-scale social integration and the transformation of everyday life. In *Social Theory for a Changing Society,* ed. Pierre Bourdieu and James S. Coleman. Boulder, CO: Westview Press, 95–130.

Cantor, Marjorie
1983 Strain among caregivers: A study of experience in the United States. *The Gerontologist* 23:597–604.

Chapleski, Elizabeth E.
1989 Determinants of knowledge of services to the elderly: Are strong ties enabling or inhibiting? *The Gerontologist* 29(4): 539–545.

Chapman, Nancy J. and Diane L. Pancoast
1983   Working with the informal helping networks of the elderly: The experiences of three programs. Portland, OR: Regional Research Institute for Human Services, Portland State University.

Chavez, Leo
1994   The power of the imagined community: The settlement of undocumented Mexicans and Central Americans in the United States. *American Anthropologist* 96(1): 52–73.

Clark, W. A. V. and Suzanne Davies
1990   Elderly mobility and mobility outcomes: Households in the later stages of the life course. *Research on Aging* 12(4): 430–462.

Cohen, Carl and A. Adler
1984   Network interventions: Do they work? *The Gerontologist* 24(1): 16–22.
1986   Assessing the role of social network interventions with an inner-city population. *American Journal of Orthopsychiatry* 56(2): 278–288.

Cohen, Carl and Jay Sokolovsky
1980   Social engagement versus isolation: The case of the aged in SRO hotels. *The Gerontologist* 20(1):6–44.

Cohen, Carl, Jeanne Teresi, and Douglas Holme
1983   Social networks and adaptation. Revised version of a paper presented at the 36th Annual Meeting of the Gerontological Society of America, San Francisco, CA.

Comptroller General of the United states
1977   *The well-being of the older people in Cleveland, Ohio.* Washington, D.C.: Comptroller General of the United States.

Connidis, Ingrid Arnet and Lorraine Davies
1990   Confidants and companions in later life: The place of family and friends. *Journal of Gerontology* 45(4): S141–149.

Daatland, Svein Olav
1990   What are families for: On family solidarity and preference for help. *Aging and Society* 10: 1–15.

Daniels, Norman
1988   *Am I my Parents' keeper?* New York, NY: Oxford University Press.

Dyrud, Keith P.
1981   East Slavs: Rusins, Ukrainians, Russians, and Belorussions. In *They chose Minnesota: A survey of the state's ethnic groups,* ed. June Drenning Holmquist. St. Paul, MN: Minnesota Historical Society Press, 405–422.

Eames, Edwin and Judith Goode
1977   *Anthropology of the city*. Englewood Cliffs, NJ: Prentice Hall, Inc.
Eckert, J. Kevin
1983   Dislocation and relocation of the urban elderly: Social networks as
        mediators of relocation stress. *Human Organization* 42(1): 39–45.
Edelman, Perry and Susan Hughes
1990   The impact of community care on provision of informal care to
        homebound elderly persons. *Journal of Gerontology* 45(2): s74–84.
Fisher, Gene and Richard Tessler
1986   Family bonding of the mentally ill: An analysis of family visits
        with residents of board and care homes. *Journal of Health and
        Social Behavior* 27:236–249.
Froland, Charles, Diane Pancoast, Nancy Chapman, and Priscilla Kimboko
1981   *Helping networks and human services*. Volume 128, Sage Library
        of Social Research. Beverly Hills: Sage Publications.
Fuehrer, Tim
1991   Known for streetcar development, Lowry was also a wheeler-dealer
        in real estate; much activity NE." *Northeaster* (May 15): 7, 15.
Gallagher, Sally K. and Gerstel, Naomi
1993   Kinkeeping and friend keeping among older women: The effect
        of marriage. *The Gerontologist* 33(5): 675–681.
Gallo, Frank
1983   The effects of social support networks on the health of the eld-
        erly. *Social Work in Health Care* 8(2): 65–74.
Gans, Herbert J.
1962   *The urban villagers*. New York: Free Press.
Gies, Frances and Joseph Gies
1990   *Life in a medieval village*. New York: Harper and Row.
Greene, Vernon and Deborah Monahan
1982   The impact of visitation on patient well-being in nursing homes.
        The Gerontologist 22:418–423.
Gutkind, Peter
1974   *Urban anthropology*. New York: Barnes and Noble Books.
Hawkins, Beth
1997   The Polish Inquisition. *City Page* (February 5): 7.
Hayes-Bautista, David E.; Werner O. Schink, and Jorge Chapa
1988   *The burden of support: Young Latinos in an aging society*. Stanford,
        CA: Stanford University Press.

Hazel, Robert
1977   Notre Dame de Minneapolis: The French-Canadian Catholics. Minneapolis, MN: Post Publishing Company.
Holmquist, June Drenning (ed.)
1981   *They Chose Minnesota: A survey of the state's ethnic groups.* St. Paul, MN: Minnesota Historical Society Press.
Humphrey, Robin
1993   Life stories and social careers: Aging and social life in an ex-mining town. *Sociology* (27)1: 166–178.
Ingersoll-Dayton, Berit and Toni C. Antonucci
1988   Reciprocal and nonreciprocal social support: Contrasting sides of intimate relationships. *Journal of Gerontology* 43(3): 565–573.
Jabbour, Alan
1993   Ethnicity and identity in America. *Folklife Center News* 15(2): 6–10.
Johnson, Collee
1988   Fairweather friends and rainy day kin: An anthropological analysis of old age friendships in the United States. *Urban Anthropology* 12(2): 103–123.
Johnson, Colleen L. and Lillian E. Troll
1994   Constraints and facilitators to friendships in late late life. *The Gerontologist* 34(1): 79–87.
1996   Family structure and the timing of transitions from 70 to 103 years of age. *Journal of Marriage and the Family* 58: 178–187.
Johnson, Hildegard Binder
1981   The Germans. In *They chose Minnesota: A survey of the state's ethnic groups,* ed. June Drenning Holmquist. St. Paul, MN: Minnesota Historical Society Press, 153–184.
Jones, Delmo
1987   The "community" and organizations in the community. In *Cities of the United States: stories in urban anthropology,* ed. L. Mullins. New York, NY: Columbia University Press.
Kane, Lucile M.
1987   *The Falls of St. Anthony: The waterfall that built Minneapolis.* St. Paul, MN: Minnesota Historical Society Press.
Kaszuba, Mike
1985   A hardy community begins to change. *Minneapolis Star and Tribune* (December 26): 1A, 8A, 10A.
Keefe, Susan E.
1980   Personal communities in the city: Support networks among the

Mexican-Americans and Anglo-Americans. *Urban Anthropology* 9(1): 51–74.

Laslett, Peter
1985   Societal development and aging. In *Handbook of Aging and the Social Sciences*, ed. Robert H. Binstock, and Ethel Shanas. New York: Van Nostrand Reinhold Company, 199–230.

Lupton, Robert
1996   The gospel of community. *Urban Mission* 14(1): 3–5.

Martin, Judith A. and Anthony Goddard
1989   *Past choices/present landscapes: The impact of urban renewal on the Twin Cities.* Minneapolis, MN: Center for Urban and Regional Affairs.

Megets, Lyuba
1996   Letter to editor. *Northeaster* (June 10): 3.

Merry, Sally Engle
1981   *Urban danger: Life in a neighborhood of strangers.* Philadelphia, PA: Temple Press.

Miller, Baila and Stephanie McFall
1991   Stability and change in the informal task support network of frail older persons. *The Gerontologist* 31(6): 735–745.

Minneapolis City Planning Commission and City Council
1965   *Northeast community: Analysis and action recommendations.* Minneapolis, MN: Minneapolis City Planning Commission.

Minnesota Republican
1857   *Minnesota Republication.* St Anthony and Minneapolis.

Mitchell, J. Clyde
1969   The concept and use of social networks. In *Social Networks in Urban Situations*, ed. J. Clyde Mitchell. Manchester, England: Manchester University Press, 1–50.

Moen, Phillis; Donna Dempster-McClain, and Robin M. Williams, Jr.
1992   Successful aging: A life-course perspective on women's multiple roles and health. *American Journal of Sociology* 97(6): 1612–1638.

Morrison, Peter A.
1990   Demographic factors reshaping ties to family and place. *Research on Aging* 12(4): 399–408.

O'Brien, J., and D. Wagner
1980   Help seeking by the frail elderly: Problems in network analysis. *The Gerontologist* 20: 78–83.

Olson, Gail
1996   Masons groups enjoy long history NE. *Northeaster* (August 26): 10, 11, 13.

1997   Edison High: The community's school. *Northeaster* (September 22): 5–8.

Olson, Laura Katz (ed.)

1994   *The graying of the world: Who will care for the frail elderly?* New York: Haworth Press.

O'Rand, Angela M.

1996   The precious and the precocious: Understanding cumulative disadvantage and cumulative advantage over the life course. *The Gerontologist* 36(2): 230–238.

Pearlman, Deborah N. and William H. Crown

1992   Alternative sources of social support and their impacts on institutional risk. *The Gerontologist* 32(4): 527–535.

Peterson, Evan T.

1989   Elderly parents and their offspring. In *Aging and the family*, ed. Stephen J. Bahr, and Evan T. Peterson. Lexington, MA: Lexington Books, 175–191.

Polish White Eagle Association

1981   *Polish White Eagle Association: Polskiego Bialego Orla, 1906–1981 Diamond Jubilee.* Minneapolis, MN.

Regan, Ann

1981   The Irish. In *They chose Minnesota: A survey of the state's ethnic groups,* ed. June Drenning Holmquist, St. Paul, MN: Minnesota Historical Society Press, 139–152.

Redfield, Robert

1947   The Folk Society. *American Journal of Sociology* 52: 293–308.

Renkiewicz, Frank

1981   The Poles. In *They chose Minnesota: A survey of the state's ethnic groups,* ed. June Drenning Holmquist, St. Paul, MN: Minnesota Historical Society Press, 362–380.

Rice, John G.

1981   The Swedes. In *They chose Minnesota: A survey of the state's ethnic groups,* ed. June Drenning Holmquist, St. Paul, MN: Minnesota Historical Society Press, 248–276.

Rosenbaum, Walter A. and James W. Button

1993   The unquiet future of intergenerational politics. *The Gerontologist* 33(4): 481–490.

Schreck, Harley C.

1996   *The elderly in America: Volunteerism and neighborhood in Seattle.* Lanham, MD: University Press in America.

Settersten, Richard A. and Gunhild O. Hagestad
1996   What's the latest? Culture age deadlines for family transitions. *The Gerontologist* 36(2): 178–188.
Simonson, Jennifer
1994   Religious references slowed book's trip to classroom. *Northeaster* (October 26): 1, 7.
Smithers, Janice A.
1985   *Determined survivors: Community life among the urban elderly.* New Brunswick, NJ: Rutgers University Press.
Sokolovsky, Jay and Carl I. Cohen
1978   The cultural meaning of personal networks for the inner-city elderly. *Urban Anthropology* 7(4): 323–342.
Steinmetz, S. K.
1981   Elder abuse. *Aging* 2:6–10.
Stolcke, Verna
1995   Talking culture: New boundaries, new rhetorics of exclusion in Europe. *Current Anthropologist* 36(1): 1–24.
Stoller, Eleanor P.
1990   Males as helpers: The role of sons, relatives, and friends. *The Gerontologist* 30(2): 228–235.
Sun Newspapers
1976   *Northeast: History.* Bloomington, MN: Sun Newspapers.
Sussman, Marvin
1985   The family life of old people. In *Handbook of Aging the Social Sciences,* ed. R. H. Binstock and E. Shanas. 2nd ed.. New York: Van Nostrand Reinhold, 415–449.
Swierenga, Robert P.
1994   The religious factor in immigration: The Dutch experience. In *Immigrant America: European ethnicity in the United States,* ed. Timothy Walch. New York: Garland Publishing, Inc., 119–140.
Taylor, David Vassar
1981   The Blacks. In *They chose Minnesota: A survey of the state's ethnic groups,* ed. June Drenning Holmquist, St. Paul, MN: Minnesota Historical Society Press, 73–91.
Taylor, Robert Joseph and Linda M. Chatters
1986   Church-based informal support among elderly Blacks. *The Gerontologist* 26(6): 637–642.
Urban Coalition
1996   *Trends in Northeast Minneapolis, 1980–1990.* St. Paul, MN: The Urban Coalition.

van Baal, J.
1981   *Reciprocity and the position of women.* Assen, The Netherlands:
        Van Gorcum.
Vecoli, Rudolph J.
1981   The Italians. In *They Chose Minnesota: a survey of the state's eth-
        nic groups,* ed. June Drenning Holmquist. St. Paul, MN: Minne-
        sota Historical Society Press, 449–471.
Wang, Yue-Eng
1979   *Natural support systems and the rural elderly: A Missouri case.*
        Ph.D. dissertation, University of Missouri-Columbia, Columbia,
        Missouri.
Welsh, Most Reverend Lawrence H.
1997   Letter to the congregation of Holy Cross Catholic Church in
        Northeast Minneapolis from the Auxiliary Bishop of the Bishop
        of the Minneapolis Vicariate of the Archdiocese of Saint Paul
        and Minneapolis, St. Paul, MN.
Wenger, G. Clare
1990   The special role of friends and neighbors. *Journal of Aging Stud-
        ies* 4(2): 149–169.
Wiberg, Glen
1995   *The other side of the river.* New Brighton, MN: Salem Covenant
        Church.
Wirth, Louis
1975   Urbanism as a way of life. In *City ways,* ed. J. Friedl and N. J.
        Chrisman. Harper and Row, 26–45. First published in *American
        Journal of Sociology* 44(1938): 1–2.

Index